363.1798 Esposito, Richard.
ESP
Bomb Squad.

$24.95

BOMB
SQUAD

BOMB SQUAD

A YEAR INSIDE THE NATION'S MOST EXCLUSIVE POLICE UNIT

Richard Esposito and Ted Gerstein

HYPERION

NEW YORK

Library of Congress Cataloging-in-Publication Data
Esposito, Richard.
   Bomb Squad : a year inside the nation's most exclusive police unit / Richard
   Esposito and Ted Gerstein.
      p. cm.
   ISBN 1-4013-0152-5
   ISBN-13: 978-1-4013-0152-1
1. New York (N.Y.). Police Dept. Bomb Squad.   2. Bomb squads—New York
(State)—New York.   I. Gerstein, Ted.   II. Title.
   HV8080.B65E87 2007
   363.17'98—dc22
                                                        2006049678

Hyperion books are available for special promotions and premiums.
For details contact Michael Rentas, Assistant Director, Inventory Operations,
Hyperion, 77 West 66th Street, 12th floor, New York, New York 10023,
or call 212-456-0133.

Design by Renato Stanisic

FIRST EDITION

10   9   8   7   6   5   4   3   2   1

For Chris
&
For Chris

At the end of the day it always comes down to a man in a
Kevlar suit . . . it's man versus bomb

—LIEUTENANT MARK TORRE, COMMANDING OFFICER,
NYPD BOMB SQUAD

In my mind it's all business; I don't worry about my family, I don't
worry about a function that I'm doing after work, I just worry about
what's at hand. And what's at hand is that package; I don't want that
package to hurt me or hurt the public, so I treat that package as being
live, or being an explosive device, no matter what it is.

—DETECTIVE FIRST GRADE JOE PUTKOWSKI,
SENIOR MAN, NYPD BOMB SQUAD

Contents

A Preface

They are a small group of thirty-three pointedly relaxed, decidedly suburban, offhandedly humorous men who are partial to wash-and-wear pastel shirts and pleasant, just-good-enough ties. They are the current members of the New York City Police Department Bomb Squad. The watches they wear tend to be the kind with thick bezels, clear numbers, and easy-to-read sweep hands.

Measured in precious seconds and eternal minutes standing over a bomb, time is surgically important to these men. Of course they also measure it in all the ways that other police officers measure time—in hours on duty or in years on the job. But for them time can suddenly come to an end with a blast wave moving at 26,000 feet per second—an incomprehensible, invisible, soundless force. It smacks and compresses with such speed and such violence that it is not until after it is followed milliseconds later by another wave that bystanders can hear the deafening sound and see the shrapnel-filled fury of the killing force. For the man kneeling over the bomb, this is a requiem. Yet each day they must reach inside themselves in the same offhanded manner in which they draw on their blue Bomb Squad windbreakers, and call on a stillness that allows them to face this destructive force with steady hands.

In existence for 101 years, the NYPD Bomb Squad is the oldest bomb squad in the nation. During those 101 years nearly 500,000 police officers have served New York City. From them, 225 were selected to join the Bomb Squad ranks. Beginning with a surge in domestic terrorism in the late 1960s, these bomb technicians have headed out to an average of more than 2500 stress-filled "bomb runs" a year.

On December 31, 2003, the authors were invited to join the NYPD Bomb Squad as full-time observers. With the gracious permission of the New York City Police Department and the unanimous consent of the squad members, we were given unprecedented access to the life of their squad room. It was a chance to observe day to day, for three hundred and sixty-five days, an elite unit in action. It was an opportunity to explore what made these ordinary men so willing to take on such extraordinary risks.

This book is a result of that year on the Bomb Squad. It is not a book about the grander themes of a war on terror, or a book about the mechanics of building or taking apart bombs. It is simply a book about bomb technicians.

In the course of a year, the squad thought we should attend the same courses they did, try on the heavy protective suits that they wore, and read the files of past cases that they kept in their basement. To allow us to get a better feel for the rigors of the craft, the United States Army and the Federal Bureau of Investigation invited us to audit the basic training course at the Hazardous Devices School in Huntsville, Alabama. The FBI also allowed us to participate in a Large Vehicle Post Blast forensic course that the Bureau conducts for law enforcement officers and members of the military. The International Association of Bomb Technicians and Investigators invited us to their conventions and to listen to the technical briefings they offered their members. We drove robots, hid behind bunkers as bombs were detonated, and stood behind our hosts so that we managed to return home with all of our fingers. But this book it is by no means our personal account—these were simply the tools the squad gave us to enable us to tell their stories. That is what we have tried to do.

At a time when "Improvised Explosive Device" is a phrase heard on television nightly, it might come as a surprise to discover that those devices are nothing but bombs, the kind of bombs that bomb technicians across the United States take apart every day. It certainly was a surprise to us. Also surprising was the discovery that there are a lot of bombs planted and defused each year in the United States and that this has been going on for a very long time. In one year, now forgotten but just over twenty-five years ago, extremists planted 384 bombs in New York City. A handful of bomb technicians went out to defuse them.

This book is about those individual bomb technicians—the ones who work in the squad today and the ones who took apart those bombs in the past. As such, it is part oral history. Many living retired members of the Bomb Squad provided us with their memories and their personal files.

The culture of the bomb technician, we came to learn, is not to be found in the five-inch-thick NYPD rule book—the Patrol Guide—or in the regulations of any other police department. Nor is it explained in the volumes of explosives training material. It is a culture that has evolved over the ten decades of trial and error on the part of police officers who donned protective gear, knelt down, said a prayer, and attempted to cut the correct wire, sever a circuit, remove a blasting cap, and defuse a bomb.

The public rarely sees a bomb technician up close. And that is what this book attempts to offer—a close-up.

Normally, it isn't until a package has been identified as suspicious and an area several hundred to a thousand feet square completely cleared of civilians that a bomb technician will step from behind a big blue and white response truck and into his silent arena. What the public sees is a hooded man behind a ballistic faceplate inside a bulky ninety-pound khaki green Kevlar suit. He lumbers slowly toward danger. The suit cuts off most outside noise so the technician is accompanied only by the sound of his pumping blood. The suit is so hot that he can lose three pounds on a twelve-minute walk to a suspicious package and back. As he walks, he empties his mind of extraneous thought, of useless bravery, and of as much fear as he can. His fingers appear from beneath the cuffs of his armor. Free of any armor themselves, their unimpaired nimbleness is valued more greatly than their potential loss.

The bomb technician plays chess with an opponent who conceals his moves from view inside a fried chicken box, a thermos, a lead pipe, a briefcase, or a backpack. The bomb tech prefers to play the game with no spectators because each disclosed move is removed from his arsenal and added to the opponent's. The bomb technicians accepted our word that we would not expose important elements of their craft. Even if certain solutions or tools or bomb-building methods can be found in texts or online, we made our own decision not to add to the propagation of this information.

Something that you might not think a big risk is the willingness of the bomb technicians to allow us to put their names in a book at all. In countries outside of the United States, bomb technicians themselves have been the target of terrorism. The logic behind that is as chilling as it is simple: If the person who can defuse the bomb is eliminated, then the bomber has a greater chance of success. The trust the NYPD Bomb Squad placed in our word was an important part of what made the access they granted us to their lives so special. We hope we have lived up to it.

—*Richard Esposito and Ted Gerstein*
New York, 2006

BOOK ONE

The Red Zone

1

TIMES SQUARE, NEW YORK
DECEMBER 31, 2003, 4:31 P.M.

Detective Brian Hearn, on the verge of forty-three, stood at the center of the Times Square crowd and blessed it with his Irish smile.

Hearn, to look at him, actually resembled a block of weathered granite. From his steel-and-snow brush-cut hair straight down to his boots, at five foot eleven and 190 pounds, he was a neatly squared off, if well-worn, man.

His sometimes-moody blue eyes sparkled tonight. The ashen stubble that marked the end of his frequent midnight tours was gone. He was close shaven and his cheeks had appeared, colorful as Christmas ornaments. The overall effect was to ruin his familiar sternness and replace it with a perfectly good face. During the rest of the 225 tours of duty he worked in an average year, at its daily best Hearn's face was marked by a squint and waves of worry surfing his broad forehead. He was always hunting for something wrong with a technique, a protocol, a tool, a rule; just about anything that a police chief, equipment salesman, or private contractor—anyone in fact who was not actually a bomb technician with hands-on experience—had come up with and tried to foist onto the squad.

"The Job has changed. It really has changed. There is really too much of that 'me' generation that's hanging around."

Detective Second Grade Brian Joseph Hearn was old. *Viejo.* Worn. A curmudgeon. He had been pinned to the hands of the police clock for more than twenty years. If you have not lived on a duty chart year in and year out, appearing for work mornings, evenings, midnights, and weekends, you might find it curious to consider someone old when his forty-third birthday was still twenty-seven days away. It takes some explaining. These are long years in the weather, long years examining what no one else really wants to look at. They are filled with hard days strapping on a gun belt and risking your life. Long years, and tough days, as the noir novelists are fond of saying, of picking up and putting out society's garbage. Hearn could retire with a full pension. He had served ten years out of his twenty on the Bomb Squad clock and was the third longest serving member. He was the senior man of the A Team of Squad 228. Squad 228 is the official designation of the New York City Police Department Bomb Squad.

"I grew up in Staten Island. I was born right around the corner from where I live now. I never came to the city until being on The Job. Going over The Bridge was very threatening to me."

The island where Hearn grew up is claimed by New York City, according to the city charter, but its residents view themselves as a people apart. Although the long span of the Verrazano—The Bridge, the Staten Islanders call it—has linked the borough to Brooklyn since 1964, it remains an island of ponds, of 1930s bungalows purchased from a Sears catalogue and assembled on site, of mafia mansions, golf courses, and for New York, large expanses of open land. It sits offshore, where it rises over a gray green Atlantic. When a Staten Islander heads for Manhattan to work, the Islander invariably describes the journey as one to "The City."

"It was like a small town on the south shore. It was Small Town USA. We used to pick chestnuts, go-kart race; we had a softball league."

By 2003 Hearn had become sentimental. He struggled to reconcile his sepia memories with the rush of the present. But he was not in any hurry to retire to Staten Island's idealized shores. A father of two daughters, at times he seemed a father still in search of sons. He had come to be the squad outsider, and this satisfied him. He had the pay of a sergeant, since his promotion to second- from third-grade detective. He could act like an army lifer. He was an *alter kaker*, an old head, and he saw his work in police as a craft.

"My father was a phone man, a lineman, a repairman for forty years. I was good with my hands, I like working with my hands just like my dad. I have been on the Bomb Squad since '95. We do our own thing. You keep your mouth shut."

Hearn loved a crowd and he had one tonight. All the marvelous faces of New York flashed by in a luminous dusk. It sparkled with police torches, blue strobes, and lightning white spotlights. New Year's Eve, Hearn said, was his favorite night of the year. He had prepared all morning. Before leaving the squad garage, he telephoned his wife to tell her he loved her; and yes, he said, he was wearing "the thermals." The thermals were his lucky red long johns, the ones he had worn every New Year's Eve since he joined the squad ten years earlier.

Three minutes had passed since muster at the center of Times Square's bow tie of streets. It was now 4:34 P.M., and the A Team had moved into the second half of a sixteen-hour day. There were still four more minutes before the official setting of the sun and the end of a nine-hour-and-nineteen-minute-long squirt of daylight. But in Times Square the sun's set and night's rise were overwhelmed by the jaw-dropping brilliance and the wave of sound that breaks like a frothing surf when a million voices speak excitedly and at the same time. Wearing floppy orange hats and oversized sparkling silver 2004 glasses, and flanked by Jumbo-Tron TV screens, they gathered, already dazed by loud music, as television crews and stagehands carried out the last-minute chores of checking the aluminum pipe frame and extruded aluminum seats of the bleachers for loose bolts and clearing the stage platforms of building materials. Among the owners of these voices were the proud romantics who would be married or propose marriage at the stroke of midnight. There were shimmery dancers and wild-eyed teenagers with jeans threatening their ankles. There were also the puzzled faces of young children ripening in the cool night air as they pressed against the lowest part of the barriers, where their parents had placed them for a six-hour wait. The Times Square crowd is a wonderful thing.

At its center, "The Crossroads of the World," Steve Lanoce, Bill Popper, Mike Klippel, and Supervisory Detective Sergeant Brian Coughlan assembled with Hearn on an asphalt island of calm. They were directly beneath Number One Times Square, a twenty-five-story tower that is topped with the Times Square Ball. They would begin 2004 here at the core of the "Red Zone," a point deep inside the frozen zone in which the festivities would take place. In August 1949, when the Soviet Union developed a nuclear capability, this intersection became a symbol of the mutually assured destruction policy of the Cold War. It became the brawling, seamy target of Soviet bombers and a dreaded intercontinental ballistic missile attack. Neither attack occurred. Fifty-four years later it had become a revitalized urban wonderland and it remained the bull's-eye for a terror attack.

Beneath the Waterford Crystal Times Square Ball, the A Team member personalities surfaced. Lanoce was a playful man with a perfect Five-O surf of hair. Popper was slightly dark in his demeanor. Klippel was wry, buzz-cut and edgy. Sergeant Coughlan was a perfectionist. He appeared to be underdressed tonight without his shirt, tie, suit jacket, and "squad coat," the dark three-quarter-length overcoat that completes detective division dress in the fall and winter. Hearn was himself. A reporter who had joined the team was given a police windbreaker to wear and instructed to leave his press card in his pocket and tell anyone who asked, "I am with the Bomb Squad."

Each team in the Bomb Squad also has what is called its team personality. In the case of the A Team it was relaxed, slightly goofy, but very efficient. This team would move quickly and without undue effort when it was time to move.

Beneath its feet the twenty-seven-inch-diameter, 195-pound manhole covers had been welded to their 395-pound frames. Trash cans and mailboxes had been removed from each intersection. Everything that could hide an attacker, a bomb, a gun, a biological or a chemical agent had been sealed, searched, or removed before the first reveler arrived. The crowd had for the most part obeyed the police directive to come stripped of excess baggage. The revelers carried little besides water and enthusiasm into the pens of the nine-by-six-block frozen zone. No backpacks. No alcohol. No glass. They had been herded by thousands of uniformed police officers through chutes made from 6,783 aluminum barriers and 3,087 of the familiar but now older and faded blue NYPD sawhorse barriers—a total of 47,481 feet of aluminum barriers and 43,218 feet of wooden ones. In all, the New York City Police Department Barrier Unit had set down a total of 17.18 miles of barricade, a total of 355,320 pounds of metal and wood.

In order to protect the crowd, the city had built a layered defense. First it sealed the streets and removed the "street furniture" (trash cans, etc.). Next it searched and observed crowd members at the entrance to the frozen zone. Inside, the security forces manned chemical sniffers, biological sensors, and handheld radiation wands and pagers. Undercover officers—as many as a thousand—blended into the crowd. Increasing the margins of safety were the explosive ordnance detection (EOD) canines—the Bomb Squad dogs. Peyton, a male black Labrador, and Tucker, a male yellow Labrador, were the A Team dogs. These dogs accompanied the team and sniffed for explosives each step of the way as they trotted the streets and avenues of the frozen zone.

The EOD dogs were crowd-pleasers. Hands reached out to pet them. Young women posed for pictures with them. They so often had been praised, for a job well done or for the simple reassurance they provided, that the bomb technicians sometimes referred to themselves as the dogs' assistants. The dogs had a usually unerring ability to scent ten thousand combinations of chemicals used to create explosives. But on a night like this the sensitive noses and the stamina of the dogs could be overwhelmed. The dog handlers would try to protect them against overwork by giving the dogs frequent rest periods in the quiet of their cages in the darkened compartments of the Bomb Squad response vehicles. These trucks were parked on the edge of the Red Zone.

New Year's Eve was a "slash and grab" night. Any suspicious item the team members encountered they would attack with hand tools. For rapid movement the heavy Kevlar bomb suit, the X-ray gear, water jet cannons, and a large array of other special equipment were left behind in the two trucks and one SUV that had carried the team to the scene.

Tonight the bomb technicians wore nothing more protective than long underwear, Bomb Squad golf shirts, chinos, and blue NYPD microfiber fleeces. This approach would allow them to keep up with a hectic pace, and it eliminated the chaos that would result from a man in a Kevlar suit walking a robot on an electronic leash through the crowd. The bomb technicians do not generally talk about this bare-handed approach. They do not want necessity to be confused with bravery.

"There is no set protocol as to when you wear the bomb suit. There are a lot of times when you have to go into a place where you can't wear the suit. Besides that, whether you wear the suit or not, you can be dead," Hearn explained.

There is one other reason for approaching a bomb unprotected. When there is an immediate risk to a civilian life, the Bomb Squad ethos suggests that a bomb technician take the same risk, skipping the protective gear. The techs believe this is reassuring and that it reduces the chance of a panicking victim. This maximizes the chance of success in defusing a suspicious device. If more equipment was needed, one of the response vehicles could race in with it. In seconds, they joke, knowing that seconds and bombs are a perverse mix.

There is no odor of the bravado of a warrior when the bomb technicians describe their methods. There is no action-oriented, danger-seeking adrenal drumbeat. An officer who had those characteristics would not have made it through the selection process and unanimous vote required for acceptance into the squad. Bomb technicians do not run toward danger. They walk there, straddle it, and when they step back from it, they also do so slowly, never taking their eyes off of the suspicious package or device. Bomb suits are designed with this in mind. The maximum armor is in the front. The maximum cushion for a blow that could knock the occupant down is in the back, protecting the spine.

Mike Klippel had ventured away. He returned after giving an operational security reminder to Transit Bureau police officers stationed in a trailer at Forty-fourth Street. These officers were the radio and video link to the hundreds of officers working belowground on subway lines leading into the Times Square station and at the station's thirteen entrances. "If anything happens, and you need us, don't transmit your message over the radio. Call my cell phone, and remember, do not use the words 'Bomb Squad,'" Klippel told had told them.

With Klippel back, the A Team split in two and the security sweeps began. Six minutes had passed since the team's arrival. Hearn, Klippel, and Hearn's dog, Tucker, had one set of assignments. Lanoce, Popper, and their dog, Peyton, had another. Everyone had a gas mask and each team had a radiation detector.

Each team member had his favorite or lucky hand tool nestled among the knives, clippers, hooks, scalpels, tape, crimpers, and forceps they all carried on their belts, in their pockets, and in the small nylon pouches attached to their belts. One man also carried a record of municipal inefficiency—his paycheck, which arrived dated December 2004. No one in America can survive for two weeks between paychecks, so this headache would need to be resolved before his next pay period, in January 2004.

There were twenty-six bomb technicians and fourteen dogs on duty. There were two teams in Times Square and one team stationed north of the festivities. That team regularly patrolled the perimeter of the zone. Another team stood ready in Brooklyn. Another was in the Bronx, and two were kept in reserve at the Bomb Squad's Greenwich Village base. The design of their deployment enabled the teams outside the frozen zone to avoid the crowds and fly under lights and sirens down sealed-off streets to reach a "suspicious package" anywhere in the city's five boroughs.

A second reporter had joined Lieutenant Mark Torre. The commanding officer of the Bomb Squad, Torre would spend his night directing its movements. The squad seemed a small one for such an immense task.

"When the squad is called out," Torre explained, "it means that the entire nation's and the city's prevention resources, border checks, airline checks, and the entire intelligence gathering apparatus, have failed. At that point it is 'Break glass, call Bomb Squad.' It only takes a small group to respond even to dozens of suspicious packages or actual devices.

"And when the threat turns out to be nothing, we are put back in our box." Elite units, he said, became unwieldy and inefficient when they become too large. At that point there are too many team members to keep them training hard enough and running on "bomb jobs" and security sweeps. This is the necessary combination of hard work and hard training required to keep their knowledge current and their skills sharp. It is the only guarantee that each squad member is at a constant state of readiness. Torre's is the logic that drives this breed of specialists to excel at their mission. Nationwide there are about 2500 full-time bomb technicians among roughly 700,000 law officers. In their way of thinking they are last responders—the last line of defense before an explosion occurs and the ambulance teams, doctors, aid workers, and morgue attendants have to be brought in. Their mission requires them to confront an unknown and lethal enemy.

Think of it this way:

When an X-ray technician takes a picture and a doctor interprets it, they are studying a light- and dark-gray transparency in a climate-controlled room. It is a picture of a part of the human body each has seen thousands of times before. When a bomb technician takes a picture of a bomb, he is taking it lying on his stomach in the middle of a street and peering through his own sweat. When he gets up to his knees, stands, and then waddles back to his partner to interpret it, what they study is an image of something that neither of them has seen before. The bomb tech faces a unique challenge; his interpretation of the gray tones of an X-ray is the first interpretation of them.

This is a key reason why rank carries very little weight in the field. The technician's life depends on the technician's interpretation. Nothing more and nothing less. In the squad room itself, the squad operates in a limited democracy, with Lieutenant Torre holding a commander's absolute right to veto. In the field, neither Torre, nor his sergeants, nor a police executive who arrives as the technicians are at work, can interfere with the approach to the suspicious device.

2

A Squad Room in New York
Greenwich Village, December 31, 2003, 3:29 p.m.

Lieutenant Mark Torre had been at his scarred and cluttered desk for several weeks now with very little rest. The forty-year–old commander looked up, wiped his unruly black hair from his forehead, and with his eyes sparkling at a possible challenge said:

"Are thirty-three bomb technicians enough? Does thirty-three sound slender? You don't need a thousand techs, you don't need a thousand dogs, and you don't need a thousand dog handlers. What you need is dedication."

Short, agile, but carrying a small paunch as he stood at the gates of middle age, Torre was an engineer. He was precise by disposition, by education, and by constant practice. He could be ruthlessly Jesuitical in his logic. And he could snap the fuzed top off a small explosive at fifteen yards with a single shot from a sidearm.

Torre had a fierce passion to protect his squad members. When a decision passed down through the police chain-of-command could add an unnecessary risk to their well-being, this passion would burst into operatic rage. That rage was satisfying and provided amusement for the squad, but for a lieutenant to win an argument with chiefs requires guile and tact. Although he was short of both qualities, Torre would complete his arias, fight down his anger, and apply himself to finding viable but diplomatic solutions to the challenges. His checks and balances on his temperament required that before he wrote a memo, proposed a plan, or attended a meeting, he would closet himself with his sergeants and his senior men and allow them to take apart his logic and help him to put it back together. They then would rehearse his presentation.

On December 31 Torre's day began in the early morning hours. The senior men and sergeants came in through his open door and flopped down on the black vinyl couch and set of dusty club chairs that surrounded his desk. They had gathered to make last-minute adjustments to the duty chart for the final night of the squad's hundred-year anniversary. Torre had worked on this duty chart since early November. For the forty-eight hours that had begun at midnight of the thirtieth every squad member had been assigned a double tour of duty. But the chart Torre had constructed made sure that everyone who was married got time off with his family during the holiday weeks from Thanksgiving to New Year's Day. The younger, single guys could get their time later. Some may not have liked his logic, but it was hard to fault it. Still, there was no way around the fact that the duty chart was stretched thin. It had been that way since September 11, 2001. Since then the squad had needed a full presence at every major public event, including the opening day of the baseball season, the opening session of the United Nations, the entire U.S. Open tennis tournament, and every Fleet Week, Memorial Day weekend, and Thanksgiving Day parade.

The tempo of the run-up to New Year's had been fierce. It began in November with a concern that bombers would target the shoppers as they began their annual holiday journey up the aisles of malls and department stores. This had been prompted by convincing intelligence reports that indicated terrorists were shifting from attacks on hard targets—embassies, landmarks, and official buildings—to soft targets—hotels, shopping centers, and rail lines. The concern escalated in mid-December. As the retail sales numbers began to roll in strong, New York, Los Angeles, Washington, D.C., and Las Vegas were alerted by federal authorities to an intelligence "packet" of very specific information. Pieces of that packet and other intelligence were reported in the news media:

- *December 9—New York.* U.S. counterterrorism officials say that new overseas information has surfaced concerning attacks on subways. New information has also surfaced concerning attacks on malls.
- *December 10—Washington.* ". . . the concerns will likely intensify as we head toward Christmas."
- *December 19—New York.* Police officials deny there is a specific, credible threat of a suicide bomber attack on the city. . . . U.S. officials confirm the threat and say, "We are in the process of trying to determine its credibility."
- *December 21—Washington.* Tom Ridge, head of the Department of Homeland Security, elevates the national threat level from yellow to orange. He cites a volume of threat-related intelligence higher than at any time since September 11.
- *December 24.* Authorities fear terrorists have infiltrated foreign airline crews. Their intent is to hijack a plane in flight and use it to kill "more than 100,000 people." Times Square is at the top of the target list.

With the escalating tension, there came repeated meetings at Police Headquarters. Torre reviewed for his superior officers the squad's capabilities and discussed how the squad would mesh with other agencies should a full-scale response to a threat become necessary.

It had been two months of a steady, draining, constant pressure. Torre had to be sure that no squad member's eye, instinct, or intuition let a single suspicious event go by without a complete and thorough check. They had to be right 100 percent of the time. A bomber only had to be lucky once. Tonight, despite the months of pressure on his men, the commanding officer of the Bomb Squad—the COBS—knew he had to put his protective instincts aside and pull out all the stops to give the city the highest level of protection he could. His precautions included making mutual aid arrangements with bomb squads in surrounding counties—on Long Island, in Westchester, and in New Jersey. They all agreed to rush in any teams they could spare should they be needed.

"If you think of a bomb as a large gun, that can shoot a lot of people, all at once, without you even being there to pull the trigger, it makes kind of a handy tool for terrorists," Torre says.

"They have lots of weapons at their disposal, but certainly bombs are very effective at accomplishing their mission; they're very dramatic, they get a lot of media attention, and as a result, they certainly put people on edge."

Media attention spreads fear, and the spreading of fear is the terrorist's primary immediate objective. It is of far greater importance than the spreading of death and destruction. It is fear that can create the conditions of chaos that terrorists seek. Despite more than a hundred years of resounding historical evidence that the terrorist will virtually always fail in his mission to use violence to achieve political change, each new group mixed a new batch of ideologically charged explosives in the hope that it could. For a bomber, a New Year's Eve crowd watched over by a very large media presence made a perfect venue.

3

TIMES SQUARE
DECEMBER 31, 2003, 6:31 P.M.

Torre wheeled his pristine black Ford Crown Vic into the frozen zone and found a spot for it on Fifty-third Street. He parked there in the side-street shadow of the Marriott Marquis Hotel, inside of which the police had set up their command center. Torre adjusted himself into comfort behind the wheel and settled in for a wait. Through the windshield, Seventh Avenue's broad, black length shimmered in refracted neon.

The Crown Vic interior was dark gray and as comfortable as a men's club. It was fitted with a police equipment package of telephones and radios and switches and buttons for the flashing strobe grill lights, the traditional revolving red ball on the dash, the sirens, and the hailer. Highlights of hilarity now bounced off its smoke gray tinted windows. The lieutenant's car was part of a twenty-vehicle Detective Division support "package." To any developing danger, this convoy could rapidly transport with all their gear several dozen Crime Scene Unit technicians, Arson and Explosion investigators, lab technicians, senior detectives, and field commanders, including lieutenants, captains, inspectors, and assistant chiefs. While the convoy moved, the seat of Command and

Control would remain implacable in the hotel suites, and the top chiefs would be kept from getting too close to any scene. This strict procedure maintained discipline and a chain of command from the lowliest uninformed rookie to the top of the department. It was designed to minimize casualties, prevent panic, and preserve control of the outcome of a crisis, and it's a reason NYPD officers in the past had suffered fewer casualties than personnel from other rescue agencies.

Inside the Crown Vic, chatter and static spit from across the high-frequency police radio bands in the 800-megahertz range. Reports from the Traffic Division took up airtime with discussions of tows, plate checks, and traffic flow. Torre squeezed the wheel in frustration as he waited through these for cell phone and radio calls from his own sergeants and senior men. He repeatedly took out and replaced a cigar from his breast pocket. It would stay unlit until the night was over. Instead, he grimaced and muttered and listened for his two squads in Times Square to begin their sweeps. Beside him in the passenger seat—the recorder's seat, in police radio car terminology—was Detective Tommy "Sack" Sullivan, who made notations in his steno pad as the calls from the runs and sweeps started to come in. When the time came for Torre to brief the senior commanders, the notes would serve to refresh the lieutenant's memory.

The first sweep for the A Team was at the Millennium Hotel on Broadway, a regular layover for commercial airline flight crews. Hearn's Lab, Tucker, leapt from the doors through the lobby and into the gift shop. Nothing, not a sniff.

"I trust the dog," Hearn said as he turned on his heel to walk out.

Leaving the hotel, the team came across an unattended black and orange knapsack across the street. Klippel headed for the package. Hearn turned to the crowd and said:

"Back up, back up please. Clear this area while we make sure everything is safe here."

"I'm just gonna 'slash and run,' " Klippel said.

"Slash and run" should not be taken literally. Unless Klippel could run faster than an explosive blast wave—somewhere between 3000 and more than 20,000 feet per second, a blast would win. It would suck the air from his lungs, the lungs from his chest, and then turn around and try to shove it all back in again. It is a crushing force. In the highly improbable event that he survived the most lethal effects of a blast at close range, he would suffer permanent hearing loss, vertigo, lung tissue damage, and a lifelong trauma. "Slash and run" is simply a term of art. It captures the combination of common sense, experience, a cop's sense of the environment, plus all the training and science that go into the bomb technician's job—and it allows the technician to reach into a suspicious bag with a pocketknife and a prayer.

Klippel sliced the knapsack. He extracted a blanket and a water bottle and placed the slashed package and its former contents prominently in plain view. It was a success. It was a relief. It was deflating. It was time to move on.

Klippel used the Handie-Talkie feature on his Nextel cellular phone to report the outcome of the incident to Sergeant Coughlan. The sergeant was supervising the A Team's actions from behind the wheel of his Ford Explorer, an SUV in NYPD white and blue livery, parked at the southern perimeter of the Red Zone. Coughlan then used his cellular phone to notify the lieutenant.

"Nothing at the first hotel. Just a knapsack on the way out, Loo," he reported. Sullivan took notes.

By now the A team was on its way to perform another sweep. This one was at the 1,282-seat Al Hirschfeld Theatre just over three blocks away on Forty-fifth between Eighth and Ninth Avenues, a Byzantine confection erected in 1923. New York's mayor, billionaire Michael Bloomberg, would begin ringing in his New Year there by attending the night's performance of a musical called *Wonderful Town.*

Hearn's half of the A Team began to walk there, straight up the middle of the Broadway. The dogs were cheered. Hearn waved his arms and brightly bellowed, "Louder," as he winged up his arms to orchestrate cheers from all sides.

"I'm having fun tonight," he said. "I like it. You meet good people. I have a good life. You see, in this job, you see everything, it's amazing. It's like when we testify in court: You hear from us on everything from fireworks to a device; we go from one gamut to another. Same thing with being a policeman; you go from death to birth."

Flashlights aided Tucker as the ten-year-old Lab bounded and wagged and drooled through the theater aisles. A detective from the mayoral detail arrived and was told the theater was clear. He would secure it against any entry until the mayor arrived. Hearn, Klippel, and Tucker headed a few doors east on Forty-fifth, toward the Milford Plaza. They then walked a little more than another city block east to the Ambassador Hotel. Both hotel sweeps were routine. They had been planned in advance and posted earlier in the week on a white assignment sheet hung from a clipboard at the entrance to the squad room kitchen. The sheet contained just the bare bones of the dozens of assignments for New Year's Eve. It did not include sensitive details as to who might be staying at a hotel or whether some specific intelligence had singled it out as a high-risk location.

"We go in cold," said Brian Hearn. "We aren't told anything."

In the car, Lieutenant Torre explained this point of view. "A bomb is a bomb. From our point of view, we shouldn't care whose bomb it is, or to some degree what size it is. Our job is to stop it from blowing up.

"Whatever intelligence we had about who planted it didn't stop it from getting planted—so fundamentally, it failed."

What the bomb technicians crave is information useful to prevent a bomb from exploding. They crave news of the types of devices typically or currently planted by various terrorists. They care about who planted a device insofar as it might allow them to anticipate how the device might have been constructed. To get that information they probe law enforcement databases, swap pictures, and build replicas of successful terrorist devices to familiarize themselves with the mechanisms.

"A bomb," the lieutenant said, "is a large gun. If you can see it, it can see you; if it can see you, it can kill you."

It is six-thirty, and Hearn's team heads back to Number One Times Square, at the direction of Sergeant Coughlan. Unsure why he was being summoned, Hearn explained, "It's a job; you go where you are told."

On the way, two young women reached over the barriers to pet Tucker. A young man asked whether a dog could smell a bullet. Whenever the massed bodies became so thick that crossing an intersection seemed impossible, Hearn shouted, "Dog coming through," and the crowd parted. It was a few blocks, but it was a long walk. Along the way, a police officer's radiation monitor alarm went off, and Hearn, Klippel, and Tucker were diverted to investigate. The Emergency Service Unit officer who wore it said, "I bet someone took a barium test today."

"Did anyone take a barium test?" shouted Hearn.

A man sheepishly answered yes. He was isolated from the crowd, the radiation detector was placed next to him, and its digital readout soared. When it was pointed at the larger crowd, the numbers retreated. Smiles. Handshakes. Good-bye. Situation cleared.

Sergeant Coughlan had summoned his team after receiving a call from the FBI. He had used his cell phone rather than his police radio to limit the chance of his call being overheard. He had kept Hearn in the dark rather than take a chance that even a stray bit of information over the cell phones could be overheard. So it was not until everyone was gathered beneath the scaffolding that wrapped the base of Number One Times Square that he gave the full report: The FBI had received information through Canadian authorities that there might be poison gas inside the pyrotechnics in New York. The pyrotechnics were the fireworks that would mark the arrival of the New Year. They were housed on the roof of Number One Times Square. The team would climb to the top of the 395-foot building to investigate.

4

The Past
1 Police Plaza, December 31, 1982, 9:30 p.m.

Tony Senft had been on the Bomb Squad for just about two years, and a cop for just about seven, when the call from Police Headquarters came in to the squad room at 9:30 p.m. on New Year's Eve 1982. He answered it, and a chain of events began that altered his molecules and his brain waves, and cost him his eyesight and his dexterity.

"I lost my right eye. I was broken here and here." He pointed to his face as he spoke. "I've had face . . . facial work done; I've had new eardrums put in. They cut your ears down and skin graft new eardrums in. My right hip was broken. My whole face was reconstructed. I'm a little scarred up. I suffer a severe case of vertigo and a severe case of post-traumatic stress disorder.

"I crouched over, and that was the end of it. All I remember is a loud explosion. According to witnesses, I was blown fifteen feet off the ground."

Senft's call to action had come on crisp, fatally dark New York night. For a little over a decade the city had been the target of a set of sustained bombing campaigns by groups including antiwar extremists, black nationalists, right-wing anti-Castro groups, right-wing Zionists of the Jewish Defense League, foreign nationalist factions from Croatia, Puerto Rican separatists, and countless other groups with a grudge and access to explosives. The wave of explosions had begun in earnest in 1970, a year in which there had been 384 bombs planted in New York City. These were planted largely by antiwar activists, but they became part of a national wave of terror.

In the sixteen months between January 1969 and April 1970 the federal government recorded more than 35,129 bomb threats, 4,330 actual bombings (the vast majority small "incendiary" or fire bombs), 1,175 attempted bombings, and 43 lives lost from bombings across the United States. Over time the political motivations behind the individual bombings by domestic groups began to blur. As pressure from the law thinned their ranks, the remnants of several groups evolved and found common ground in each other's revolutionary struggle and new strength in their combined resources. The bombings that were against the war, against the draft, and for black separatism by now were simply against society and all it represented.

Many of the bombs were triggered by the Weathermen—later called the Weather Underground—a far-left student activist group committed to militant overthrow of the U.S. government; by the New World Liberation Front, comprised of survivors of the Symbionese Liberation Army, an urban guerrilla group dedicated to the same goal; and by various splinter groups sharing some and disagreeing on other elements of this ideology. Most of the lives lost were office workers, diners, and travelers.

At the same time these bombing campaigns were under way, other domestic terrorists targeted police. The Black Liberation Army and Black Panther groups used assassination as their weapon, gunning down cops in New York, Georgia, Connecticut, Chicago, and New Jersey.

Determined to stand out—and succeeding—were the practiced bombers of the Fuerzas Armadas de Liberación Nacional

Puertorriqueña—the FALN. Their bombs were reliable and they were very often deadly. With each attack came their clear and simple message—the Armed Forces of the Puerto Rican Nation wanted a Puerto Rico free from American "colonial oppression." An unspoken part of the message was a desire to align the island with Castro's Cuba. While the messages of the other bombers became lost in a glutinous mass of arguments, the FALN, in the terms of modern political spin doctors, stayed on message.

At 9:27 P.M. on New Year's Eve, the FALN had struck. A bomb had exploded at FBI Headquarters. Within three minutes the Bomb Squad rookie Senft had taken the call from Headquarters, and he and his senior partner, Richie Pastorella, were rolling. Senft's explosive ordnance detection canine, Hi-Hat, was with them as they took the straight shot downtown from the squad room to the scene of the blast, 26 Federal Plaza, headquarters for the FBI New York Field Division.

They pulled up short in their blue and white Bomb Squad station wagon. Their headlights revealed that several of the forty-one stories of the glass facade of 26 Federal had curtained down in a crystal rain onto the fortunately empty streets.

"Obviously we saw devastation," Senft recalled. "There were several stories of glass on the ground. There were Emergency Service Squad people there. There were fire engines.

"Our department priest came and blessed us. . . . I was the handler. Richie was the technician. It was simple. We found the seat of the bomb, and thank God there wasn't a secondary device to kill or maim anybody.

"About fifteen minutes later a second device . . . a . . . second explosion. That was at Police Headquarters. We took the station wagon. What we found there was more devastation. We found a uniformed man down on the ground. His leg was blown off. He was ripped up like someone took a box cutter and shredded his face. His name was Rocco Pascarella. We really didn't even know he was a uniformed man until we found his weapon, that's how badly he was injured."

Twenty-eight minutes had passed since the call. Senft and Pastorella were on adrenaline-fueled time. Their body clocks had gone from resting in the squad room, to fast on the run downtown, to faster on the four-block screech to this redbrick plaza in front of Police Headquarters. Fast, fast, fast, faster. Time was being squeezed. Until finally it would stop.

"The doors on Police Headquarters were all twisted . . . like Superman came in and twisted all the steel," Senft said. "I mean, that's exactly what it appeared to be when we were there that evening." At the same time, he explained, the big S on his own chest was shrinking fast.

Officer Rocco Pascarella, meanwhile, blinded, missing a leg, bleeding profusely, managed to make his own superhuman effort.

"This guy gets up on his elbows, as severely injured as he is, and says to us, 'It's in a Kentucky Fried Chicken box.' Now, imagine a man who's that severely injured getting on his elbows to warn someone else to be safe. That's what that man did."

Within the next five minutes, a third device exploded. This one shook the foundation of the Federal Courthouse in Cadman Plaza, Brooklyn, directly across the East River from Police Headquarters and the Manhattan office of the FBI, and a half a mile away.

"I don't know how far exactly the distance is between Police Headquarters and the Cadman Plaza, but it shook the glass above our heads," Senft said.

The Fuerzas Armadas de Liberación Nacional was eight years into its bombing campaign. It had already claimed credit for more than 110 bombings in New York and 30 others in cities that included Chicago, Philadelphia, and San Francisco. Its deadliest bomb had killed four and wounded fifty-three in 1975 when it exploded inside Fraunces Tavern off Wall Street, during the lunch hour.

It was 9:55 P.M. when the bomb at Police Headquarters exploded. It was 10:00 when the one in Brooklyn shattered the glass in the courthouse. Time, which had been going fast, fast, faster, was now on a slow crawl through the carnage. The magnitude of the event was growing and starting to sink in. For Senft, the second hand was creeping across the dial of his wristwatch. Five minutes had become an eternity; the events were so large, each one was so arresting, that twenty years later when he described the time between the Police Headquarters explosion and the Brooklyn explosion, it still felt to Senft like twenty minutes had elapsed between the two bombings. In listening to him, you also realized that for him no time at all had passed between when he felt the final blast and his recounting of it in your presence.

An Emergency Service officer had come over. " 'We think we have a little package on the side of the building. We want you to check it,' " Senft recalled him saying.

"So I brought the dog and searched it. I put the dog on that and he didn't sit. It turned out to be McDonald's hamburgers. There was no indication of any explosive material."

Less then two more minutes had passed. Senft had already notified his supervisory sergeant, Hugh McGowan, who was at home for the holiday evening. McGowan had begun his own set of radio and telephone calls to squad members.

Now a sergeant from the Intelligence Division was summoning Senft, Pastorella, and Hi-Hat. The time was 10:04.

The location, the ESU cop said, was the federal prosecutor's office at One St. Andrews Plaza, a few hundred yards of redbrick away. The reason: Two bombs had been found there.

The bombers had chosen well. The intersecting lower Manhattan blocks and nearby Brooklyn plaza held the FBI offices; the city, state, and federal court complexes; a church; Police Head-quarters; a city jail; and a federal prison. It was a compact piece of geography containing all the apparatus of state, law, and justice that they were rebelling against. The targets and the timing of the attack on New Year's Eve were designed for symbolic value and to bring maximum attention to their demand for Puerto Rican independence. The FALN was not averse to inflicting civilian casualties, but in this case, such casualties would have detracted from their goal. So the deserted streets of official Manhattan were the perfect landscape.

When Senft, Pastorella, and Hi-Hat arrived at the U.S. Attorney's Office, they found the two bombs resting against columns about thirty or forty feet apart. The bombs were concealed in shoe box–sized bundles wrapped in newspaper.

"I put Hi-Hat on the first package," Senft said. "He snapped his head back and sat down. Because he was doing his job, I fed him.

"I looked into the package. There were four sticks of dyna-mite, a slew of wires, a pocket watch, and apparently there was a blasting cap, which I didn't see at the time.

"We put a bomb blanket over it. Went to the other package. Same thing. We had two packages working at the same time, approximately eight sticks of dynamite. Twenty feet. We were wearing fire-retardant jumpsuits that said 'BOMB SQUAD' on the back. We went and we put our bomb suits on."

Senft and Pastorella did not, however, put on the heavy Kevlar hooded helmets. "We made a critical decision that night not to put on the helmets. We felt the helmets were inferior. They would fog up. We had a cream but that didn't work. We felt it would be more dangerous to have the helmets on than to not have the helmets on."

The dog's job was over. Senft put Hi-Hat behind a wall for safety until another Bomb Squad detective could come over to take care of him.

"And we went to the one package. My partner knelt down. I crouched over, and that was the end of it. All I remember is a loud explosion. According to witnesses, I was blown fifteen feet in the air. He was blown back. We were both on fire."

In a movie, at this point the hero—clothing torn, face grimy—gets up after having been blown back by the bomb, grabs a gun, and goes out to hunt down the bomber. At this point, Detective Tony Senft, Shield Number 160, and Detective Richie Pastorella, Shield Number 1527, had begun a very long journey home.

5

The Story of New Year's Eve 1982 was the squad's operational history lesson for tonight. The explosions that critically injured Senft and Pastorella were a reason Lieutenant Torre's deployment of units across the city was a necessity. To predict where an attack could take place—in Times Square, for maximum casualties, or at some landmark that seemed a softer target, for maximum symbolic effect—was impossible.

The idea that poison gas would be unleashed when fireworks bloomed at midnight was as unlikely upon examination as it had seemed fiendish at first glance. The intense heat and light of the explosions would neutralize any chemicals or biological agents.

But in a post–September 11, 2001, national atmosphere, nothing was too absurd: not anthrax-laden crop dusters attacking Manhattan, or bombers attacking obscure malls, or armies of al Qaeda sleeper agents rising up in the night, or thousands of millions of dollars budgeted for untried gadgets designed to protect the unprotectable.

There was also genuine risk. The police and FBI adopted the

only wise approach: a zero-tolerance stance on threats. Each was taken seriously, each run down.

FBI Supervisory Special Agent Bill Zinnikas—weapons of mass destruction coordinator, according to his business card—arrived beneath Number One Times Square to brief Sergeant Coughlan and his team. Zinnikas sported a salt-and-pepper mustache and a demeanor reminiscent of Peter Falk's character Columbo, as well as a job title the likes of which would not have existed just a few years earlier.

Zinnikas said that the Royal Canadian Mounted Police had passed on a bit of threat information: A man in Toronto had called the Mounties and claimed that his friend in Hungary told him there was poison gas in the fireworks; not in Times Square, just "in New York."

Sergeant Coughlan took a moment to alert the security detail at the Statue of Liberty, where a second fireworks display was planned. He then informed Lieutenant Torre.

Torre's tension filled the Crown Vic like a veil of cigar smoke. "This is nuts, nuts," he said, turning his head to his aide, Tommy Sullivan. Every bomb technician knew why the scheme could not work, so no other explanation was needed. Torre would now have to walk the report up his chain of command.

At the foot of One Times Square, Zinnikas remembered something, and he dipped back into his vehicle to get it. He extracted a MultiRae Plus. The MultiRae Plus is the Cadillac of explosive and chemical detection protection. Rugged, encased in bright yellow rubber, and lithium ion battery–powered, the MultiRae is an "assay device," a microsensor that weighs in at just sixteen ounces and uses an array of photoionization sensors and electrochemical cells to analyze the air. It samples for the presence of volatile gases that indicate a chemical or explosive threat. It can do so rapidly and repetitively; sucking air and pulling the gases across a lightbulb, the heat and light of which break up the sample into its components. If the gases indicate a blood agent, blister agent, or nerve agent, the technician on the scene will know immediately. By plugging the assay device into a laptop a neat digital log containing the evidence could be switched across the Internet and downloaded to a database outside the area of attack.

The response to a chemical or biological attack, like the threat itself, is designed to be initially invisible. No alarm bells. No lights and sirens. Instead, health officials, decontamination teams, and medical teams encircle an area and bring potential victims out of the Red Zone into quarantine zones. As the evacuation gets under way, previously selected command sites go operational. They and the quarantine areas are upwind of a threat. Each has one way in and one way out. Both are heavily guarded. Containment is the first step—stopping the threat from spreading from person to person—a real concern in the case of several biological agents, such as anthrax.

In Times Square the uniformed cops manning the metal and wood barriers would don their gas masks and begin using the paths formed by their barricades to rapidly push a million people to safety.

For the bomb techs, the possibility of contamination was another risk to be confronted in shirtsleeves. The time it would take to put on biohazard gear, squeeze into cramped elevators, and climb the metal catwalks to the top of the twenty-five-story tower would pretty much run out the clock. The risk, as Senft and Pastorella had learned, is all a part of the duty chart, the shift, and The Job.

They were a team of fifteen at the foot of the tower. The professionals included Arson and Explosion detectives; Emergency Service Unit officers with their machine guns; Fire Department Hazardous Materials men; and FBI Special Agent Bomb Technician Bill Davitch, the assigned liaison to the NYPD Bomb Squad. Among them also was Christopher Carlino, the Grucci fireworks company's chief technician.

On Fifty-third Street the Crown Vic idled quietly as Torre and his aide waited for Coughlan's cell phone calls and listened for pertinent radio traffic. Torre knew as well as Grucci's Chief Technician Carlino that there was no chance that the fireworks had been tampered with since they were made, shipped, and installed. He knew they had been securely under guard by police since the day they arrived at Times Square from Grucci's nearby factory. In the past he had held a side job at Grucci to supplement his police salary, so Torre also knew how carefully the firm controlled access to their explosives before they left their warehouses. He knew how unlikely it was that this incident would pose any risk to the public, but he knew responding to it posed a risk, however small, of an accidental injury to his men.

"My job is to first protect my men. They are good men, they know what to do and they will do it. But it is my job to make sure they are not made to take stupid risks," Torre explained. The night was busy enough without the stress of this job, and the explaining of it to Torre's superiors. But he and Coughlan both knew they would respond to it exactly as if it were real, and even though they knew the answers as to where the fireworks were made, how they were installed, and how they were secured, they would ask each of those questions again.

Coughlan was a perfectionist and Torre knew he would execute a flawless response. Any slim chance of a real threat would be ruled out before Coughlan logged the incident as unfounded and moved his team back out onto the streets, where they would be needed.

"Is there any possible connection between the explosives and Hungary?" Torre asked, addressing first the source of the threat information.

"No, there is no connection between the fireworks and Hungary," Coughlan answered. "None." Grucci's fireworks did not originate there and had not been stored there.

"Have the fireworks been guarded, have they been secured?" Torre asked.

"Yes, the fireworks have been secured and under guard since yesterday." They each knew the answer, but they each had asked the question again, Coughlan at the scene, and Torre of Coughlan. And soon Torre's superiors would ask him. Detective work is a methodical, repetitive business. The rechecking to see if all questions have been asked was standard police procedure.

"What are you going to do now?" Torre asked.

"I guess we will go to the top and check it out."

"Keep me posted."

"I better head upstairs," Torre said and started to ease out from behind the wheel. He stepped from the car to the curb, and as he did he adjusted his gun, his sport coat over it, and the knot of his tie. Then he walked into the hotel. A bright, brassy elevator took him up to the command center. Chiefs of Detectives, Counterterrorism, and Intelligence collected him, and he briefed them. Men used to crisis, they sipped coffee and water and smiled as they listened. No one was going to bite a fingernail over this.

Coughlan, Lanoce, Popper, the Arson experts, the Grucci technician, two FBI agents, and seven others headed up to the top of One Times Square. There is a moment of surprise at the discovery that the building is simply a shell. Anything inside—walls, floors, doors—not needed to anchor a skin of advertising to the exterior walls has been removed. It is this skin that gives the tower its world-famous brilliance.

The elevators are small. It takes two trips to bring all the experts to the room just below the ball.

The ball itself is something special. A geodesic dome that weighs 1070 pounds, it contains 504 Waterford Crystal triangles and is illuminated by 600 lightbulbs, 96 strobe lights, and 90 rotating mirrors. It was assembled and installed by Neil Mazzella of Hudson Scenic Studios. It has ten seconds of fame each year.

Two flights of stairs lead up to a square mesh catwalk—it's called the lower roof—right beneath a final platform at the base of the ball, draped in a web of thick and thin electrical cable and fitted with a video monitor to keep an electronic eye on the ball above. From the platform, one by one the bomb techs climbed a ladder the rest of the way. The telephone calls between Coughlan and Torre continued.

"Yes, they definitely have been sealed since they left the Grucci factory," Coughlan reported.

"Double-check," Torre said. He half whispered so the chiefs wouldn't overhear.

"Yes, they definitely have been under surveillance since they arrived," Coughlan replied.

The MultiRae, he added, showed no indication of a poison. But three sample fireworks were removed and taken for testing at a mobile lab operating in the frozen zone below. There were 1257 individual pyrotechnics scheduled to explode in the midnight display. "Will anybody miss three shells?" It was an idle question.

"Yes. Mr. Grucci," Carlino replied.

The report from the mobile lab was negative. The long climb down began.

No sooner were they down than the entire squad was on the move. An unverified report had come in from the Special Operations Division dispatcher. A caller stated, the dispatcher said, that there were bombs packed inside one or some of the cars in the 250-space parking garage of a Times Square hotel.

As his team made its way to this search, Torre reached for a bottle of water. He had arrived at the Bomb Squad as a young sergeant a week after the February 1993 attack on the World Trade Center. One thousand five hundred pounds of urea nitrate mix, stuffed in a rental van and driven into the garage of one of the towers, had blown a hole several stories deep through the garage and claimed several lives. A new enemy was using increasingly aggressive tactics. Like the few flakes of snow that fell that day, the event's significance quickly melted away: For the most part the public forgot about it; for the most part counterterrorism experts missed its implications for an escalating war against the United States. The significance was not lost on the bomb techs. For them it spelled out the increased magnitude of the devices they might have to render harmless and the number of lives that could be lost if they failed.

6

The Surgeon Does His Job
CHINATOWN, DECEMBER 31, 1982, 9:36 P.M.

The ambulance sirens had barely faded. Nine minutes had passed since the explosion. Senft and Pastorella were on their way to Bellevue Hospital. Sergeant Charlie Wells, Shield Number 2636, pulled up. He had headed in to The City from his in-laws' celebration on Staten Island. "I get the radio, put it on, and now there's an explosion at Headquarters, which is Rocco losing his leg.

"So I jump in the car and I'm racing for Manhattan."

"At some point, the one in Brooklyn goes off. Now I hear the guy from Emergency yelling to Central, 'Explosion! And!! Injuries!' The dispatcher asks him how many members of the service are injured. He goes like eleven or something.

"So, I know: Man, it's Richie and Tony that are there. They're our guys. They know what to do. Right, yeah.

"So I'm thinking, 'All right, the bomb was still sitting there. They got the bomb blanket on it. They're off suiting up or something and the Emergency guys are hanging around smoking and standing too close as usual and it goes. So they got some smoke in their eyes.' So that's what I'm thinking. Then I get there."

Sirens and lights—rescue rigs—were running back and forth across the river. The crime scene smelled of burned flesh and smoldering clothing and the odor of too many cigarettes. It was a familiar greeting to Wells. So were the blood, and the gauze, and the remains of first aid kits.

Wells had come to the PD in October 1968, six months after he left Viet Nam. His tour in the Third Marines had been as a tunnel rat and an explosives demolition man, a demo man. In 1967 he had spent thirty days under siege in a place called Leather Neck Square, up north by the demilitarized zone. His small unit had been surrounded by a battalion of Viet Cong regulars—at the time a new sight for U.S. forces used to fighting guerrillas farther south. The unit was pounded each night by their mortars and artillery. In the morning, Wells would climb out of his hole and clear the unexploded shells. Then he crawled back in and waited for the next volley.

Wells's time in Viet Nam was served under constant fire. He probed and swept for mines as company after company of marines around him were decimated each time they were ordered, morning after morning, day after day, company after company, to march up what he described as the same damned road. The road was freshly mined each night and waiting for them each morning. Wells greeted those who remained from yesterday's unit, noticed the newest members, shook his head, and then began to sweep the road. He had no electronic metal detector. He probed the earth with a bayonet, listening for metal touching metal and ignorant of the nonmetallic mines the Russians had developed and sent to Viet Nam. The zone he worked was soon so filled with deaths that the Marine Corps simply started over: They changed the name of the zone from Prairie Four to Hickory One.

"Yeah so, I figured if Charlie didn't get me, I was ahead, and nothing else was going to get me. You have to be overconfident, or how can you go out day after day?" Wells, when he said this, was fifty-five. He had already defused dozens of bombs and was as fit, lean, tough, and tough-minded as Martin Sheen's character in *Apocalypse Now*. Wells was the Surgeon. He and his partner had been summoned to deal with the remaining time bombs.

"Frank DeCecco gets there the same time—to this little alley between the U.S. Attorney's Office and the church. We're the first two there.

"Our sergeant tells us there's one bomb left. There it is right there against the thing that holds the building up.

"'So what's the plan?' the sergeant, Hugh McGowan, asked.

"So I say, 'Me and Frank will take that.' So we go over there and look and there was a lot of blood and skin and whatnot.

"Richie had one of these detective rings, which are pretty substantial, heavy. I saw it on the ground there. It was, like, egg-shaped. So I don't know for good luck or for safekeeping, instead of leaving it in a puddle of blood, I take it. I put it on my finger. So I'm actually wearing his ring when I take the fifth bomb apart."

This fifth device, like the other devices that night, was in a Kentucky Fried Chicken box, wrapped in newspaper: thirty-one pages from the New York *Daily News*. They concealed four sticks of dynamite, wires, a blasting cap, and a pocket watch wrapped in a paper bag.

Wells approached. What he faced was a Hang Fire, a bomb with a timer that had run down, completing the electrical circuit that should have triggered a blast. In this case, although the metal clock hand rested on a metal contact point—a screw set so that it protruded through the watch face and wired to complete the electrical circuit—a malfunction somewhere in the loop between battery and blasting cap had caused the device to fail. These malfunctions were unpredictable, and a wrong move could complete the circuit. This, Wells figured, was what had happened to Senft and Pastorella.

During his ten years on the Bomb Squad, Wells had so far rendered safe seventy-five explosive and incendiary devices.

According to Police Department records, they had included three Jewish Defense League pipe bombs placed at the UN when the Security Council met with the PLO, and many placed by the FALN. He had conducted post-blast investigations into the 1975 LaGuardia Airport bombing that killed eleven and was believed linked to Croatian "freedom fighters," and the Fraunces Tavern 1976 FALN bombing that killed six. Wells knew what he was doing. He produced a scalpel.

It was eleven o'clock, 2300 hours, when he donned the MK II Galt bomb suit and approached the package. According to the police record of the incident:

> 10. After several approaches . . . it was decided to hand enter and attempt to render safe the device. The newspaper was cut away a layer at a time until a Kentucky Fried Chicken box was encountered. This chicken box was then entered and found to contain four (4) sticks of Hercules Dynamite. Further inspection revealed that a Hercules electric blasting cap or detonator was inserted into one of the four (4) dynamite sticks. . . .
>
> 11. Next, the brown paper bag was opened and found to contain a timing device consisting of a Westclox pocket watch wired to a 9 volt transistor battery.

"It was a painstaking operation. To sum up our procedure, we used a scalpel to slit this newspaper package open layer by layer, being careful not to tilt the package or cause any unnecessary movement.

"Subsequently we examined the timing mechanism on a volt ohm meter and determined that there was a loose connection where one of the wires connected to one of the alligator clips. We determined you could move this package horizontally, but if moved vertically, a positive contact would occur, causing the device to explode."

Wells left the scene. He headed to the hospital to check in on the uniformed cop, Rocco Pascarella, and take down a statement of his recollection of the explosion at Police Headquarters. Wells could and would bear witness that the device had pretty much exploded in Pascarella's face with only the slightest touch by the officer. From the hospital, Wells went to the squad room and began to type up his incident reports; he remembers smoking another pack in an endless line of cigarettes. As the pages piled up beside his typewriter, he became satisfied that he had set down everything pertinent. Pascarella, Pastorella, and Senft, he reflected, were wrapped in bandages, their pain for the moment dulled by intravenous morphine, and their feeble signs of life monitored constantly. Wells and his colleagues now would hunt down their attackers.

7

TIMES SQUARE
DECEMBER 31, 2003, 10:30 P.M.

"**H**ow do we know that there are bombs in the parking garage?" Lieutenant Torre asked.

"Actually we don't," Coughlan said. The original report, he explained, came from a guest. Headed to the lobby, the guest had met a stranger in the elevator and the stranger had told him it might be a good idea to "stay out of the elevator." Hotel security had passed on the information to police.

Asked whether the hotel would shut down the garage when the sweep was completed—ensuring that if no bomb was found, none would be brought in after the squad left.

"No, Boss," Coughlan said as his telephone call continued. "They do not plan to secure the garage when we are done."

"So there is really no point to this at all," Torre replied. This, he said, was a classic problem with sweeps. Everyone wanted the sweep. But no one wanted to then freeze the swept area from traffic. It is the equivalent of buying an umbrella and then puncturing a few holes in it before venturing out into a thunder shower.

When they arrived at the hotel, the A Team split up again. One team headed to the mechanical rooms for the elevator, the other to the two-story garage. They intended to make this search quick, dirty, and done.

"Don't worry, Boss," Coughlan said. "Hearn says he has got it under control."

"Ask him to report direct."

"Ten-four."

Hearn's team walked each floor of the garage, and on each Tucker was unleashed and pointed from car to car. A commercial garage is a damp, gray world of rebar and poured concrete, tinged with the smell of fumes, spilled coffee, soda, chips, and whatever else is dropped on the floor, locked in a trunk, or picked up by a tire. By the time he was done searching, Tucker's sense of smell was shot.

Hearn phoned in to Torre.

"All done, Boss."

"The dogs checked, Brian?"

"Of course, Boss."

The lieutenant paced the command center as he spoke.

By the time the A Team exited the hotel into the pleasant forty-degree night, it was eleven-fifteen. People had begun to hang out of windows. Cyndi Lauper sang "At Last." She then invited the revelers to join her in singing "Until You Come Back to Me (That's What I'm Gonna Do)."

11:15. Time was starting to move fast. Brian worked the crowd, a maestro of the street orchestra.

"Come on, louder. Happy New Year!" Hearn stretched the word. Laaaaaaaaaaaaoooouuddddddddddeer.

"Come on, you came all the way here and that's the best you can do?"

11:30. Confetti started to stream from windows. Dr. Dre filled the JumboTron.

11:56. Hearn, Klippel, Popper, and Lanoce telephoned home.

"If something happens now, there is nothing we can do about it, except go down and pick up the pieces," Hearn said.

Nothing did. Lieutenant Torre lit his cigar, called his bride, rode the elevator to the street, and enjoyed the temperate overnight breeze. By morning sixty-five sanitation workers had picked up a very different set of pieces: Twenty-eight tons of party hats, noisemakers, confetti, and paper streamers were hauled off in the big gray-streaked white trucks that looked as grimy as gulls as they waddled away weighed down with the festive scraps in their bellies. The trash cans went back in place. The streets were swept and watered. The barriers were collected and the city slept late.

8

Senft's Long Journey Home

Each time Detective First Grade Tony Senft turns on his television set he takes the risk that a stray piece of news will transport him back to that moment twenty-three years earlier when he faced a bomb for the first and last time. His long road back began in a hospital bed. It will continue until the day he dies, with another bout of vertigo or post-traumatic stress always around the corner.

After thirty days in a hospital, Senft sat on his couch for ten months without moving.

"Loud noises really hurt him. Bright lights hurt him. He really couldn't do too much and he really couldn't walk that much," his son, Brian Senft, remembers. "He needed someone to help him walk to the bathroom, and the bathroom was right there in his room. After a while of just bed rest, he made it to the couch."

Vulnerable. Defeated. Senft had become an invalid. He felt self-pity and he felt useless. His wife wanted her husband back— not Tony the hero, not Tony the detective, not Tony the bomb technician, but Tony Senft, the man. His children wanted their father back. For a long time, Senft refused them.

"I was in trouble, I was in real trouble. I went and got some help. I worked on things. Thank goodness that my marriage was intact prior to getting seriously injured, and it's still intact today, thank God."

Senft's wife, Carole, forced him into the Police Department Self Support Group. One of the first persons he met was a Puerto Rican officer, Angel Poggi. Poggi was one of the FALN's first victims. On December 11, 1974, Poggi, twenty-two, was maimed and blinded by an explosive booby trap. He had been lured to an abandoned tenement building by a false report of a dead body on the premises. Afterward, the FALN apologized, saying it had not meant to maim a Puerto Rican officer. For Senft, meeting Poggi was an awakening. He no longer felt alone. He felt needed. He became active in the Police Self Support Group, and later he became its president.

"When I look back at New Year's Eve of 1982," he says, "there's a couple of lessons: You realize that you're not invincible. You realize that you're vulnerable. And, most important, I realized it was my lucky day, because I survived. There's police officers out in this country that are very, very severely injured, who have to live off a respirator, who are crippled and can't do the things that I can do, that can't see their children get married.

"I'm fortunate, I have grandchildren—two more on the way—I have a son and a daughter-in-law that are both on the Police Department. Matter of fact, my son Brian made me very proud. He's now junior man in the Bomb Squad."

"I was awake," Brian Senft remembers. He was twelve at the time his father was injured. "It was New Year's Eve so I was trying to stay awake to see the ball drop. It was me, my mother, and my younger brother.

"They showed a picture of my father and I think Richie running up a staircase. They were in their jumpsuits. The back of the jumpsuit said 'BOMB SQUAD.'

"The phone calls started. My mother was unsure what was going on, so she told me and my brother to go to bed. I remember hearing a car pull into the driveway. When I looked out, I saw it was an unmarked police car.

"I knew something was up at that point. I knew it wasn't good. When a police car pulls up in front of the house, it's not good. It's bad.

"They took us into Bellevue in the morning. I remember pulling up and there were maybe fifteen cops in front of the door. They made a big circle around us because the press was trying to get at us and the lights were flashing and everything in the world. The cops surrounded us and just rushed us in, up to the room."

Brian followed his father onto the police. One day he drove home to ask his father's permission to join the Bomb Squad.

"I said, 'Brian, if that's what you want to do, then you go do it,'" Tony Senft says now. "I was very proud. Obviously I want him to be safe, but I'm confident that my son is much, much safer where he is than when he was an undercover narcotics cop."

Brian remembers asking for his application to join the squad.

"They just looked at me kind of weird and said, 'Does your father know you're here?' I said, 'Yes.'"

Brian Senft's presence in the squad today is a reminder of how police work is a family affair. At the bottom of the Bomb Squad Roll Call for each week there is the notation: "Rank: Detective. Name: Senft. Assignment: Mayors Exempt."

Tony Senft is not retired. He remains on the roster by an exemption granted in 1983 by Edward I. Koch, then mayor of New York.

BOOK TWO

Who Are These Guys?

1

SPRINT REPORT 1305 HOURS
BOMB SQUAD JOB #001, 2004

"UNDERNEATH WHITE AUTO—[CALLER] STS PACK-
AGE IS ATTACHED TO HIS AUTO—SOMETHING—
UNDERNEATH—HAS ELECTRICAL—TAPE AROUND
IT—BOMB SQUAD RESPOND TO LOC—"

Listening to the excited radio traffic, Kenny Dean and Paulie
Perricone had heard enough. The two young techs had just
finished up a security sweep. They notified Bomb Squad Base,
tossed their gear back into their response truck, pointed it east,
and headed out to Whitestone, Queens, under lights and siren. It
appeared someone had rigged a homemade bomb to the undercarriage of a man's car. The new year had begun.

Their sergeant, Mike Walsh, signed out at Bomb Squad Base
and also headed to Queens. The new guys were determined to
get there first and have something accomplished before their boss
arrived.

"We had done a marathon; worked the overnight on New

Year's Eve into New Year's Day; started at three P.M., worked until seven A.M., and then began a day tour. The job came in at five
minutes to two, just before we were scheduled to go off," said
Perricone afterward. He and Dean, along with seven other new-
comers, had joined the squad in February 2002. It had been a
massive influx of new blood for such a small unit; a unit that had
had less than 225 members in its first one hundred years. They
had been rushed into place to bolster a squad depleted by a wave
of post-9/11 retirements. After the World Trade Center attack,
many of the most senior squad members had been faced with a
choice. They had completed a year fat with hard-earned overtime, and if they elected to retire, their pension would be figured
against the swollen earnings. If they elected to stay, they would
later retire on a much smaller pension. Security and family came
first, and eleven sets of retirement papers were sent to Police
Headquarters.

"We were brand-new. On the way there I called my buddy
working on Emergency Service that day, and he says to me,
'Paulie, you know that I open everything and I'm the last guy to
call the Bomb Squad unnecessarily, but if I had to guess what a
mercury switch looked like . . . this would be it.' So we had a bit
of pucker action on the way there.

"This was the first time. We were a little nervous, but Kenny
and I were a little excited to have a real bomb. We shot over quick;
I suited up Kenny quick—and I wanted to have at least a picture
in our hands before anybody showed up. Kenny went down and
took an X-ray, and you could see a mercury switch, a battery, you
could see what looked like a load. The can was packed.

"It was just as we were peeling open the X-ray that Sergeant
Walsh arrived. I peeled it open and we were all 'Oh, shit, look at
that.'"

The suspicious package was a Red Bull energy beverage can.
The X-ray showed it was packed with match heads and attached
to the car's gas line. Starting the car was supposed to trigger the

switch and complete the circuit that ignited the match heads—a crude incendiary device designed to set fire to the car's fuel supply.

Perricone and Dean set up their water disrupter, loaded a shotgun shell, and pulled the trigger. The force of the shell pushed a jet of water, hard as steel and at the speed of a bullet, straight into the heart of the improvised bomb. The speed and force of the strike was faster than the device itself. The water severed the power supply, disrupted the electrical circuit, and sprayed parts of the device all over the front lawn of the attacker's intended victim. Before its switch had been able to flip and send the message of destruction along its electrical path, the bomb had been rendered safe. It took a split second.

"Now, we have been on for twenty-five hours. And after we collect all this evidence, we have to go to the lab and voucher all of it. Both of us were slap happy and neither of us could type by the time we got over to the lab. It was pretty funny to us, but then, we were exhausted."

2

Bomb Squad Base is a suite of three shabby rooms behind a plain beige steel door on the second floor of a Greenwich Village police precinct. A large, finned, khaki green military bomb hangs nose down from the ceiling above it. Mischievous eyes and a red and white sawtooth grin painted on the nose point the way inside. Behind the door the mood was relaxed.

Lieutenant Mark Torre was at his desk sipping his morning coffee from an oversized dark blue Bomb Squad mug. He had a steel watch on his left wrist and a gold wedding band on his left hand. The year's first pile of paper was already in front of him. A pen rested on the top sheet. Winter light came in through small, streaked, aluminum-framed windows. Behind Torre the American flag and the Police Department flag rode on their staffs, the bases of which were covered by a clutter of parts, tools, training manuals, videotapes, and memorabilia. Above Torre's head on the NYPD-blue walls were five official portraits. The portraits were of the police commissioner, Raymond Kelly; the first deputy commissioner, George Grasso; the chief of department, Joseph Esposito; the chief of detectives, George

Brown; and the chief of the Field Investigation Division, Dennis McCarthy.

Paulie Perricone and Kenny Dean sat outside in the squad room. They were finishing up their paperwork on the energy drink bomb. The most prominent feature of a police squad room is always its collection of scarred desks and broken-backed swivel chairs. The Bomb Squad's was no exception. There was also a wall of lockers covered with every imaginable police warning or quip that could be reduced to a sticker- or decal-sized cliché. A clipboard of upcoming security assignments was nailed to the wall at the door frame to the kitchen. The squad sign-in book rested on top of a battered two-drawer file cabinet just inside the front door. The sign-in book was a thick green ledger with hand-drawn columns containing a neat record of each sign-in and sign-out for meals, sweeps, and runs, as well as for the beginning and end of each tour.

The commercial coffeemaker was on inside the kitchen, pushing piping hot water through the grinds. Every hour or so the standing coffee would be tossed and a fresh pot brewed. It was the squad's pride that it had the freshest, strongest coffee of any Police Department office, including that of the police commissioner himself.

The kitchen served as conference room, confessional, dining room, TV room, and study hall. It held a fridge, a stove, a cutting board, a dishwasher, a VCR and large-screen TV, and like the mess on a ship, it was home to all the gossip that was a part of the life of a squad. At the far end, a metal pipe coatrack was hung with uniforms, should they be needed. A collection of seven or eight bright blue swivel chairs surrounded a long conference table. Everything was functional. Everything was battered.

Two flights of metal stairs down from the squad offices was the basement. Detective Joe Putkowski could usually be found there tinkering with practice devices amid gray metal shelves filled with bound histories of many past cases and cardboard boxes of many others. Joe had the battered ears and scarred-over cheekbones of the champion boxer he had been. He had the twinkling ice blue eyes of the earnest man that he had become.

Kenny, a tall, gentle man with a soft, husky voice, stepped into the lieutenant's office. He sat on the edge of the black vinyl couch that was jammed against one wall. Joe Putkowski wandered in and got comfortable on the other side of it. His knuckles rested comfortably in his lap. Paulie stood in the doorway. His gold shield and Glock automatic were clipped to his belt. It was time for the postmortem.

"Right up until the picture came back we were sure it was a hoax," Kenny said. "It comes back and I see the battery, the switch, the filler, and the hot wire." He handed over a pale gray and milky white X-ray picture to Torre.

The energy drink bomb that Dean and Perricone had rendered safe was a bomb attached to the undercarriage of a car, not a car bomb. Car bombs are designed to cause mass casualties and mass terror. The car is stuffed with explosives and becomes the container for the bomb; its metal becomes the shrapnel traveling at an ungodly velocity into whatever flesh or bone it can find.

Bombs attached to cars are the devices of assassins: mobsters, spouses, competing businessmen, CIA operatives, terrorists, and political opponents. They are devices of vengeance. The victim in this case was an Italian-American man who the Arson and Explosion Squad said had been singled out for revenge. This is a story as old as the squad itself, which had its beginnings in 1903 as the five-man Italian Squad. The Italian Squad had been formed by the Police Department to quell a wave of extortion bombing against Italian immigrants by the Black Hand, a parasitical secret society of criminals whose members had emigrated from Sicily and Naples. The reason for targeting this particular man in 2004 was unclear. It would be the job of Arson and Explosion and the precinct detectives to figure that out. The squad's remaining task was to review the procedures used to defeat the bomb and see if a safer or more efficient approach could have been used.

Kenny explained the device. Its trigger mechanism was designed so that when the car door was opened and the front seat sat in, a motion switch was flipped and a jolt of electricity snapped down a hot wire stripped of insulation and rigged over the fuel line. The idea was that the sparks would ignite the fuel and send the flames down into the gas tank, triggering a satisfyingly lethal explosion.

"I'm not sure it would have worked," Torre said.

Joe Putkowski didn't think it would have ignited either.

Lieutenant Torre added that it seemed doubtful that even if the switch had worked, the match heads would have burned hot enough to ignite the fuel. In any case, the younger men had taken the proper precautions. Joe might have just cut the wire. He was old school. New school taught bomb techs to defuse devices from a distance whenever possible and go hands-on only when necessary. That was why they used the water disrupter.

At 10:12 the Special Operations Division radio crackled. A suspicious person had been spotted as he opened the trunk of a parked white sedan, dropped something in it, slammed it shut, and departed, leaving the keys dangling from the trunk lock. Brian Senft, Jeff Oberdier, Sergeant Brian Coughlan, and Sergeant Bobby Duke stood up, stretched, and went into in motion.

Even as Duke signed the team out, the dark blue garage doors below them motored open. A dog was taken from his kennel and loaded into his cage inside a truck. Gear was checked. Coughlan headed to his Ford SUV. Traffic was halted on the quiet side street. The response vehicle, as the trucks are called, was backed out. The two-vehicle convoy dodged through Greenwich Village and raced across the Williamsburg Bridge into Brooklyn.

Yellow police tape was strung to clearly define an inner and outer perimeter. The outer one was marked by lines of tape strung several hundred feet in all directions from the vehicle. The inner one was a compact rectangle about a hundred feet away from the car. Emergency Service officers stood there ready to assist in suiting up the bomb tech if needed. The operating procedure called for the ESU officers to assist in getting the tech into his suit and to deploy their heavy weapons if needed for force protection. A big diesel ESU truck was parked between the team and the target, completing the preparations by providing maximum uprange protection should the car downrange suddenly explode.

Senft led his dog from its cage. He let him familiarize himself with the smells of the scene. Jeff Oberdier, the squad's training officer, stood beside him, his Air Force EOD wings with their dull gleam on his left lapel. An Ohio farmer, Jeff had been an Air Force EOD man—an explosive ordnance disposal technician— before joining the NYPD and coming to the squad. He would go downrange with Senft, who was the newest man on the squad.

Senft and Jeff and the dog took their walk down to the car. Everyone else stood ready. The dog sniffed around—hood, sides, trunk lid, and bumpers. Senft handed Jeff his coat and crawled under the car for a look. Everything was clear. At 10:30 ESU opened the trunk. At 10:45 Coughlan informed the base, "We're good." Back to Manhattan. No lights. No sirens. A quiet drive home. There had been no explosives, but that was not a surprise to the techs. Similar scenarios would be repeated over and over again each day throughout the year. One of the challenges for the bomb techs was to keep repetition from dulling their senses to the reality that the device only had to be real once.

It was two days into the New Year and the workload was already coming in steadily. In 2003 there had been 2634 bomb runs, sweeps, and disposals. There was no reason to expect a sharp reduction in 2004. As jobs came in and were disposed of, the most important would be noted in department Unusual Occurrence Reports—a Form 151. The "151s" were circulated throughout the Detective Division. On January 6 the twelfth case report was added to a clipboard in the kitchen:

Det. Sqd. BOMB SQ
Day/Date of Original Report: 1/6/04
Time: 2100 hours.
Place of Occurrence and Type of Premise: C/O Stillwell
   & Ave V
Crime/Condition: Hoax Device
Case #: 012/04

On 1/6/04 at approx. 2100 hrs the Bomb Squad
was requested to respond . . . to a suspicious package on
a phone booth . . . A 911 call was received from an
anonymous caller stating a bomb was at the location.
Subsequent investigation . . . determined that the
package, which consisted of a black plastic cased 6 volt
battery, wrapped in brown plastic packing tape, pieces of
brown, black, green and clear wire, a black watch body
with a white face, and a piece of circuit board was
deliberately configured to resemble an improvised
explosive device. The above evidence was removed . . .
for latent print analysis and the case was referred to [the
precinct detectives].

The job of a detective is to detect. The job of a bomb technician is to stop a bomb from going off. Despite the fact that the Bomb Squad officers hold the rank of detective, they prefer the title "bomb technician." Their job stops with the field investigation of the suspicious package or device. For the tech each day starts with a clean desk. The introspection of figuring out who did it and why; the building of case folders; the slogging through the time-consuming construction of a court case is left to the other detectives in the Detective Bureau.

The bomb technician, like other highly skilled mechanics— microsurgeons, test pilots, Formula One race car mechanics, or astronauts—is completely focused on his field. Practice is second nature. Reading technical journals is a steady activity. Reviewing each bomb that explodes anywhere in the world is the subject of daily squad discussion. Duplicating and disarming the most inter- esting devices goes without saying. Testing new tools; improving techniques; attending seminars on robot handling, disruption techniques, large vehicle bombs, booby traps, and the use of vari- ous kinds of detonators and explosives are the subjects of sched- ules posted on a chalkboard. The board also includes notices and sign-up lists for training with other units in the Police Depart- ment and with bomb squads in neighboring jurisdictions. Bomb technicians work in teams, and those teams have to be as smooth and efficient as a NASCAR pit crew. Jeff Oberdier, the training officer, kept track of who needed to be sent down to the Haz- ardous Devices School for the triennial recertification of basic skills. All in all, this creates a steady backbeat behind the daily calls to action.

The Bomb Squad is a part of the NYPD Detective Bureau's Forensic Investigative Division, which includes the police lab, the latent print section, the firearms analysis section, and the Crime Scene Unit. In other words, the FID is a group of field investiga- tive units backed by laboratory forensic science.

Once a device is rendered safe, the Bomb Squad role is to lend forensic support to the unit assigned to follow the case through. The squad helps Crime Scene identify and properly tag impor- tant evidence. Its members explain the technical aspects of how the device was made, why it might have been made that way, how to identify similar devices should they be found—all of the elements the detectives or intelligence officers might need to formulate an analysis, or a context. Should a court case develop, a squad member supplies the expert testimony.

The Bomb Squad prided itself in being what its members call "The Forgotten Unit." It preferred to quietly go about its job. But recently the unit had been discovered. With improvised explosive devices and terrorist attacks a daily occurrence, its members had become concerned about being tarnished by the glamour of personal risk that commentators attach to the defusing of such devices. The quiet approach—one that protects the craft of the technician from prying eyes—had become increasingly difficult to maintain. The possibility of bombings in the United States was very real, and 2004 had begun with a sudden a proliferation of "bomb experts" appearing on television, in news articles, and as lecturers.

Even inside the New York City Police Department—arguably the most sophisticated in the world—by early 2004 the commanders of various special units had begun to want to incorporate a portion of the Bomb Squad's mission into their units. They did not understand that defusing bombs was not a part-time job. It required an ethos of doing one thing, constantly and quietly and well. One commander wanted to consider using plastic explosives to blow doors off of hinges, without necessarily being aware of the refinements of shaping charges, the storage of explosives, or the need to maintain skills; not to mention what would happen when it turned out to be the wrong door, which past experience dictated would happen during a raid sooner or later. Another police boss wanted to build a unit of "explosives mitigation experts." This unit would take untried and uneducated detectives and supervisors and plunge them into the arcane world of tracking the transfer of bomb-making skills, the building of bombs, the ease with which terrorists could acquire the needed materials in hardware stores, and what equipment a Bomb Squad ought to consider using. This quixotic unit would a year later so embarrass the Police Department by its inept interaction with British bomb technicians that in 2006 the damage had still not been undone. In observing bomb technicians at work, well-meaning officials became confused about the skills behind what appeared to be done with such ease. It was a dilemma that newspaper reporters summed up, when told by earnest outsiders how to do their jobs, as a confusion of the ability to read a newspaper with the ability to write for one.

Lieutenant Torre was now forced to learn how to explain to the larger Police Department what the squad did and why they did it the way they did it. This was a struggle. Bomb techs were problem solvers, not process explainers. They preferred to hand in a job well done, rather than explain it to death and then have it go wrong on them. The idea of having to defend a turf that until now no one wanted any part of seemed strange. Worse, anyone outside the squad who learned a technique meant one more person who could accidentally share it with the enemy. While not averse to taking risks, the squad members were averse to taking unnecessary risks. Loose lips cost lives. The Bomb Squad had unexpectedly become a victim of its own silence and its refusal to welcome one and all into the "black art" of defusing devices, transporting devices, detonating devices, and the "positive use of explosives," which simply means blowing things up—doors, cars, buildings, and other explosives.

As the year went on and more bombs exploded and a Republican convention in New York loomed, a series of police executives offered Lieutenant Torre proposals to increase the NYPD Bomb Squad size. Several of these were based on ideas about what a Bomb Squad does, which included deterrence, boosting public confidence, teaching bomb awareness courses, and creating an omnipresence. Within two weeks after joining the squad, we understood the explanations of why not only were more officers unnecessary, but having too many reduced the chance that each officer would get enough time in the field—time on packages, to stay sharp. Meetings were scheduled to consider whether the squad ought to at least have another dozen dogs—at these meetings the costs of training, feeding, and housing the dogs were discussed. And Lieutenant Torre explained that the number of dogs in the squad was designed to complement the number of teams in the field. More dogs were not needed to detect bombs.

A Bomb Squad's job, its only job, was detecting bombs and rendering them safe. For this, a few dozen men and a dozen or so dogs were a far more efficient unit than one that had increased its size to encompass secondary roles. The lieutenant did not want anyone in the squad to take his eye off of the job of defusing bombs or the requirement to maintain his own skills through rigorous training. For the younger bomb technicians, the training process takes two years. It began months before any NYPD apprentice bomb tech was even sent to the U.S. Army–FBI Hazardous Devices School in Huntsville, Alabama, where he would earn his "license to die" in a five-week basic course. It continued for months afterward to ensure that the techs knew more than just enough to get blown up. Post-HDS, training was relentless, even though many of the NYPD bomb techs had already been hardened as Marines with tours in Afghanistan and the Gulf, or as Air Force EOD men, Army Rangers, and Navy SEALS, specialties where explosives detection and defusing often were at the center of the job.

In-service training was not only the job of Jeff Oberdier, it was also the job of the senior men: Sergeant Hearn, Detective Joe Putkowski, Sergeant Anthony Biondolilo, and Detective Jimmy Carrano, the range officer. Since 9/11 their jobs had become more important then ever. A unit that had seen roughly 225 officers in one hundred years had an influx of sixteen new officers in the year 2002. This meant that by 2003 more than half the squad members were in the earliest stages of their Bomb Squad careers.

3

The Senior Man

"What you see me do, you may not do yet. To you they are shortcuts. But not to me. You may first have to do it a little more by the book." Detective Second Grade Joseph Putkowski was speaking. When he began, his ice blue eyes twinkled as if he were sharing a private joke. But then they hardened and his voice became even and deadly earnest.

Joe had been speaking to a younger tech even as he was suiting himself up in a Harlem subway station. It was well after dark, but people still streamed home from work and up onto the busy sidewalks and bright lights of Lexington Avenue and 125th Street. Emergency Service had been waiting to assist him when he pulled up, and two of those officers now helped him into the Kevlar suit. Lieutenant Torre arrived and saw that the transit officers who had reported the suspicious package had not shut down service. Trains were still coming through and passengers were exiting. If this suspicious package did turn out to be a bomb, then all of this was too close for comfort. He ordered the subway officers present to clear both platforms and stop service.

"Do you guys draw straws and the short straw gets to put this suit on?" one of the ESU officers asked Joe. He was strapping on the chest plate.

"No. The short straw guy doesn't get to wear the suit," Joe laughed. "We all want to put it on."

"Loo, I think it's probably nothing," Joe told Torre. "I mean I can probably just go and cut it open, but since we're all here, we'll take some pictures first. And if the lieutenant wasn't here," Joe said sotto voce, "I would skip the suit too. But . . . rules . . ." He smiled. He now looked like a blue-eyed turtle, peering from a dull green shell.

A pulley was rigged and lines run down the stairs to the package. Once the area was clear, the ropes were used to gentle the package into position for an X-ray. The picture showed baby wipes, a bottle, and baby food. Joe went down and cut it open.

Joe was a senior man. A senior man has neither a particular rank nor an official standing. What he has is his personal authority. He doesn't need any other. He and the other senior men are the institutional memory of the art and the science of rendering bombs safe. Part oral historian, part master craftsman, and part medicine man; each represented a piece of the knowledge, tradition, and history of the squad. Each team of bomb techs, from the A Team to the F Team, that goes from Bomb Squad Base into the field has a senior man as well as a sergeant attached to it. The sergeants command. The senior men teach by example. They exhibit a confidence and deep-rooted modesty that a junior tech must someday possess. They are mentors, judges, and harsh taskmasters. They joke about the bomb scenes in Hollywood movies where the hero goes in and cuts the red wire in the nick of time, or fails to and blows up but walks away with only his clothes tattered, and then they still go in and "cut the red wire" with hand tools. They do it with the economy that only training, intuition, practice, and the experience of defusing hundreds of actual devices permits.

.　.　.

Private, quiet, a family man who walked each morning to the ferry terminal at St. George on Staten Island to come into Manhattan and face his own dragons, Detective Second Grade Joseph Putkowski had been on the Squad for fifteen years. He was its most senior member. The path laid down for him to get there was the most unusual of any member since 1940, when the squad and its protocols became fully modernized.

The Police Department faced a particularly difficult challenge in 1988: The Fire Department had a champion boxer they dared the police to beat in a charity bout. None of the known challengers seemed up to the task. The interagency rivalry was fierce.

A rookie with just twenty-one months on the job, Joe was approached by the four-star Chief of Department and asked if he thought he could do it. Joe, a former Marine champion middleweight, replied he thought he could.

If you do, you can have any assignment you want in the entire department, the chief, Robert J. Johnston, Jr., told Joe, who went on to win. He asked for the Bomb Squad. Chief Johnston was taken aback and said so. The Bomb Squad, he told Joe, was an assignment that insisted on senior officers as candidates. Joe quietly said that nonetheless it was the assignment he wanted. He would do a good job and not disappoint the chief. Chief Johnston was true to his word, and Joe was transferred into the squad on November 18, 1988.

By 2004 Joe insisted that others approach him for help. If he was not asked, it was not offered. Joe would just continue quietly practicing his own skills; re-creating bombs inside fire extinguishers and letters and then timing himself disarming them. A bout with a bomb was not one Joe or any other senior man was prepared to lose.

"We . . . have to respond to a lot of devices or events. We have to try to figure out what's inside the container. The container could be a vehicle; it could be a small box. We may have to open up the box and render the device safe by cutting a wire.

If there are lives at stake . . . we have to act right away. So we might not be able to use the tools that are assigned to us."

Whatever technology was available, a fully accomplished tech had to be able to approach a package with his two hands and a scalpel or a folding knife and have the confidence to unwrap it and defuse it. Senior techs like Joe worried that an over-reliance on technology could ultimately be the cause of a bomb tech's death.

"The best training tool I have to offer a new guy is time on the street," Joe explained to a reporter. "In the one hundred years of the Bomb Squad, we have lost six bomb technicians. We have probably approximately twenty-five members that were wounded." His other training tool was shelved in the basement. It was a history of thousands of devices successfully defused, carefully documented and kept in a set of boxes and binders and folders on the gray metal racks there.

"From the beginning in 1903 you had the Italians that used bombs for extortion. During World War One the Germans came in as saboteurs . . . the Hell's Angels . . . the Ku Klux Klan, the FALN . . . the Cubans . . . the Weather Underground, the Black Panthers. They all used explosive devices to further their cause. You can look back at their case folders and see the way they operated. In the case folder . . . or case booklet, the kids see why a device went off . . . why it didn't. . . . This is the meat and potatoes of the job. The past members of the squad, they're the very wealth of the squad. . . .

"These are the records dating back to 1918, records of prior explosive devices, prior explosions. I come down to this room about three times per week. I look at old case folders; I read old case folders. I would say if I put together all of the time I've spent down here, I've spent two years to learn about past improvised explosive devices, past explosions, how they handled past explosions, how they rendered devices safe, why devices went off, why devices didn't go off, what group set the devices off; the signatures of these different groups.

"When a young member comes into the Bomb Squad, I bring him down and I explain that here he can learn the history of improvised explosive devices; how they were made, how we rendered them safe or handled past explosions, and how the techs vouchered their evidence or did their paperwork."

To Joe, this is all a part of his discipline, like walking to the ferry. He grounds himself in his mundane day-to-day squad routines. "He will never leave five minutes early," Sergeant Anthony Biondolilo explained. He and his wife live in a modest home, they share one car, and he would walk down to the ferry, cross to Manhattan, and walk down a street to his death if his job required it.

"Joe knows if it means he has to die, he is still going to do it," Sergeant Biondolilo explained. "That is his call to duty."

4

History Lesson

New York has been bombed far more often and with far less lasting impact than might be thought.

There were 384 bombs by antiwar activists in 1970. The Puerto Rican Liberation Army, FALN, planted and detonated another 134 between 1974 and 1982. Croatian nationalists killed dozens in the mid-1970s with an airline bomb and an airport locker bomb. The Palestinian Liberation Organization has sent letter bombs to the UN. The subway has been targeted by bombers at least a dozen times, beginning the year after it was built at the turn of the twentieth century. Tens of thousands of patrons were evacuated from movie theaters when union activists bombed them over and over again. Italian shop owners were bombed relentlessly by the vermin that followed their migration to America. The Bomb Squad history spans 101 years of combating terrorism and extremism in the United States.

> My name is Salvatore Spinella. My parents were of honest station in Italy. . . . I am an American citizen fifteen years. My children, as they are big enough, all go to school. I educate my oldest daughter to be a teacher. I make a little

money. . . . Last winter I think I am prosperous. I own
houses at 314 and 316 East Eleventh Street. I lease a house
at 326 East Eleventh Street where I live. The Black Hand
come and demand $7,000. I tell them to go to hell. They
try to blow up my house. I go to the police and fight them
as well as I can. They set off another bomb; two, three, four,
five bombs. My business is ruined. My tenants leave, all but
six of thirty-two families. . . . I am a ruined man. My family live in terror day and night. There is a policeman in
front of my house. . . . How long must this endure?

—*New York Times*, July 24, 1908

The "Black Hand," a loosely organized group of thugs, mur-
derers, and gangsters, preyed on the Italian community of New
York City's Lower East Side. Their preferred tool for extortion
was dynamite.

To combat them, the police turned to its only Italian-
American detective, Giuseppe Petrosino, an immigrant from
Salerno, Sicily. He was assigned to head a new five-man unit.

Beginning in April 1905, Petrosino and his "Italian Squad," a
team of Italian-American undercover cops, arrested and deported
thousands of members of the Black Hand and reduced crime
against Italian-Americans by half. Petrosino was murdered in
March 1909 in Palermo, Sicily, where he had gone to gather intelligence about Black Hand members. His funeral was attended by
250,000 people, and the procession lasted five and a half hours. He
is the only NYPD officer killed in the line of duty outside the
United States. Someone had leaked news of his trip to the mafia.

By 1915 the squad's mission had changed. Now it was hunting German spies. Bomb Squad Sergeant George France, fluent
in German, infiltrated a cell of German saboteurs as they plotted
to dynamite ships in New York Harbor.

In 1920 the mission was anarchists. A horse cart filled with
dynamite and packed with hundreds of pounds of sash weights to

act as shrapnel exploded on Wall Street near J. P. Morgan's bank and killed some forty people. It was the nation's first large vehicle bomb. The description is one that will sound familiar to anyone who keeps up with Middle Eastern and southwest Asian conflicts.

"I saw the explosion, a column of smoke shoot up into the air, and then saw people dropping all around me, some of them with their clothing afire," one eyewitness reported.

Bomb Squad detectives were there to carry out one of the few pieces of evidence, a blackened horseshoe. They took it to some four thousand blacksmiths in hopes of finding the culprits.

In 1919 the squad intervened in a plot to dynamite St. Patrick's Cathedral. They've been called there several times since.

In 1935 the Bomb Squad prevented one of the nation's first suicide bombings. That was the year the Bomb Squad and the United States Secret Service arrested Clarence Cull before he could get close enough to the President and blow himself up.

The squad's past was not all glory. Its beginning was checkered by stints as a "Red Squad" and a "Radical Squad." Those units did not focus on the explosives either of these groups might have used. Instead the squad became a tool of intimidation. It used searches for explosives as reasons to raid the homes and meeting places of activists. It used blunt force to wreck their furniture and files. It was not above abusing the suspects. It was forced to grow more professional in 1940 when two Bomb Squad detectives where killed in a massive explosion while attempting to dismantle a suitcase bomb left at the British Pavilion at the New York World's Fair. The Irish Republican Army has always been suspected, but the case has never been closed. Prior to 1940, there was very little equipment at the disposal of bomb technicians. They had their eyes, their hands, and a pair of pliers. Since then they have worn increasingly effective body armor.

5

Paulie Perricone on this Tuesday night had a white T-shirt and a white apron on over his gun belt. He kept up his end of the conversation while moving from the four-burner stove to the knives on one of butcher blocks flanking it, the pots stacked on the other and the fridge at the end of the row. Although he was young, Paulie, thirty-six, would soon have twenty years on the job. At twenty, he could retire. Before he did, the squad members wanted him to train a replacement.

"He's a great chef." Sergeant B leaned into the kitchen to extol Paulie. Wearing a silvery tie over what we will learn is his habitual black shirt, he continued into the room and filled it with life. "We ought to do a cookbook: *One Hundred and One Years of Bomb Squad Meals.*"

Everyone felt at home in this room. A half dozen techs sprawled in swivel chairs clustered around the Plexiglas-protected top of the conference table. A couple of others leaned back onto the black vinyl cushions of a bench built against the farthest wall.

Paulie's menu featured double stuffed oven-baked pork chops,

RICHARD ESPOSITO AND TED GERSTEIN

broccoli with sauce and cauliflower without, biscuits, and iced tea. The meal started off as usual with gossip about firemen.

"Why is it they act like they are the only ones who can cook?"

"Maybe because they have nothing else to brag about since there are hardly any fires?" There were three dozen bomb techs and thirteen dogs to cover more than 2500 runs and incidents. There were about seventeen thousand firefighters. They fought 3202 serious fires in 2003. The bulk of their work—and there is much more to the job than fighting serious fires—was responding to other emergencies, from minor blazes to malicious false alarms. But the bomb techs did not count this when it came to teasing.

Around the table were Paulie, Sergeant B, Ray Clair and Andy Rea from the D Team, as well as a couple of guests from the earlier shift. At the head was Lieutenant Torre.

After dinner, inside Lieutenant Torre's office, the talk turned to suicide bombers.

"Why hasn't it happened here?" Sergeant B asked.

"They see the resources. The resources look impressive from the outside. For whatever reason, they overestimate us," speculated Lieutenant Torre.

There had been one recent attempt that could be loosely linked to overseas terrorists. It was a lucky break and an alert and persistent new immigrant that saved the city from three would-be martyrs.

On July 30, 1997, a man flagged down a passing patrol car in Park Slope and warned the officers that three men were building suicide bombs inside their apartment. He told police that they planned to strike within hours. The officers drove the man to their station house and questioned him. As his story unfolded, it became clear he was telling the truth. The FBI Joint Terrorism Task Force, an NYPD Emergency Service Unit, and the Bomb Squad were called in.

Surveillance of an apartment above the Family Car Service on

Fourth Avenue and President Street in Brooklyn confirmed that the frightening story was true. At 4:30 A.M. on July 31, as Brooklyn slept, helicopters swooped in, and heavily armed police teams burst through the apartment door. Two of the men inside attempted to reach their five pipe bombs. They were shot. The men admitted readily that they had planned to blow up the station at Flatbush and Atlantic Avenues. Trains from ten different lines stopped at that station throughout the day. The station was joined to the Atlantic Terminal of the Long Island Rail Road, a major commuter line bringing suburban workers into the city. The apartment contained materials suggesting the men were sympathetic to the terror group Hamas. What appeared to be a martyrdom letter was also found.

Hamas had never orchestrated a bombing inside the United States, and within hours it had disowned the men and their intentions. U.S. officials moved quickly to term the men lone wolves; dangerous, but based on the devices themselves, amateurs whose devices might have in the end failed to explode.

"I think we were close to a disaster," FBI Assistant Director James Kallstrom said afterward. "It didn't happen, and that's the good news."

In 2004 the subway system, hotels, and department stores in New York and the nation's other major cities remained vulnerable. Neither this 1997 incident, nor repeated warnings that transportation would be a key target had prompted an overhaul of subway security or most rail security across the country. There were studies going back to the 1960s—when the U.S. Army analyzed the damage a chemical or biological attack on the subways could cause—that pointed the way to improvements. What might have seemed a distant concern at that time was now part of a pile of information that continued to be ignored. The lack of an in-depth physical defense against an attack after September 11—more than any intelligence failure before it—was the real disaster, on par with keeping the entire fleet closely anchored in

Pearl Harbor on a sleepy Sunday morning in December. The United States now had the intelligence that it was under attack, but by January 2004 the nation remained defenseless in areas—mass transit, port security, airline cargo—where security could have been methodically improved. The New York subways alone had more than 2000 separate entrances and exits through 31,180 turnstiles at 468 stations along 230 miles of track that included 68 bridges and 14 underwater tunnels. There were few video cameras, no education of workers, and no provision of gas masks to those workers. There was no increased security at the many important weak points, including the entrances to underwater tunnels. Many of these same vulnerabilities would remain unaddressed two years later.

Amateurs like the Brooklyn men, in the very worst case, might have taken lives and prompted a temporary scare. But an organized suicide attack could send the city into a panic and the city economy into a tailspin. This was the kind of attack that Torre and Sergeant B were discussing. The two Bomb Squad bosses knew that the far more dangerous religiously devout, ideologically determined, almost exclusively Muslim homicide bomber, the *shaheed* (or martyr), who plagues the Middle East and threatens Western Europe, came well equipped and with a well-thought-out plan. The *shaheed* wears a suicide vest or belt packed with explosives and rigged in a fail-safe manner that virtually guarantees that the bomb and its cargo of nails and ball bearings will explode into mayhem and murder. Hundreds could die. Several rail lines would shut down. And the city would certainly wait in anguish for a follow-up attack.

Within a few months of January 2004, an attack in Madrid would bring home these points.

6

They claimed they did it for art, but that did not stop a massive response to the loud explosion in a three-story walkup in Red Hook, Brooklyn. The walkup was hard by the Gowanus Canal, an as yet unreclaimed industrial sewer and a historical mob dump site.

The Special Operations Division call to the squad came in at noon. The report was of a large explosion, possibly terrorist-related.

When firefighters and uniformed patrol officers responding to the blast entered the building at 217 Butler Street, they had found an assortment of small arms, ammunition, and explosives. It looked to them like a possible bomb factory, and that information was relayed to SOD, to the squad, to the FBI Joint Terrorism Task Force, and to the NYPD Intelligence Division. It appeared that a device under construction had exploded in the bomb maker's hands. A man injured by the blast, probably the bomb maker, had been transported by Emergency Medical Services under police guard to nearby Lutheran Hospital. He had suffered burns and a broken jaw.

The blast damage was limited to the area where the man had been working. But scattered in the post-blast debris was anarchist and survivalist literature, including a homemade weapons makers' bible: "A Poor Man's James Bond."

The investigation at the crime scene was already under way when Bobby Duke, Brian Hearn, and Detective Mike Klippel arrived at twelve-thirty.

"When we got there, the FD and Patrol were in the building. We went in and saw what it was that they had, and then we asked everybody to step out in front," Duke explained. A newly minted supervisory sergeant, Duke spoke quietly, sparingly, but with confidence in his sense of command. He was single, so a great deal of the squad's sexual fantasy life revolved around speculating on his exploits. He kept his secrets. He was the son of one of the greatest living detectives and detective supervisors in the NYPD, barely retired Inspector George Duke. He had a brother in narcotics and a lot to live up to, and a lot to live down if he let down the squad.

The Fire Department had already ensured that the lights and power had been turned off in the building to prevent an electronically triggered secondary blast. Duke's search team used flashlights. On the first floor was a welding shop. It was later determined that it was used by a number of artists in the Madagascar Institute, a guerrilla performance art group whose tagline was "Fear is never boring." The second and third floors of the building were a combination apartment and art studio.

Inside the apartment the search team found a homemade machine gun that resembled a World War II Sten gun, a duffel bag of rifles, 9mm ammunition and shotgun shells, three rolls of "hobby fuze" (the gunpowder-impregnated twists that are stuck into fireworks), an assortment of fireworks, seven one-pound cans of black powder, and a book on the making of zip guns.

"We were in the home of gizmo man," said Klippel when the search was completed. Gizmo Man turned out to be Christopher

Hackett, who represented the Madagascar Institute as a team member of the Brooklyn Benders. Hackett and his Brooklyn Benders designed a paintball tank, replete with compressed-air-propellant cannon, and competed against a group of FDNY fire-fighters in an event dubbed the Junkyard Wars.

"His forte was compressed air and compressed gas. The apartment contained propane tanks," Hearn said later that day. "The guy does a lot of pyrotechnics; still, he's an artist."

In a world filled with bombs, the NYPD had by 2004 witnessed an explosion of art featuring representations of bombs, guns, and the violence they caused. The art was a natural outgrowth of the pain of world events. The techs understood art as the opposite of violence. But sometimes they wished the artists would understand just what havoc the materials they worked with could cause.

This explosion had taken place when Hackett attempted to test fire a homemade black-powder-charged starter cannon.

"The fugazy starter cannon kicked like a mule," Hearn explained. Hackett, who could only speak with great pain, nonetheless was able to tell police that the blunderbuss was going to be used to fire confetti at the starting line at the opening of the "Idiotarod" challenge, a tongue-in-cheek New York version of the great annual Alaskan dogsled race, the Iditarod.

"Except, instead of dogs, it's people. Instead of Alaska, it's New York City. And instead of sleds, it's shopping carts," one of the event's founders had earlier explained to New York University's Journalism School news service, Livewire.

While the squad and the counterterror officials were pretty sure that Hackett was a whacky artist, in addition to the explosives and weapons another pile of news clippings and articles had also been found. "Ghost Stations of New York" and "Underground Tunnels" were among them, as well as maps and documents about the Brooklyn Bridge and Croton Reservoir. It took a little longer to get an explanation for those materials.

Detectives stationed at the hospital with Hackett reported that they had interviewed Hackett's friend Sasha Wizarsky and gotten an answer. She ran an organization called Dark Passage, which specialized in taking journeys into off-limits places. The maps were guides to those places. Once the answers were in hand, Deputy Chief of Counter Terrorism John Colgan addressed the media gathered outside the crime scene tape.

"It appears this gentleman is an artist and uses these devices in the course of his work," Colgan said.

Hackett had built a gun, and it had misfired, but he did it for art. The cops were sympathetic, certainly more so than any cop would have been who did not work in the art capital of the United States. But New York has remarkably tough weapons laws, and Hackett faced numerous charges. By the end of 2004 several had been dismissed, but others were still pending.

7

Fifty-three diners were injured and four men died when a lunchtime bomb exploded at 1:25 P.M. in the harborside tavern. It could have been Tel Aviv or Jerusalem. Instead it was New York's Fraunces Tavern, a relic of the colonial port at the narrow tip of lower Manhattan. Revolutionaries had met there to plot against the English. George Washington had said good-bye to his officers there on December 4, 1783. It had since been expanded and become a watering hole for Wall Street's moneyed classes and a dining club for anglers. It was a perfect target.

"Victims in the tavern restaurant and the second-floor dining room of the adjacent Anglers Club were hurled from their tables in a confusion of screams and flying debris," wrote Robert Mc-Fadden in a report spread across five of the eight front-page columns of the *New York Times* on Saturday, January 25. "Thousands of Wall Street workers thronged into the area as police cars, fire apparatus, and other emergency vehicles converged. . . . Witnesses told of victims bleeding and falling in the street outside or groping in the darkness of the shattered interior."

The carnage was America's wake-up call to a terrorist

campaign. A telephone call to the Associated Press and United Press International wire services claimed credit for the Fuerzas Armadas de Liberación Nacional Puertorriqueña, the FALN, and directed authorities to a note, three copies of which were found in telephone booths nearby:

The note said that the FALN had in the past injured no innocent person. That was not true. On December 11, 1974, Police Officer Angel Poggi, twenty-two, on his first day on the police force was lured to a booby-trapped East Harlem apartment by an

FUERZAS / ARMADAS

de LIBERACIÓN NACIONAL PUERTORRIQUEÑA

Comunique No.3   January 24, 1975

We, FALN, the Armed Forces of the Puerto Rican Nation take full responsibility for the especially detornated bomb that exploded today at Fraunces Tavern with reactionary corporate executives inside.
We did this in retaliation for the CIA ordered bomb that murdered Angel Luis Chavonnier and Eddie Ramos, two innocent young workers who suppoorted puerto Rican independence and the concienceless maiming of ten innocent persons and one beautiful Puerto Rican child six years old in a Mayaguez, Puerto Rico dining place on Saturday the eleventh of January of 1975.
The Yanki government ■ is trying to x terrorize and kill our people to intimidate us from seeking our rightful independence from colonialism. They do this in the same way as they did in Viet Nam, Guatemala, Chile, Argentina, Mexico, the Congo, Algeria and in many other places including the United States itself. But this CIA/Colby method will fail.
In our comunique number 2 we warned the North American Government that to terrorize and kill our people would mean retaliation by us. This was not an empty warning.
The bombs exploding in Puerto Rico and the United States in support of striking workers, in demand of the release of our political prisoners and our independence and to protest the Rockefeller - Kissinger visits, have avoided any injury to innocent people. The attacks on our people have been elevated vicious criminal brutality and murder of hungry hard working people. You have unleashed a storm from which you comfortable Yankis cannot escape.
Release OScar Callazo, Lolita Lebron, Rafael Cancel Miranda, Andres Figueroa Cordero, and Irving Flores.

FREEPUERTO Rico RIGHT NOW !

COMANDO GRISELIO TORRESOLA

anonymous report of a dead body inside. Poggi suffered a broken arm, facial injuries, and lost the sight in his right eye. The event did not capture lasting public attention beyond New York City itself.

"At the time, in the seventies, we had from time to time ten or eleven different terrorist groups operating simultaneously," recalled Charlie Wells, who at that time was one of the two newest members of the Bomb Squad, the first of the Viet Nam War era to join a squad of Korean War and World War II veterans.

Congressional testimony stated that from January 1969 to April 1970—sixteen months—there had been 4,330 bombings in the United States, 3335 incendiary and 975 explosive. Those devices alone claimed forty-three lives. There were 1175 attempted bombings and 35,129 reported bomb threats, according to the record of that testimony. These attacks riveted the nation, one torn asunder over war and racial inequality, and a target for foreign terrorists seeking attention to their cause.

An adolescent nation when it had entered the Viet Nam War, America seemed to grow no wiser emerging from it and from the firestorm inside its own borders. In a few short years a national amnesia settled in, and it was as if this lost war, these bombings, and dozens of cop killings by radical groups never happened.

"In 1993, when the World Trade Center was attacked and they said this is the first foreign terrorist attack on American shores, I wondered what the hell all those bombs were," Wells said. He had by then defused more than a hundred.

From 1974 through 1986 the FALN did its best to stand out from the Weathermen, the Students for a Democratic Society, the Black Liberation Army, the Black Panthers, the John Brown Anti-Klan Committee, the New Movement in Solidarity with Puerto Rican Independence and Socialism, and the Revolutionary Armed Task Force—all the slivers and factions of the radical left. The FALN did so by a maintaining a steady and successful campaign in which most of their bombs went off and most of the time the credit for the bombings was clearly attached to their cause— Puerto Rican independence.

"We were young then, although we didn't think so at the time," Wells said. "In that period from '76 to '82, we had eight guys blown up in that six-year period. And there were less than twenty guys on the squad. So that's like a Marine Corps casualty list. It was a very dangerous business to be in the Bomb Squad in those years."

The FALN campaigned night and day. By night incendiary bombs in cigarette packs were timed to explode after department stores closed, in order to cause maximum damage from the five-foot fireball that would erupt from the pocket of a jacket hanging on a crowded garment rack, before firefighters could get inside the locked store. These incendiary attacks occurred inside Macy's, Gimbel's, Ohrbach's, Lord & Taylor, Woolworth's, Korvettes, B. Altman & Co., and Bloomingdale's. Several stores were struck multiple times.

By day the FALN favored larger, difficult-to-defuse incen-diaries—pipe bombs packed with black powder, their timers sealed inside and their screw caps rubbed with powder so that the friction of unsealing them could create a spark and trigger the bomb. These time bombs exploded at Chase, Citibank, the Hilton, the GM Building, American Express, Gulf & Western, and the Pan Am Building. High-order explosive devices—bombs containing several sticks of TNT or dynamite—also took their toll. The FBI was bombed; so was the old Police Headquarters on Centre Street and so were New York Life, Bankers Trust, Metropolitan Life, and the Department of Defense offices in Manhattan. A partner in an employment agency was killed when an FALN member posing as a woman job seeker filled out an ap-plication in a fictitious name and left, forgetting her umbrella on the coatrack. The bomb was concealed inside. She did, however, leave a fingerprint, and later it would prove her undoing. But that was years later.

Five persons were injured when four FALN bombs exploded in June 1976 in downtown Chicago. On June 4, 1976, a bomb went off inside a Cook County, Chicago, building that housed the office of the city's acting mayor. One person was injured. Riots soon broke out in the city's Puerto Rican neighborhood. By the end of the day, police had shot and killed one person and eighty-one people in all had been injured. Not a glorious day.

On July 12, 1978, at 5:20 P.M. law enforcement officials got a break. There was an explosion in an Elmhurst, Queens, apartment. The Fire Department arrived quickly. They smelled gas and assumed a gas line had exploded.

But moving about in the wreckage, they spotted several lengths of galvanized pipe. The pipe was not blackened and the galvanized steel was not the stuff used for gas lines. They stepped backward from the wreckage and called for the Bomb Squad. But not before they did what firefighters are trained to do at the expense of their own lives—they checked for victims. Behind a curtain in a corner of the apartment they found the FALN master bomb maker Willie Morales. Bloodied stubs were all that remained of his hands. Half of the bomb maker's face was blown off. Morales was stretchered into an ambulance, and a detective from the nearby 110th Precinct climbed in beside him. When questioned, he refused to talk, or at least to say anything worth hearing.

"What happened in there?"

"Fuck you. Fuck yourself."

"Fuck me."

"Fuck yourself."

"It's you that are fucked, pal. You'll be wiping your ass with your elbows."

As this lively colloquial discussion ensued, Charlie Wells and his Bomb Squad colleagues began their search of the apartment. But first, the three pipe bombs the firemen had found were

82

wrapped in bomb blankets, gingerly placed in a containment vehicle, and rushed to the Bomb Squad range across the river in the Bronx. Morales had already set their timers for an attack that day. The accident occurred as he put the finishing touches on a fourth device. The containment vehicle made it to the range. The bombs were unloaded and deposited in a pit. Then the timers ran down and they detonated.

The search of the apartment yielded an assortment of cheap watches, nine-volt batteries, battery holders, spools and coils of insulated and bare copper- and tin-plated wire, machine screws, and flashbulbs used as igniters in the incendiary bombs. The detectives found sixty-six sticks of dynamite, two hundred pounds of chemicals, smokeless and black powder, and FALN letters. There was blood on the stove's knobs, and investigators speculated it had dripped there when Morales turned the gas on, possibly with his mouth after the accidental blast. He knew police and firefighters would respond, so he had tried to turn the apartment itself into a suicide bomb, ready to ignite with a stray spark when they entered.

When the search was complete, it fell to Detective Ludwig Sabatino, Shield Number 2478, of the Crime Laboratory to prepare a thirty-six-page report that compared the evidence in the apartment with the evidence from dozens of bombings claimed by the FALN. In almost every instance, right down to the color of the insulation on the wires and the manufacturer's codes stamped onto that insulation, there was a perfect match.

A federal trial was held before Judge Eugene Nickerson in the Brooklyn Federal Courthouse. The atmosphere in the court was charged. One side of the aisle was packed with cops and FBI agents, the other with FALN members, Black Liberation Army members, and Weathermen. Fistfights broke out repeatedly, Wells recalled.

The evidence was persuasive to the jury, and Morales was convicted on five charges carrying a ten-year term each. It could have been fifty years in prison if the sentences were ordered served consecutively.

"But Nickerson decided the charges could be served concurrently," Wells said. "And you know they were basically 'bomb-making without a license,' 'attempting to place bombs while wearing sneakers.'" With parole, which they had at the time, and good behavior, Morales could be out in three years. In such a charged atmosphere Wells said it was easy to understand Judge Nickerson deciding not to take the less usual step of ordering that the sentences be served consecutively. "Still, we weren't happy and we ran across to state court." The state court judge ruled that a trial on state charges would start that same day, in just a couple of hours, at one o'clock. Normally justice delayed is justice denied. In this case, had the evidence not been so clear, and the weak nature of the Queens state prosecutor not so well known, the rush to trial would have been unseemly.

In the hours he had, that prosecutor—the district attorney for Queens, John Santucci—did everything he could to prevent a trial. He also did everything he could to impact its outcome. He went so far as to pull Jack Ryan, one of his top prosecutors, off the case. He instructed his lawyers that no FALN letters or logos or reference to the group's revolutionary agenda could be mentioned in court. With snipers perched on the roofs around the court, the trial went forward. The state court judge had none of Nickerson's gentle manner. Morales was sentenced to eighty-nine years. There was a riot in the court; Morales's wife was taken into custody, and afterward Morales was sent to the Bellevue Hospital prison ward, where he was to be fitted with prosthetic devices before being sent upstate to a maximum security prison.

Morales's lawyer, Susan Tipograph, visited him dozens of times over the course of several months. After one of those visits, Morales had come into possession of a pair of eighteen-inch bolt cutters. He used them to snip away the mesh from the ward's windows. He then unrolled an ace bandage and shimmied down to within thirty feet of the sidewalk. He dropped the rest of the way, suffering a few more injuries. Three vans of FALN and Black Liberation Army members raced away with Morales inside.

It would be years before Morales was heard from again. But the FALN continued to speak through the bombs he had designed and through hostage taking. In 1979 two bombs exploded at Chicago military recruiting offices and another at the naval armory. In 1980 Carter-Mondale headquarters in Chicago were taken over by the FALN; seven workers were bound and gagged. In New York, in March 1980 the FALN bound and gagged ten inside George Bush's campaign headquarters. Also in March the FALN used a Colombian newspaper to threaten an attack on the U.S. nuclear reactors. (In 2001 authorities made it sound as though al Qaeda was the first group capable of considering such a threat. They promised to upgrade security. In some instances they have. In others they still have not. And university nuclear research facilities that used high-grade ore were still unprotected by 2006.)

On April 4, 1980, authorities got another chance at Morales. Eleven FALN members were arrested in Evanston, Illinois. A suspicious resident had tipped police to their presence after spotting a group of men in jogging suits who were standing beside a van smoking cigarettes. The arrests yielded fourteen weapons and forty-one criminal charges. The arrests led to the discovery of FALN safe houses in Wisconsin, New Jersey, and Milwaukee. Ten of the eleven were tried and convicted of "seditious conspiracy," an old law, but the one that carried the stiffest charges. One of those convicted, a new recruit named Freddie Mendez, decided to cooperate. He identified the already convicted FALN members as having participated in specific violent attacks and the planting of several bombs. He told authorities that Willie Morales had been in the Chicago area, and had held a pointer under his arm while outlining the strategy for a thwarted plan to hijack an armored car to fund FALN activities.

Following the trial, surveillance was set up on other FALN

members in the Chicago area. It continued for a full year and led authorities to more arrests and the seizure of large amounts of explosives. The surveillance enabled cops and federal agents to thwart plots to rob a Chicago Transit Authority mobile safe, to bomb military sites, and to free imprisoned FALN members from a prison, using bombs set off in public buildings as a distraction.

While eavesdropping on telephone calls at one FALN safe house, authorities soon discovered that each Tuesday a call came in from a pay phone in Mexico. The caller was Willie Morales. In order to get him to safety in Mexico after the Evanston fiasco, he had been smuggled from one radical safe house to another, until his associates managed to get him across the border.

When the location of the calls was pinned down, Mexican authorities were alerted. But they underestimated the FALN and sent just two cops in a patrol car. Morales had five armed guards. In the shoot-out, one officer was seriously wounded and the other fatally wounded. But the officers managed to kill all of Morales's bodyguards. As Morales tried to flee, a final shot from the wounded officer knocked him to the ground. The wounded officer picked up the wounded Morales, locked him in the trunk of his patrol car, and then hoisted his fatally shot fellow officer into the backseat. It was too late for the officer by the time they got him to the hospital.

The Mexican methods for dealing with cop killers and those who aid them are vengeful. They raided a nearby village known to support the FALN and killed twenty inhabitants, according to Wells.

There interrogation of Morales was no less harsh, according to the verbal report of an NYPD detective sent to observe. Detective Elmer Torro reported that the police had clipped electrodes to Morales's testicles and slowly extracted a confession from him. However, a request for an extradition to the United States was denied. Mexican politicians ruled that the "escape" charge was not covered by the extradition treaty between the two nations. But Morales was allowed to depart for Cuba, the nation he had hoped would become a free Puerto Rico's communist ally. He continued to reside there in 2006.

On December 31, 1982, Detectives Senft and Pastorella and Police Officer Rocco Pascarella were maimed by FALN bombs.

On August 11, 1999, while the legislature was in recess and the vast majority of the nation's police union leaders were attending a convention, President William Jefferson Clinton offered clemency to sixteen of the FALN terrorists, including those convicted following the Evanston arrests and also including Dylcia Pagan, Morales's wife. In the past, Clinton had granted just three of the 3042 requests for clemency before him.

It had been a year and a week since the August 7, 1998, terrorist bombings of the U.S. Embassy in Kenya and in Tanzania, and a Clinton promise to be tough on terror. Twelve U.S. citizens and thirty-nine foreign nationals had been murdered in those attacks, and more than five thousand were injured.

"These acts of terrorist violence are abhorrent. They are inhuman. We will use all the means at our disposal to bring those responsible to justice, no matter what or how long it takes," Clinton said immediately afterward.

"There will be no sanctuary for terrorists," Clinton said in announcing attacks on a purported terror training camp. "We will defend our people, our interests, and our values."

Eleven of the sixteen FALN members accepted the clemency offer, which required them only to renounce future terrorism. They walked out of their prisons on September 10, according to the *New York Times* of September 11, 1999. Several found sanctuary in Puerto Rico.

BOOK THREE

The Bomb

1

What Is a Bomb?

The job of the terrorist is to spread terror. The bomb is simply a tool. The newspaper, the television network, the radio network, the text message, and the Web site compound the power of the blast. In the twenty-first century its instant reverberation is felt around the world. Each time a significant terror bomb explodes in Israel, Kenya, Madrid, or London, in the twenty-first century global fear is the result. The terrorist's message spreads faster than the bodies can be carried to the morgue and the hospitals; faster than the scene of the blast can be washed clean.

This digital age combination of the bomb and mass media is even more important than the increasing size and lethality of the bombs modern terrorists use in enabling terrorists to punctuate religious, political, and ideological debate. By the late nineteenth century, the terrorist message as delivered by bomb or gunfire was already understood as "propaganda by deed." It has simply become more effective propaganda.

Terrorists sell ideology. With the power of bombs, they possess the power to manipulate mass media as cynically as a tabloid newspaper editor. Although the FALN failed to turn Puerto

Rico into a Cuban protectorate, to this day it is romanticized in the Puerto Rican community as an organization seeking independence for the island. The IRA maimed and injured 58,000, but in 2006 graffiti praising these "freedom fighters" graced buildings in Manhattan. Al Qaeda, or the false perception of al Qaeda, has helped spread its message to second- and third-generation Muslim immigrants, creating an al Qaeda myth that glosses over the calculated cynicism of its mass murders.

The bomb itself is a simple thing that requires very few parts: a power source, a switch, an initiator, explosives, and a container. In one form or another it has been with us for more than a thousand years. The incendiary low-explosive or high-explosive mix can be liquid, jelly, powder, or solid. It can create blinding light, searing heat, toxic gas, and blast waves moving at thousands of feet per second. Low explosives such as black powder combust relatively slowly, in a process called deflagration. They explode at subsonic speed. High explosives detonate and release their energy at supersonic speeds. The blast-wave energy released and the shocking and shearing effect that results, known as brisance, make them the most lethal bombs of all. They include nitroglycerine, dynamite, TNT, ammonium nitrate–based explosives, and military and commercial plastic explosive compositions.

High explosives are used by the ton commercially, in operations including mining, drilling, and demolition. Some 5 billion pounds are used in this manner each year. Security in this commercial sector is very strong, and theft is kept to a minimum. However, the sale of ammonium nitrate for fertilizer remains virtually unregulated, and about 18 billion tons of fertilizer-grade ammonium nitrate are produced in the United States each year. It is the same basic material used in about 98 percent of U.S. commercial explosives. Anyone can buy it with relative ease. Enough plastic explosives have been stolen or sold to nations that have supported terrorism to ensure that an ample stockpile exists outside the explosives magazines of the world's militaries and commercial firms.

Mines and hand grenades, artillery shells and mortar rounds, blocks of plastic explosive and sheets of plastic explosive—all are military ordnance that can be combined and buried, hooked to trip wires and aimed at soft spots in armor, packed into vehicles, and driven into compounds or hidden in plastic rocks to kill and maim passing troops. Used this way the ordnance is turned into new devices—improvised devices with staggering explosive power. Essentially, these improvised explosive devices are bombs made from found objects—the detritus of war, the unexploded munitions stolen or found by the side of the road.

Whether made with commercial explosives or explosive ordnance, the creation of improvised explosive devices (IEDs) is limited only by the imagination and materials at hand. IEDs can be assembled quickly. Their effective use since the mid-1980s has had a chilling effect on military and civilian transportation in Chechnya, Bosnia, Afghanistan, and Iraq. Packed into cars, trucks, backpacks, suitcases, guitar cases, birdcages, books, or letters, IEDs, especially large car bombs, are effective tools to spread the desired message. Large bombs, delivered by vehicle, by projectile, by human or boat or plane, and aimed at economic centers, civilian populations, or symbolic targets, can have a long-term impact. The most successful devices, containers, and routes for delivery have been shared among the global terror fraternities. In learning to effectively create homemade high explosives (HME), the Palestinians have sacrificed a good number of youths to maiming and death. And the bomb recipes and patterns for sewing the suicide vests have been sent in digital clips and videocassettes to political and fundamentalist extremists throughout the world's conflict zones.

The method of initiating a device or IED and setting the explosive train in motion can be as complex as a remote-controlled laser trigger, a multiple booby-trapped delay fuze, an X-ray-sensitive timer, or a combination of these incorporated with a motion switch. It also can be as simple as a rag or piece of paper soaked in flammable liquid or twisted with gunpowder, or a pressure plate set in the ground that is triggered by the weight of a vehicle driving across it. Bomb makers have refined the pressure-plate triggers so that a small vehicle can drive over them while the devices remain inert—until a heavy vehicle, a tank or a heavy military truck, tries to pass. High explosives, with all their lethality, have a fascination that even the Lawrence Livermore National Laboratory can wax poetic over. This is from the introduction to a Livermore paper "Unraveling the Mystery of Detonation":

In the brief instant of a high-explosive detonation, some remarkable events take place: the shock wave produces pressure up to 500,000 times that of Earth's atmosphere, the detonation wave travels as fast as 10 kilometers a second (32,808 feet per second), temperatures can soar to 5,500 kelvins (more than 9440.33 degrees Fahrenheit), and power approaches 20 billion watts per square centimeter (129 billion watts per square inch).

Nonetheless a pipe bomb filled with black powder and fuzed with a Timex watch, while it may only spew death at three thousand feet per second, kills as effectively if not as dramatically as an airliner filled with jet fuel or a knapsack filled with sixteen kilograms of plastic explosive and a small explosive timing pencil to detonate it. A black-powder pipe bomb with an improvised detonator has a virtue that experienced bomb makers appreciate and experienced bomb technicians respect: When well made, they are very reliable. Their use is the reason why the FALN bombing campaign was so successful.

Why do bomb technicians stand over these devices so willingly? Thirty-three times that question was asked of the NYPD Bomb Squad members and thirty-three times the Bomb Squad member's answer was the same: "Somebody has to do it."

2

A few scattered flakes of snow fell. Pools of ice spotted the sidewalks. The New York sky was a cool blue and it was very cold, that February cold that makes spring in New York seem very far away. It was 12:18 P.M. When the blast occurred, its reverberations rocked the foundations of the twin towers of the 110-story World Trade Center. Black smoke insinuated itself through the ventilation system of the buildings as the blast wave punched down through three garage levels of fourteen-inch-thick steel-reinforced concrete floors, leaving jagged, 150-foot-wide holes in each. The lights went out, and the flames from dozens of burning automobiles illuminated a hellish spectacle. Six died, and more than a thousand were injured in what would turn out to be the second large vehicle bombing in the city's history. (The first large vehicle bombing in the city—and the nation—took place at 12:01 P.M. on Tuesday, September 16, 1920. A horse-drawn wagon, filled with dynamite and metal chunks, exploded in front of the JP Morgan Bank, killing 40 and wounding 200.)

Within four hours 50,000 were evacuated from the World Trade Center towers above. For the moment, though, no one was entirely sure what had happened. Newspaper editors ran back from lunch. Reporters were dispatched to the morgue and to several hospitals. The lower Manhattan police bureaus, courthouse press rooms, and City Hall press room were emptied. The reporters went on the run to the World Trade Center site just a few blocks south and west. Fire, police, and ambulance radio dispatches clogged the airwaves.

Lieutenant Walter Boser, commanding officer of the Bomb Squad, ordered all his technicians on duty to put on their blue overalls and grab their black bags. An initial inspection team was sent racing south from the Sixth Precinct squad rooms to the Twin Towers. "It looks like a large industrial accident," Boser's detectives recall being told before they left. But no one was sure. The earliest media accounts and law enforcement telephone calls suggested the possibility of a generator explosion.

By 12:28, when the first NYPD bomb technicians arrived, the streets were gridlocked with rescue vehicles. The sidewalks were crowded with fire and police personnel. Broken glass and ice crunched underfoot. Looking back, it was a chillingly familiar scene. Already the word was spreading that it had to be a bomb. It did not smell like an electrical fire, and although no one was certain, there appeared to have been no mechanical equipment capable of exploding in the area where it appeared the blast had occurred. The time of the explosion was evident to the first firefighters laden with heavy bunker gear and Scott air packs who descended from the street-level entrance into the acrid smoke of Level B-1, where they could peer down into the epicenter of the blast on Level B-2 through a sixty-foot-wide hole punched up through the ceiling. The clocks thrown from the walls all had stopped at 12:18. These clocks would stare investigators in the face for the next several days as they worked frantically to find evidence, first to prove it was a bomb and then to learn how the bomb had been delivered. The firefighters began to pour tens of thousands of gallons of water from their unruly two-and-a-half-inch pressure hoses—the force so fierce that a team of four men was needed to direct the water onto the flames below.

Although a full inspection of the scene and the recovery of any evidence was at least a day away, it did not take more than a couple of hours for the NYPD bomb technicians; FBI special agent bomb techs; Alcohol, Tobacco and Firearms explosives experts; and retired or former bomb technicians summoned from home and other posts to conclude that only a bomb could have caused this destruction.

"They called me in to take a look and I looked," said Charlie Wells, by then a captain of police. "Yeah, I said, it looks like a big hole, but then I started to see the twisted metal, the pattern, I was pretty sure it was a bomb. What kind? they asked. A big bomb. What else could I say, I was just looking at the way things were pushed and shoved and twisted." The inspectors retreated and the firefighters continued their wet, cold, dangerous work. Lieutenant Boser ordered all hands to the scene.

On Saturday afternoon, February 27, Bomb Squad Detective Donald Sadowy and Investigator Joe Hanlin of the Bureau of Alcohol, Tobacco and Firearms led a team of six from the NYPD, ATF, and the FBI into the dark hole to begin digging for evidence. Sadowy was unaware that his mentor, Charlie Wells, had even been to the scene.

It was Sunday afternoon at 3:30 P.M. when "Everything started to come together. Most of the cars are crushed and burned but basically except for the plastic intact. Then we see debris at the edge of the crater." Sadowy had been a student in a technical school, and while not the best student in the class, he had studied auto mechanics. Something was odd about the way the parts he spotted had come apart.

"I'm looking at the differential broken open. I'm looking at a stress crack in the hardened steel pinion gear. I start picking up the pieces and rolling them together. Looking at the top, the drive train really took some hit. All the other cars are basically intact."

Sadowy and Hanlin stood on a swaying concrete ramp, forty-five feet long, twelve inches thick, and held up by steel reinforcing rods, rebar, and dipping over an open crater. Below them was the seat of the blast.

"There is a piece of twisted, charred metal, mangled chassis. I pull it up." Below that, on Level B-2, is what is now beginning to look as though it is the seat of the blast. The garage is now cold, dark, wet, and still smoldering. Sadowy takes off his glove and starts to run his finger inside the chassis rail.

"I can feel it, a diamond shape, a series of numbers and a star shape. This was the hidden VIN number." The Vehicle Identification Number was the key to hunting down the bombers.

At that moment, the FBI radio dispatcher alerted the team to clear out. A commuter train that had been stuck under the rubble for the past two days was about to be moved. That movement could trigger a further collapse. Although the rules for preserving a chain of evidence explicitly include not moving the evidence in an unauthorized manner, Sadowy decided he needed to take a risk. His team—ATF, FBI, and NYPD investigators—agreed. This piece of chassis was the only way to locate the vehicle that delivered the bomb. Now the team needed to get it out to a lab for analysis without anyone noticing what they were doing. The fear was that if the media saw their movements, the bombers would guess that a clue had been found and they would scatter. A Stokes rescue basket—a rigid, body-sized platform used in precarious situations—and two body bags were lowered down the ramp. A Crime Scene Unit station wagon backed up carefully along the crumbling garage ramp. A body bag was laid on the bottom of the basket, the seventy-six-pound chassis rail was set on top of it, and everything was covered with the second bag. Aboveground, agreed-on streets were blocked to prevent the media from following the Crime Scene wagon as it roared out of the tunnel, lights blazing and sirens blaring.

The metal was twisted and carbonized. It was impossible for the FBI and ATF agents to get anywhere in terms of reading the numbers. They were in the Police Department lab on Twentieth Street in Manhattan. One of the PD lab technicians suggested, "Let me take that inside and see what we can do." His name was Detective John Sardone. He took the piece of chassis away and closed and locked the door behind him. Inside the lab, he used a vise and heavy tools to unbend the chassis. Next, his team poured acid on it to raise the numbers. Then they photographed them.

The FBI agents were furious when they learned what the lab had done. The twisting and acid wash violated every guideline for evidence collection and preservation. Later that night, an FBI supervisor reamed Sadowy out at the top of his lungs. He did it in front of all of the agents and officers assigned to the case. He called Sadowy a cowboy and an idiot. Sadowy went home to a sleepless night and the waking nightmare that his career was over. He returned to work the next day and was greeted by cheers. "You did it! You did it! You broke the case."

Sadowy really was in no mood for any more public humiliation. He hadn't slept. He was uncertain of his career and in generally bad humor. He did not appreciate his own team members making fun of him, and he turned his back.

"No! Donald, you did it. They are making arrests right now," he recalled being told. The hidden vehicle identification number had led the FBI to a rental van company in New Jersey.

"The bosses came over, and by now I have realized this was

no joke," Sadowy recalled. At the evening briefing for the large team of investigators working on the evidence collection, the FBI supervisor who had publicly humiliated Sadowy publicly apologized to him—fully and well, Sadowy said.

The VIN number had led to a yellow Ford Econoline van, Alabama license XA 70668. It had been rented in Jersey City, New Jersey, by a man named Mohammed Salameh. He had left a $400 cash deposit in lieu of a credit card. In the hours after the bombing, Salameh filed a police report that the vehicle had been stolen, and attempted to collect his deposit from the rental agency. By Thursday Salameh and two of his accomplices were under arrest and their bomb-making material and equipment were in evidence lockers. One of the men, Ibrahim Elgabrowny, forty-two, was arrested at his Brooklyn home at 57 Prospect Park Southwest, the address used by Salameh to obtain his New York driver's license. The address was also used by El Sayyid Nosair, the man accused and acquitted of the Manhattan murder of militant Rabbi Meir Kahane three years earlier but sent to prison for twenty-two years on gun possession charges and since forgotten. A larger pattern was emerging.

The documents, tapes, and other transcripts that had been seized after the November 1990 murder of Rabbi Kahane had been left dormant in their boxes. The NYPD chief of detectives at the time ordered the case to be treated as a simple homicide. The detective commander who suspected the murder was terrorist-related, Lieutenant Ed Norris, was told to mind his own business, box all of the documents not directly related to the homicide, and ship them to the FBI. The boxes now were reopened and the documents pored over, and the Kahane case, once classified a simple homicide, could be seen as the lieutenant had envisioned it, a first hint of the terror to come. The links had emerged between Mahmud Abouhalima, one of the Trade Center bombers; Rabbi Kahane's murderer; and Omar Abdel-Rahman, the blind sheik linked to the Trade Center bombing and to a group that had murdered Egyptian President Anwar el-Sādāt. Law officers could now see that the global pattern of violence, terrorist support, and the spreading of terrorist doctrine had reached the United States. The pattern that emerged, much like the milky gray and white X-rays a bomb technician views in the field, was a pattern no one had seen before.

Sadowy, Hanlin, and the FBI set out to reconstruct the fuzing mechanism for the device. When they completed it, they had determined that the bomb makers had taken lengths of hobby fuse—the kind used in cherry bombs or other fireworks—twisted at least four fuses together, and slid the thin cable inside a length of clear surgical tubing. The tube would limit the amount of oxygen feeding the lit fuse, slowing down the rate at which it burned down. The design was meant to give the bombers plenty of time to get away. It worked. And they escaped from the underground garage before their device—one that had been constructed of 1200 pounds of urea nitrate and three large hydrogen tanks—exploded. The cost of the bomb-making materials: under $300.

When the last shovel of dirt was removed from the evidence pile, Sadowy was asked to pose with it for a symbolic picture. When he returned to his office, Lieutenant Boser summoned him and handed him the telephone.

"Do you have a dress uniform?" the voice asked.

"Yes."

"Do you have white gloves?"

"Yes."

"In good shape?"

"They could be better."

"Do you need a fresh haircut?

"No. I mean yeah, maybe I do."

"Good. You get a fresh haircut, put on your dress uniform, and report to headquarters tomorrow. Someone will have a clean pair of white gloves for you when you get there. You are being promoted. This is Commissioner Raymond Kelly."

The failure to discover the plot before the attack was regrettable, but understandable in light of what was known at the time. The failure to act on what was learned after the blast was another

Blast Damage

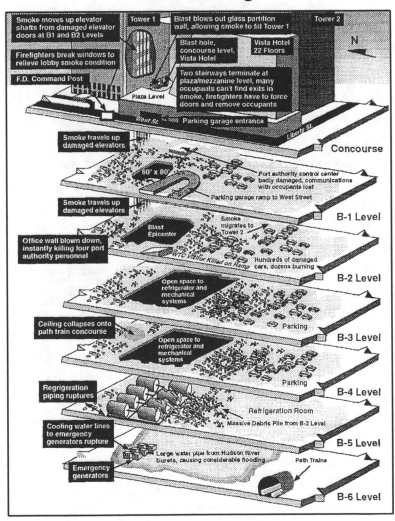

This diagram shows a cross section of the damage to the World Trade Center parking garage from the 1993 bombing.

kind of error, an inexcusable one. Those errors in critical incident management and response to potential mass casualty incidents are recorded in a 170-page report by the National Fire Data Center, based on extensive interviews with the FDNY. They were uncorrected by September 11, 2001.

"In terms of the number of fire department units that responded, it was the equivalent of a sixteen-alarm fire," said Anthony Fusco, the chief of the FDNY, in the report. "Communications were a serious problem from the outset.

"The statistics are staggering: Six people died and 1,042 were injured. Of those injured, fifteen received traumatic injuries from the blast itself. Nearly twenty people complained of cardiac problems, and nearly thirty pregnant women were rescued. Eighty-eight firefighters (one requiring hospitalization), thirty-five police officers, and one EMS worker sustained injuries. It is estimated that approximately fifty thousand people were evacuated from the WTC complex, including nearly twenty-five thousand from each of the two towers. Fire alarm dispatchers received more than a thousand phone calls, most reporting victims trapped on the upper floors of the towers. Search and evacuation of the towers finally were completed some eleven hours after the incident began.

"A major detriment to . . . control of the incident was fire department on-scene communications. Communications were a serious problem from the outset. Generally, the problems were caused by one or more of the following factors: the number of resources using channels; not enough channels for operational areas; distance problems—lost messages, construction of building interrupting signals, and the inability to contact other agencies."

Listening to the accounts in this report is a difficult job. They sound so familiar. The severe communication problem, the issue of fire code enforcement inside the towers, the difficulties of command and control on the street, the gridlock of rescuers too close to the scene of a bombing—all of these same problems would be cited in post–September 11 analyses by Kinsey consultants and the 9/11 Commission. It was as if no one had read the first report, and this despite the fact that several commanders in charge in 1993 were also in charge in 2001.

BOOK FOUR

Madrid

"When bombs on Barcelona burst
I was a thousand miles away
And yet my walls cracked wide apart
And fell on me in disarray."
—LOUIS GINSBERG

1

Democracy Derailed

Mark Torre's collar button was undone, his tie was askew, and he had his left ear tight against the beige telephone. It was March 11, 2004, and ten rail bombs of about fifteen kilograms each had exploded in rapid succession during the early morning rush hour in Madrid. One hundred and ninety-one commuters were killed and nearly 2,050 were injured. Mark had been at his desk since first light.

In Madrid the carriages of four commuter trains had been twisted and shredded into shrapnel. In New York a spring morning's calm had been twisted and shredded into an ugly thing where instead of listening for the comforting deep rumble of the subway train the ear waited for the metallic shriek of brakes and the mind filled with flying metal and hurling nails each time a train pulled in to a station. Repeated as it was in every major city, this state of fear completed the terrorists' mission.

"Madness, it's madness, and let me tell you, it's going to get worse," Torre said while fielding a torrent of calls and e-mails. Many were police logistic questions—how would he pre-position his teams to best protect New York? Others were to share bits of intelligence, and some were firm orders to produce men and dogs for display and public reassurance. The most important were the quick updates from the FBI on the situation in Madrid—practical nuts-and-bolts descriptions of what the devices had looked like, what kind of timers were used, and what kind of explosives. This was information that could be passed on to cops across the city and ultimately to the riders as items to watch for. New York's police officials had learned that the eyes of the millions of daily riders were the best early warning system. To use them effectively, detailed information was released to the public and not held close and secret. The operational doctrine was to reveal all that could be revealed as fast as it could be revealed; to protect the city first and worry about the impact of any disclosure on a court case second. It's an excellent line of defense.

From LA to Boston, from Philadelphia to Washington, Torre's peers had been at their desks throughout the predawn hours. In Los Angeles, FBI Special Agent Bomb Technician Kevin Miles had been up since minutes after the explosions. He was getting every bit of information he could from the FBI and getting it out to Mark and other commanders. Over Mark's shoulder the e-mails could be seen coming in from law enforcement agencies and bomb techs across the world. The explosive ordnance and improvised explosive device professionals were pooling their analyses, pictures, and detailed information to rapidly enhance the protection of their cities. Agency boundaries were supplanted by a common mission. This was the opposite of the vertically managed, hierarchical, insular intelligence, military, and federal law enforcement agencies, where the tendency was to keep secrets. Their failure to share information was part of what had given the terrorists their edge before 2001 and continued to give them an edge well after. For the terrorists, the World Wide Web was a tool; a worldwide, wicked weapon they were adept at using to exchange explosive recipes and launch attacks. In cities like New York, law enforcement's adaptation to the digital world and its rapid dissemination of information was a matter of survival.

Six thousand two hundred subway cars carried 1.4 billion riders down 660 miles of track each year in New York City. They hissed and slid to a stop at 468 subterranean and escalated stations that marked important intersections in neighborhoods of Japanese; communities of Koreans; sections of Hasidim; pita-sized pockets of Syrians, Egyptians, and Armenians; wide swaths of Italians; carnivals of the Caribbean; shtetls of the Slavs and other eastern Europeans; barrios of Mexicans, Ecuadorians, and Puerto Ricans; and the granite redoubts of the races of the rich. Pressed through 2100 or so entrances and exits, this was the life, the pulse, the pride of the city. Two million seven hundred sixty-seven thousand five hundred and nine trips a year were made recently, covering a total of 352,230,000 miles. Only Moscow, Tokyo, and Seoul had larger riderships. Mexico City ran a tie. None served a public so diverse and on a subway so old. Most of this arterial system had been laid down between 1904 and 1930, and most of the security had remained in the age of schooners and dreadnoughts.

It was three days before Spain's general elections when the Madrid bombs exploded. By the time the 191 bodies were removed and all of the injured treated, a nation's well-being had been destroyed. The next casualty would be the independence of Spain's political system. A fundamentalist terrorist group would succeed where terrorists had always failed. By election day—by March 14—their bombings and the government's response would succeed in helping to convince Spain's electorate to vote a pro–U.S. government out of office and to replace it with one that promised to separate itself from U.S. efforts in Iraq.

This magnification of the power of a group of properly placed, properly timed, compact, backpack-sized bombs was what set apart the ability of the twenty-first-century terrorists from their nineteenth- and twentieth-century predecessors. It was what made the Bomb Squad's mission more stressful than it had ever been.

Madrid was not the first rail bombing of 2004. In Moscow on Friday, February 6, at least 42 riders died and another 129 were injured when a metro train car exploded during the morning rush. In December 2003 a rush-hour bombing in the rebellious republic of Chechnya claimed 42 lives. It was apparent this spring morning that a lethal trend had developed. Successful attacks on rail transportation had spread fear, generated mass casualties, and perhaps influenced political moods. Rail transportation was soft and unprotected. An attack in New York could cripple the economy.

As a result, that morning official New York moved into high gear, increasing visible police presence everywhere and issuing reassuring public statements on a regular basis. One of the biggest strains on Mark's available manpower were the requests for Bomb Squad dogs. The city government wanted bomb dogs everywhere. Not for their primary purpose, detecting explosives, but to reassure the public that something was being done. When shown on TV, the dogs were great propaganda tools—just as it could spread fear, TV coverage could stretch reassurance far and wide. There was no image so comforting in a crisis, it seemed, as a Labrador dog, happily sniffing for bombs, led by a man wearing a smile and a windbreaker that said "BOMB SQUAD" across the back.

Torre's job was to keep the requests for public reassurance balanced against the need for resources to be free, available, fresh, and unencumbered should actual bombs be found.

"I tell you, Rich, there is no use explaining it to them. They just won't listen. Dogs cannot patrol raid yards," Torre said. This one request struck him as particularly thoughtless. "Why? Because there are too many tracks and too many trains. Because after those trains leave the rail yards, a bomber can get on at any stop in the city. And then what?"

There was ample history in New York to support the lieutenant's view of where bombs entered the New York City subway system, and where they did not. Within months after the subway system was completed, it was bombed. And it has been bombed repeatedly, unabatedly across the decades.

A few headlines:

- ATTEMPT TO BLOW UP SUBWAY FEED CABLE *JUNE 11, 1906*
  HUNGARIAN CAUGHT TRYING TO EXPLODE A BOMB . . . COULD
  HAVE STOPPED TRAIN SERVICE

- BRIDGES GUARDED; POLICE IN SUBWAYS *FEBRUARY 7, 1916*
  A TASTE OF MARTIAL LAW
  Citizens with valises, suitcases and bundles held up under threat of search

- POLICE TAKE STEPS TO PREVENT REPETITION OF EXPLOSION
  WHICH WRECKED SUBWAY STATION *OCTOBER 26, 1916*

- PUT "SCARE" BOMB IN SUBWAY STATION . . . LIKE WORK OF AN
  AMATEUR *JANUARY 22, 1917*

- SUBWAY DYNAMITER GUILTY *MARCH 10, 1917*

- SUBWAY BOMB CAUSES SCARE IN RUSH HOUR *MARCH 22, 1921*

- FINDS PIPE LIKE BOMB ON SUBWAY TRACKS *JULY 27, 1927*

- BOMBS EXPLODE IN TWO SUBWAY STATIONS HERE
  WALLS SHATTERED; MANY ARE HURT, ONE DYING; SACCO REPRISALS
  ARE SUSPECTED *AUGUST 6, 1927*

- SUBWAY BOMB SCARE OVER PACKAGE *SEPTEMBER 16, 1928*

- BOMB SQUAD GETS JOB *MAY 28, 1941*

- 2 INJURED BY BOMB IN PHONE BOOTH IN SUBWAY CORRIDOR
  MAY 31, 1966

- BOMB SCARE ON BMT HALTS SERVICE DURING RUSH HOUR
  AUGUST 26, 1970

- SUBWAY RUNS TO BROOKLYN CURTAILED BY BOMB SCARE
  NOVEMBER 2, 1970

- FIRE BOMB THROWN ON SUBWAY TRAIN; 3 PERSONS BURNED
  MAY 2, 1971

- MAN WITH FIRE BOMB SEIZED IN SUBWAY *MAY 8, 1971*

- BOMB SCARE DELAYS IND TRAIN IN QUEENS *SEPTEMBER 28, 1972*

- FOLLOWING DOG'S NOSE POLICE UNCOVER EXPLOSIVES IN SUBWAY LOCKER *MAY 11, 1974*

- BOMBS EXPLODE IN SUBWAY *AUGUST 21, 1976*

And a few quotes from behind those headlines:

"A phony bomb left at the 59th Street Station . . . prompted the Transit Authority . . . to reroute . . . leaving thousands . . . stranded."

"Thousands of subway riders . . . were delayed for more than an hour. . . . because of what the Transit Authority police describe as 'an unfounded bomb scare.'"

"A man threw a fire bomb in the subway. . . . Police said there was no apparent motive."

"Transit Authority policemen estimated that several thousand passengers were asked to leave eight trains."

"A homemade pipe bomb exploded in a telephone booth."

"A track worker discovered what was apparently a bomb . . . in the East River tube."

On Sunday, October 12, 1960, a bomb exploded on the Interborough Rapid Transit platform at Forty-second Street and Times Square. Thirty-one were injured. The next day the city went to work, on the subways.

On Sunday, November 6, 1960, at 7:18 P.M. a bomb placed under a seat on the Independent Subway System line A train exploded at the 125th Street Station in Harlem. A woman who was apparently seated above the bomb was killed; eighteen others were injured. The freshly painted gray and red IND car was warped and twisted, and a hole was blown in the floor. John F. Kennedy held a narrow lead over Richard Nixon, with fifteen states still close; in France, embitterment over Charles De Gaulle's promise of an Algiers free of French rule, was boiling over. On Monday the city went to work, on the subways.

On December 15 and December 21, 1994, two successful bombings took place in the subway. A deranged Edward Leary set off infernos that scarred and badly injured more than forty people. Leary thought incendiary devices were a good tool to extort money from the Transit Authority. On each day, with some localized delay, the subways ran on time.

On Thursday, July 31, 1997, the city had a narrow escape from a suicide bombing. Operating with a tip, police executed a predawn raid on a suspected terrorist bomb-making factory in Brooklyn, shot two men as they tried to detonate their improvised bombs, and arrested a third without injury. The bombers had plotted a Brooklyn suicide attack at the terminal intersection of the Long Island Rail Road with the Atlantic Avenue subway stop. Five bombs packed with gunpowder and large nails were recovered. There remains a question as to whether the devices would have detonated. It seemed the would-be terrorists had incorrectly wired the sequences in their circuit, in a way that would weaken rather than boost the battery charge sufficient to detonate the devices. That morning the city went to work, on the subway.

These events contained lessons about the system's vulnerabilities. They also contained a lesson about the city dwellers themselves and their remarkable elasticity and ability to accept the facts and carry on.

But in the face of an organized plot by a cell of terrorists who triggered multiple devices at the same time, or a series of devices over time, that resiliency could be worn down.

Why then, in 2004, was the lifeline of the financial, publishing, and media capital of the world so unprotected? Because democracy is inherently porous. Because freedom of movement, of people and of capital, is the essence of a meritocracy. Because excessive security restricts excessively. Because delivering a workforce to the capital markets, the accountancies, the publishing houses, and the music and entertainment and real estate businesses is what drives the subway schedule. The cost of delay could raise overhead and defeat competitive advantage both for the business and the worker eager to get to the top. Because New York has a staunch democratic tradition and the parochial notion that in its world all are free to thrive, and these concepts demand openness.

On the one hand, those are the good reasons for a relaxed system, which are rarely mentioned during those moments when the media and the public demand more and more security. On the other hand, the managers of the mass transit system failed to plan in advance to protect those rights and privileges not only from undue vulnerability, but also from undue restriction during a crisis. They had been asleep in class for a very long time. They had missed each lesson—including September 11—and had failed to implement changes—removal of trash bins, installation of a large closed-circuit TV system, protection of tunnel entrances, better security at stations, the training of track and train personnel in bomb awareness and rescue procedures. The list is fairly long.

Bomb squads, in this context, exist as society's tow trucks. They are a last line of defense. They are squads of knowledgeable men and women who are willing to place their lives in harm's way save yours; they can always be counted on to show up, if not always to succeed.

To Torre, the request to use thirteen dogs and thirteen highly trained specialists to patrol 220 miles of rail yard track was like capturing and fortifying high ground that had no strategic value, an expensive mistake that trapped your troops in the wrong place.

Torre won his point. The patrols were tabled. He turned his attention to the hundreds of reports of suspicious packages being called in by other units and the public in the aftermath of the Madrid attack. His sergeants had been handling that grueling load—deploying dogs and men across the city where and when needed. Torre's job now was to be sure his sergeants were responding only where necessary and remembering to keep as many teams as possible fresh in case an actual device was found.

By now the squad had a good idea of what they might be

looking for: the devices used—ten to fifteen kilograms; where had they been placed—on the track beds or the floors of the carriages; the probable method of detonation—the alarm clock function of cell phones; the type of explosive—high-grade plastic explosive; and the likely delivery device—backpacks or rucksacks.

Bill Davitch, the gently smiling FBI bomb technician assigned as liaison to the squad, was earning his keep that morning. In a series of telephone calls, he had steadily fed the squad that information as soon as the FBI team in Madrid passed it to the FBI Joint Terrorist Task Force. In his latest call he'd said that there appeared to be nails and other fragmentation packed around the explosives. Each piece of solid information Davitch phoned in eliminated an unknown. If a technician in New York had to kneel over a similar package, this knowledge could spell the difference between life and death.

At some point, a telephone rang inside a backpack that had been tossed in a pile of possessions found among the victims in Madrid. The backpack was X-rayed. It contained a bomb that had failed to explode. The pack was opened. The bomb was defused. Descriptions of the device, pictures of it, and X-rays of it were sent digitally to techs around the world, and the last unknowns were eliminated. By now New York City Mayor Michael Bloomberg had announced his plans for stepped up subway security. France had declared an elevated terror alert. Across Europe rail security had been beefed up.

The U.S. transportation sector produced cover-their-butts law enforcement awareness bulletins—reminders that U.S. commuter rails remained a known target for terrorists. For the most part, these recapped known intelligence. Six weeks earlier, on January 28, the FBI had issued a warning of a "Continuing Threat to U.S. Subways and Rails." That bulletin itself referred back to the earlier Bulletin No. 78 of August 13, 2003:

An attack on a subway or rail system cannot be ruled out.
An attack on a subway or rail system could cause substantial

loss of life and would have an adverse impact on public confidence resulting in massive economic loss.

Succinct. To the point. In the summer of 2004, Boston and New York City, each with a significant rail system, added a heightened concern of an attack during the July Democratic convention in Boston and the August Republican convention in New York to their security plans.

2

March Madness

The morning of March 12, Sergeant Joseph Hourihan climbed into his Ford SUV #3500, and Detectives Craig Collopy and Tommy O'Riordan, and O'Riordan's black Lab, JJ, backed their blue and white response truck out of the squad garage. It was 9:22 P.M. In New York the "Madrid Spring" had sprung, and with it suspicion.

Two "Middle Eastern" teens had been spotted taking photographs in the subway. They were cousins visiting from London. They had been detained by uniformed Transit Bureau officers. Ethnically, one youth was Moroccan, the other was Pakistani; both were British citizens, and they were visiting New York on "visa waivers." In time past they would have been viewed as youthful tourists. In time present they fit the general profile of potential terrorists. They had been taking pictures inside of subway cars; this has long been a part of the art and culture of New York. But the transit police were too nervous to care about art. The teens were nervous too. They volunteered to let police search their room.

"It's going to be an olfactory search," Hourihan said to the reporter who rode with him on a quiet ride uptown. He meant that the dog would do the work.

"No lights. No siren. There's no package. There's no need for a siren," Hourihan explained. The son of Irish immigrants, he had been a junior seminarian on a path to the priesthood before police work became his calling. He'd come to the Bomb Squad fresh from running a homicide squad in the low-rise and red-brick neighborhoods of the Bronx. He had twenty years as a cop and, he often said with a toothy grin, absolutely no intention of retiring. He lit a cigarette and palmed the wheel while hitting the YELP button on his console to move a car or two aside as he cruised along Eighth Avenue up to Fifty-seventh Street, where his team would search the teens' $33-a-night room at the Habitat Youth Hostel. The teens' room was small and spare. Like the teens in their Gap T-shirts and hoodies, it was normalcy itself—some hair gel, a Best Buy bag, an open carton of OJ. JJ sniffed and scooted and sniffed some more. Nothing. The Joint Terrorism Task Force detective who met the Bomb Squad at the scene called his office. "Nothing. This is mushrooming out of control," he said, commenting on the paranoia that prompted the stop and the sweep and was crawling over the backbone of the city. The sweep was over. It was barely eleven o'clock.

Beyond the evening-after-Madrid-bombing jitters, there was additional context for the incident. Prior to Madrid, it was already clear that modern terrorists had become particularly methodical in their preoperational preparations. Even when knowledge had been publicly available to them, they had gone out and used surveillance, complete with a video or photographic record, to gather the latest information about pre-strike conditions.

In November 2003 two "Middle Eastern" men had been similarly detained for taking photographs of tracks leading under the East River. These two men had turned out to be Iranian intelligence officers. Iran's intelligence service was seen as a key link between Iran and the terrorist groups its government was widely known to sponsor. The men were declared personae non grata and told to leave the country. But the lesson was not forgotten—especially not on March 12.

On March 14, at 8:15 A.M., boxes of green tags, yellow tags, red tags, and black tags were laid out and ready for the drill that would soon take place inside Shea Stadium, home of the Mets baseball team in Queens, New York. The green tags would be attached to the lightly injured, the yellow to the seriously injured, the red to the critically injured, and the black to the dead. One thousand volunteers, many of them aspiring actors, would play the victims.

The drill was a practice session for a weapon-of-mass-destruction incident. It was the fortieth disaster drill in New York City since September 11, and one thousand cops, medical technicians, firefighters, and other emergency workers were on hand. Fifty-five hospitals and twenty-one private ambulance companies contributed doctors, nurses, equipment, expertise, and vehicles. The Bomb Squad contributed eleven of their thirty-three members to the exercise. They were by far the smallest unit.

"There will be a secondary device," Torre told his men. "Remember. There is a big race to find this thing. Everybody is looking for it. Everybody wants to be a hero. Just do our jobs." The job would not include using their tools to approach the suspicious package. They would just observe, discuss, and note the approach they would have taken. Then they would rule the device "rendered safe."

"Hey, ya gotta do what ya gotta do," said Joe Putkowski, the senior man. To him, without bomb suits, without the use of X-rays, and without the use of water jet disrupters, the drill did not seem very real, nor did he see it as very relevant. He preferred to focus on preventing bombs from going off.

11:23 A.M. An air horn blast signified that the bomb had gone off. Smoke rose from three Fire Department smoke machines, and a loud collective moan started to rise from the section where volunteers and manikins were strewed about the $27- to $33-dollar seats.

11:38. The squad found a secondary device. They breathed a little easier. It took them seven minutes and fifty-three seconds from the moment of discovery to the moment when they decided the device was "defeated"—their term for "rendered safe."

11:47. Another device was reported.

12:00. Still another.

12:13. A device was found in one of the many stadium parking lots.

12:13. Another device was spotted, in another lot.

12:48. A report of a radiological device came in.

The squad responded to each device, and the drill ended with a post-blast investigation of the primary device. The teams from different agencies had succeeded in working together smoothly. The Bomb Squad went home. Even Joe now could see the benefit.

That was the point of these drills held inside subway cars, at stadiums, underground in rubble-strewn cellars. Multiple units from multiple disciplines trained together. Telephone numbers were exchanged. Tips and techniques were debated and shared. The intent was to prevent the lapses that had marred past rescue efforts.

Early in the morning of March 16, at 3:45 A.M., a suspicious package was discovered on the Brooklyn Bridge, that soaring symbol of New York. The Bomb Squad was called. Detective Ray Clair and his dog, Winston, the senior dog on the Bomb Squad, responded. Ray neatly summed the incident in his after action report:

At approximately 0400, Tuesday 03/16/2004 a "1044 Suspicious Package on the Brooklyn Bridge" was transmitted by central radio. At approximately 0410 hours members of

122

the Bomb Squad utilizing Explosive Detection Canines along with Emergency Service and Harbor units conducted a visual and olfactory search of the Brooklyn Bridge with negative results. Members of the Bomb Squad did locate two cardboard boxes on the bridge's roadway while conducting their search. Both boxes were empty. Bomb Squad Case #237 & 238. Detective Raymond Clair.

The next day dawned cold. It felt like thirty degrees. It was March 17, St. Patrick's Day, the day of the big parade. The squad detail had gathered at Fiftieth and Fifth, in the shadow of St. Patrick's Cathedral. When the Bomb Squad arrived, diocesan workers were erecting the cardinal's protective white awning over the entrance and anchoring it with 240-pound weights.

It had snowed the night before. At 6:00 A.M. workers were shoveling that fresh quarter inch of powder off of the broad steps of the massive cathedral. Heavy plows attached to the city's garbage trucks bounced and scraped Fifth Avenue clear. The marchers could now follow a freshly painted emerald green line up the center of the avenue.

"It's sort of like destiny that the Bomb Squad has to be here every year," Sergeant Anthony Biondolilo explained. Eighty-nine years earlier the Bomb Squad had raced into the cathedral and stopped bombers just as they were lighting the fuses to their dynamite bombs. On an earlier occasion an anarchist plot was successful, leaving a crack as thin as a dueling scar in the granite and marble of the cathedral. Once again, in 1952, another plot was laid. This time the bombs did not materialize.

St. Patrick's Cathedral was a powerful symbolic target. For decades, it was known as the "Powerhouse," and it had symbolized the wealth, influence, and power of the city's Irish Catholic voters and their church. Under Francis Cardinal Spellman, for example, the postmaster general, James Farley—who was also the Democratic Party chairman—had been told in no uncertain terms that Catholics would not vote for Franklin Delano Roose-velt unless what the cardinal saw as *Esquire* magazine's obscenity was curbed. *Esquire* deliveries were at times held up at the post office before a deal was struck between Spellman and the maga-zine's editors: The editors would submit articles to the cardinal for review. The church's influence had since dwindled, but the cathedral—like the Empire State Building, which was no longer the tallest building in the world—remained an enduring symbol of New York, and a potential target for radicals, fundamentalists, anarchists, and homegrown nuts.

So every St. Patrick's Day and every Christmas Eve, the Bomb Squad and the Bomb Squad dogs swept through the silence of the hundreds of pews, the naves, the lady altar, and the crypt below the main altar where the cardinals and bishops were laid to rest. Satel-lite TV trucks, aluminum grandstands, all of the decorations on the edges of the cathedral's skirts were subjected to the dogs' noses and the bomb technicians' flashlight-aided eyes.

8:30. The Roman Catholic Mass began before a congregation that was a sea of emerald green. The dogs were brought in for a second sweep, and they ran their noses across dark mountains of overcoats as Edward Cardinal Egan exhorted the bright faces to "keep Madrid in our hearts."

The snow flurried again as the parade marched by. Ray Clair and Winston stood on the top step of the cathedral as the cardinal stepped out at eleven o'clock to greet the crowd, and the parade halted for his blessing.

"Is the dog cold?" It was the cardinal who asked. Ray and Sergeant B stamped their feet and shoved their hands in their pockets, but they assured the cardinal that Winston was not cold. While Lieutenant Mark Torre might from time to time win a battle against the popularity of the dogs, his war itself was already lost. The dogs had God on their side. Winston, his black coat gleaming and a shamrock at his throat, stood proudly in his right-ful place on the cathedral steps.

A few days later, on the afternoon of March 25, the New York *Daily News* lay on the Plexiglas covering a kitchen table: "Human Bomb *FOR $22 AND THE PROMISE OF 72 VIRGINS, PALESTINIAN TEEN TURNS HIMSELF INTO A HUMAN BOMB.*" But dogs were all that was on anyone's mind, and the topic went around the table.

"Dogs are important," said Sergeant B, "but the guy at the end of the leash, that's more important."

"Dogs have to be given a break. While the dogs are working they are sucking in a tremendous amount of air. It's like they are doing a four-hundred-yard dash," said Detective Ray Butkiewicz.

"When you see the dogs come out, you know it's something important," said Ray Clair. He was the spokesman for Winston, the senior dog. "The point is not the dog. The point is to have the man and dog together as a team. That way if the dog smells something, the handler can deal with it. Together with their sense of smell, we are a powerful team," Ray explained.

Like Lieutenant Torre, the team members understood the real value of the dog. Unlike him, they did not have to put up with the constant pressure to use them for various other purposes. As a result, they had less frustration and more pride in their voices when they spoke of the squad's canine members.

Ray Clair and his father, who was also a police officer, had bred dogs their entire lives. "There are limitations but there is no greater asset to find explosives."

In the days after the Madrid bombing, the Bomb Squad and its dogs ran to investigate ninety "bomb jobs"—suitcases, backpacks, and other suspicious-looking packages and parcels on Metro-North, the Long Island Rail Road, and New Jersey Transit, the commuter lines from the suburbs into the city of New York. For the men and the dogs it was a maddening pace and an abrupt beginning to spring.

BOOK FIVE

Explosive
Detection Canines

"For dogs, they lead interesting lives."
—Sergeant Anthony
Biondolilo

So You Are a Dog

Sergeant Joe Hourihan's team was armoring Ray Clair into his fatigue green Kevlar bomb suit in the lee of a large, heavy police truck that was parked more than a hundred feet back from the possible bomb. For this job, Ray Clair's dog, Winston, did not need to be taken out of his cage.

Once a package was deemed suspicious, there was no need to use up time by having a dog go take a sniff. The package would still have to be opened. Even Ray Clair was forced to admit that the explosives detection canine was no more able to defuse a bomb it detected than a retriever could shoot a duck or a blood-hound handcuff a suspect. The dog could simply detect an odor that could indicate a possible bomb, but it could not determine whether or not the package contained an actual bomb, and it certainly couldn't render the bomb safe.

So in this case it was Detective Second Grade Ray Clair who examined the package, determined it contained nothing more than an assortment of barely serviceable clothes, cut it open, dumped its contents out to be on the safe side, and began the lumbering walk back to the truck in his ninety-pound Kevlar suit. He looked like he had emerged from a steam bath when the team lifted off his helmet and undid the suit. His T-shirt was soaked through. His hair was matted and his face covered with a thin film of perspiration. As a matter of note he did in fact look like a hunting dog fresh from the water, which is a compliment. It had been remarked on before that Ray Clair—Detective Second Grade Ray Clair—looked like a dog. The other bomb techs also had to admit that his hound dog face apparently had the same effect on women as Humphrey Bogart's. Still, they liked to ask whether it was Ray or Winston, with his coat as glossy as a tuxedo, who actually convinced the women they met to have dinner with Ray. But when it came to explaining how dogs worked to police bosses or to juries, Ray was the expert the squad called upon. He had never failed. So Ray, handler for senior dog Winston, was also the senior spokesman for the dogs.

It had been his love of dogs that got him onto the Bomb Squad in the first place.

"I can appreciate fully what can be accomplished when man and his dogs work together as a team," he had written at the head of his application to the squad.

Ray had made five hundred felony arrests on the darker streets of New York before he filled out that application. He was what is called a "very active cop."

He came from a cop family—his father and grandfather both had been officers—but he also came from a dog family—his father bred German shorthaired pointers. The pointers were good all-around utility field dogs. The family lived in exurban Suffolk County, Long Island, still a place of farms, open spaces, and fields that were filled with birds and small game. Ray grew up hunting quail, pheasant, duck, and deer, special times to be around dogs, and times to be with his father.

"It was our time," he said.

It gave Ray the chance to stand beside his dad, "who I thought was the coolest dad on the block because he was a police officer," and it gave him the opportunity to learn early the partnership between dog and man.

"That's when I realized you can go out hunting without a dog and see nothing, but you go out with a dog and then we did very well, and it was because of the dog." This was also an apt description of the dog's role in finding hidden explosives.

"He'd go out and find what we were looking for, and we would shoot it, and he would bring it back, and that's how we had our team."

But from the time he had become a police officer until he joined the Bomb Squad, this team work had been sidelined. The double shifts and the days away from home had made it impossible for him to even own a dog, let alone give it the life it deserved; his work kept him away from home too often and for too long.

In the early spring of 1997, a time when the Bomb Squad was swamped with qualified applicants and it was virtually impossible to join, Ray Clair was the only applicant who actually wanted the one opening the squad had—dog handler. None of the other would-be bomb technicians were interested in what they considered the hassles of being a handler—caring for a dog, working a dog, feeding a dog, and training a dog. For Ray, these were part of life's pleasures. Ray joined the squad.

Twenty-six years earlier, on May 1, 1971, Sally, a beautiful shepherd dog, had completed a full year of explosives detection training at the University of Mississippi and joined the NYPD as the first NYPD explosives detection canine. The pioneering program had been paid for under a federal law enforcement grant. It might be the best $25,000 the federal government ever invested in police research and training.

"In the category [of effluent detection] some extremely sophisticated scientific instruments have been developed [among them] the electronic sniffer . . . [however] the single most conspicuously successful effluent detector developed as of now has been man's best friend, and oldest, the dog."

With those sentences began the New York City Police Department Bomb Section's first "Information & Training Manual" for "Explosive Detection Dogs" as they then were called. Sally was soon joined by Brandy, a retriever, and the first bomb dogs were housed in newly installed Bomb Squad kennels.

By the time Ray Clair arrived at the squad, it had been well established that a properly trained dog with a properly trained handler were more flexible and able to cover a far wider area than any electronic explosive detection device. There is one area of bomb detection where the machines do have a key advantage, and that is at fixed portals—such as airport gates or post office conveyor belts—with a heavy flow of human traffic, luggage, or parcels. A dog is most effective in two- to four-hour blocks with a rest every half hour to an hour. The machine needs no rest, or food, or kennel, or trained handler, or constant care. So at the end of the day, in certain applications it is the far cheaper and far more effective solution.

"The dogs are a good thing for the Bomb Squad. I hate when they say they are a *tool* we use," Ray said. "They are a wonderful asset. There is no finer way to find hidden explosives than with a bomb-sniffing dog that knows his business. They are mobile. And that's the way to go."

There was a downside to the dogs' success. Since September 11, 2001, bomb dogs had become a growth industry for private security firms. But the businessmen often ignored the limitations of the animals or the need for highly skilled dog handlers.

"Frankly, it's very chic to have a bomb dog," retired NYPD Kennel Master Tim Dinan told the New York *Daily News*.

"I don't even want to get into that headache," Torre said. He didn't have to. On April 22, an example sailed into port on the morning tide when the *Queen Mary II* made its inaugural visit. Although the NYPD was heavily deployed dockside at Pier 92 in the Hudson, at Fifty-second Street, and the Bomb Squad had two teams and two dogs standing by, the PD was barred from bringing its dogs aboard. When they attempted to board the ship and perform a quick olfactory and visual search of the departure deck, private security halted them. Their own dogs, at a very nice hourly profit, were doing the search. But there is a flaw to this approach. Private security has no responsibility to the city of New York, only to the client. It's a delicate situation and not a comfortable one.

At least twenty-five new companies promising bomb dog security for the private sector had sprung up in the United States since September 11. There were no required certification programs for the dogs or for their handlers. Some firms provided very high-quality service. Others did not. By 2004 there was a strong chance that the dogs hired to protect a business's property or help screen its mail would be undertrained, overworked, without proper intervals of retraining, and that the handlers would be equally ill-suited for the task at hand. In New York, Ray Clair and Sergeant Tony Biondolilo sat on a state board to help write the first training regulations in the nation. But they applied only to law enforcement, not the private sector. In the private sector there still were no regulations in 2006, and firms often employed a single bomb technician and billed the clients for his services, while fleshing out the security package with three or four other far less qualified persons in the field of explosives and the craft of dog handling.

The risk of underperforming dogs was already apparent by mid-2002, when one private firm bragged that it had put on twenty new dogs since September 11 to keep up with the volume of business. There was no way to properly train that many dogs and that many handlers in that period of time. And the hunger for dogs started a price war. By 2004 the private security firms were purchasing fully trained dogs for up to $20,000 each and scouring the global markets for well-bred trainee dogs at between $3000 and $6000 each—prices that also kept rising because of the intense demand for the dogs.

The New York City Police Department has an entirely different approach to finding its dogs. It is one that humane societies applaud. The Bomb Squad and its network of knowledgeable scouts in the dog-loving community search for their dogs in pounds and shelters and in the litters of Seeing Eye pups. The squad also obtains dogs from a prison program that teaches inmates the basic skills of dog training. Experience has shown that the approach works at least as well as the purchase of a high-priced dog. And to the working-class guys in the squad, it seems fitting that their dogs are what they call "civil service dogs," recruited like the cops from the streets of the city and its surroundings. Winston's story is one example:

When Ray Clair joined the squad in 1996, it received a call from a Connecticut woman, Julie Starkweather, of the Labrador Retriever Club of Central Connecticut, a rescue organization.

"I have this Lab," she said. "I just rescued him from the animal shelter. He must have run away from somewhere. He was on the road for a long time. The pound picked him up. They had him for a week. They couldn't place him for a week. I think he's going to work out. You should come up and take a look at him."

"Basically the dog's time was up," Ray Clair recounted. "When the pound called her they said, today's the day and we have this one-year-old Lab. . . . She took him. And she couldn't place him." With that call, the dog now named Winston found Ray Clair.

"He was all skinny and wiry and he had no hair on the end of his tail," Ray recalls. "He was jumping around in the cage and climbing up the side and he was like a Tasmanian devil, flying around like crazy, so we took him. We decided to give him a chance. He was, in the words of Sergeant Tony Biondolilo 'one day from the needle.'

"I bought him back to the range. He was there for one night. I brought him to the Animal Medical Center, and he got checked out. Every day after that he came home with me," Ray explained. "Police Department rules at the time said he wasn't allowed to go home with me, but I took him home. There was no way I was leaving him in the kennel overnight. I took him home and we bonded." The rules have since changed, and every bomb dog now goes home with his tech each night.

A few short months after Winston's arrival, Ray was off to Hazardous Devices School for the four-week training course that all certified bomb technicians must take. Winston, by now a glossy black, healthy dog, was sent off on his own three-month basic training regime. By September they were both qualified and ready and back at the squad.

Eight and a half years later Winston continued to exhibit the passionate energy of a puppy. In 2004 he was awarded the Animal Medical Center "Top Dog" award in a gala ceremony at the Waldorf with many of the most well-heeled dog lovers in America in attendance—Cynthia Phipps, Pepe Fanjul, Daisy Soros, and Wendy Vanderbilt among them. Winston wore black. So did Ray. Henry Kissinger did the honors.

"So you are a dog," he said to Winston before the ceremony, in the same Germanic baritone with which he'd advised Richard Nixon. "Und you are fat."

"He is eight and a half," Ray said.

"Ah, then you are not so fat." Kissinger petted Winston. Winston sat obediently. Someone threw a ball. Winston brought it back to Kissinger. Eight hundred thousand dollars was raised that night for the Animal Medical Center in Manhattan, which provides first-class care when needed to the NYPD Bomb Squad's dogs.

"In the Bomb Squad, even the dogs are volunteers," said Bobby Schnell, the kennel master. "If they don't work out, they will make somebody a very good pet."

BOOK SIX
Spring Training

1

Rodman's Neck

At 8:00 A.M. on April 7, it was barely above thirty degrees, and an icy sheet of rain ran into the gutters of the Bomb Squad compound at Rodman's Neck in the Bronx. The compound is the squad explosives storage area, its explosive detonation range, and its training ground. It's set in the marsh grasses on a neck of land that juts into the western end of Long Island Sound. The staccato sounds of automatic pistol fire from the police pistol range outside the compound are its background music.

Today the squad was training on the latest robot—a Remotec Andros F-6A Bot, Serial No. 5506-02. Stripped down, light on its wheels, and fresh out of the industrial-sized Ziploc bags and heavy cardboard boxes it came in, the Andros F-6A was the latest in a series of robots the squad had acquired since the two that the city first cleared for purchase, immediately after Senft and Pastorella were maimed on New Year's Eve 1982. The robot and its accessories cost over $145,000.

They would be cheap at twice the price.

"If you can see the bomb, the bomb can see you." Brian Hearn was speaking. Hearn was leading today's session. He was explaining

AT WHAT PRICE SAFETY?
PRICE SHEET (excerpts)

Item	Code	Description	MFG & Model #	Unit Price
1	1340	Robot	#F6A	$86,939.39
2	1340	Controller	#M2455-8450	$9,848.48

SPARE PARTS & ACCESSORIES

2	1340	Spare Parts	#C2450-0166	$8,127.81
5	1340	Fiber Optic . . .	#M7055-8330	$15,097.50
12	1340	Video Headset	#HEADSET-003	$1,856.04
13	1340	Wireless Upgrade	#M7080 . . .	$23,829.90

that the robots with their video cameras allowed the technician to see the bomb without the bomb seeing the technician, who could be crouched fifty or a hundred yards away behind a protective wall. He was showing how, with their high-intensity lights, the robots could blind a suicide bomber for the time it took for its claws to grab him and forcefully pull his arms away from a detonator.

Hearn was wearing blue jeans, a blue shirt, a black vest, and a fluorescent orange cap that looked as bright as a traffic cone. He was sipping coffee from a Styrofoam cup as he spoke.

"Don't let the machine drive you; you drive the machine."

Hearn explained the art of driving the 3.5-mile-an-hour robots. First, he said, notice the slack in the fiber-optic cables. "Be sure to take it up. Then you'll have a better feel for it as you put the robot through its paces."

The remote box he wielded was a suitcase-sized detachable unit filled with dials and analog controls. On, Off, Tools, Video Gain, and Pan—Hearn walked the class through all of them. A joystick drove the bot. A microphone and speaker allowed the handler to communicate with an attacker, or hostage, or trapped civilian. Hearn's voice was mechanical, metallic, as it came through the speaker.

The class was held in a concrete–and–cinder-block building

across the parking lot from the low-roofed main building of the Bomb Squad compound. The building felt like an unfinished garage and smelled of the dampness that had gathered inside the cinder blocks. Yellow labels—"Heavy," "Sensitive Electronic Equipment"—were strewn about the linoleum tiled floor. Remotec "keeps danger at a distance"—the robot manufacturer's slogan—on the cover of the instruction manual, which featured a robot gently holding a hand grenade in its claws.

An entire patrol of other robots, older models already in service, was lined up and plugged in. They looked like electronic jousters ready to do battle. These belonged to the squad, and to the New Jersey cops and Emergency Service officers who were participating in the exercise. Pipe bombs, grenades, and mortar rounds lay on the floor.

Hearn explained that the new robot had great strength. Its claws could pull a mailbox off its bolts or a fireman out of a fire. He showed how the robot's infrared camera allowed it to be driven in the dark. And he highlighted the fact that a gun could be mounted on the robot. Once, an unarmed city robot was wounded when a crazed assailant opened fire with a shotgun. Now a robot could fire back. That combat-hardened old robot was in attendance.

At eleven-thirty the robots marched out of the classroom and onto the mock cityscape set up outside.

"Point it and follow it," Brian explained to the newest guys. "You can have problems with perception when working with the robot. The video monitors flatten everything down."

It was now sixty degrees and sunny. In the hands of the well-trained cops, the robots were picking grenades up off of the street and loading them into the total containment vehicle. This is a bomb disposal truck. It holds a bathysphere-like chamber designed so that if a bomb placed inside explodes, the blast pressure is slowly released through a series of valves. This is the truck used to transport devices to the range, where they are stored in heavy steel magazines until the squad has time to take them out and use a water jet or a countercharge to render them safe out on the range.

At 1:00 a manikin was strapped into a suicide vest. The class squad practiced using the robot to drag the bomber by his legs. This was an important practice session. Hearn had saved it as the final one of the day.

There exists in the United States a taboo, a healthy one, against officers of the law taking human life. But it has become increasingly apparent that law officers might face a suicide bomber and have to make an instant shoot-to-kill decision. The bomber will not be pointing a gun at the officer. The bomb itself may not even be visible. Police officers are trained to use deadly force only if they are clearly threatened. The bomber, and the bomber's hidden threat, will force a decision most police officers currently are not trained to make. There has been no public debate on the question of what an officer will be permitted to do if confronted with a potential bomber. If a judgment is made to shoot, who is responsible? The officer? What happens if the bomb is a hoax or there is nothing at all under the bomber's outerwear? There is no set of guidelines and no written policy on what is to be done in such a situation. Likely, if the past is a guide, the first individual to make a mistake will become the spark that ignites a debate. The cost could very likely be the destruction of that officer's life, his or her family, and the end of the officer's career.

So for now, the squads of bomb technicians, the ranks of snipers, and the members of the elite heavy weapons units practice for the moment that they expect will come, when they will confront a suicide bomber and make a moral decision for an entire society, without knowing what the decision of that society will be after the fact. It is unpleasant.

"The younger guys are not ready yet," Hearn said after the session was over.

"The crew that used to be here was tough," commented Jimmy Carrano, the range training officer.

They were back inside the comfortable Bomb Squad Compound offices across the street from the training area.

With coffee, cigarettes, and windows to gaze out through, they were loquacious.

"After two hundred and twenty-five guys in one hundred years, now we have sixteen news guys in one year. I've got to be sure they are safe." Hearn leaned against a case filled with defused hand grenades as he spoke.

Jimmy is broad-shouldered and buff as well as blunt. He runs a spotless compound right. His own appearance is spotless down to the dull gleam of his black boots and the trim of his mustache.

"Some of these guys might be new on the Bomb Squad, but they're not new on The Job, so you got to get your points across with respect," he added.

"One of the old-timers said to me when I first got to the Bomb Squad, 'You better know what you're doing when you go up on that package and you better do something with that package. If you got a clock on it and the time is running down, don't come back to me and say I don't know what I'm doing; because if that bomb goes, it was meant for you. It wasn't meant for me.

"Teaching the guys how to use the robots is like teaching them how to work with the dogs; you've got to teach the guys what's on the other end of the leash," Hearn said.

"But with the robots, unlike the dogs, they don't know what's on our end of the leash," said Carrano.

So it went. And so it goes. On-the-job training that never stops. A discussion that takes place each day, one that occasionally is leavened with humor.

Joe Putkowski, the senior man, offered one final lesson for the day.

"I asked one of the new guys which he would rather be: blown to smithereens or blown to kingdom come," Joe Putkowski said.

"So he answers, 'Smithereens.'"

"Wrong answer. Kingdom come. You want to be blown to kingdom come. If you are blown to smithereens, who knows where you are? If you are blown to kingdom come, at least you are in heaven."

Clarence Cull—potential suicide bomber—arrested in 1943 for threatening to explode nitroglycerin he carried in order to kill President Franklin Roosevelt.

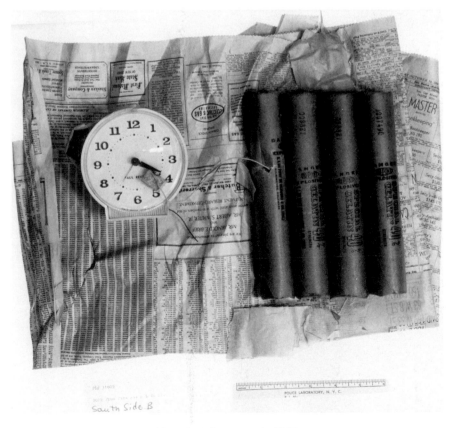

Bomb discovered on New York's posh Park Avenue in 1969.

Left: Saddle retrieved from the rubble of the horse-drawn cart used in the 1920 Wall Street bombing—the first large vehicle bomb in U.S. history.

Above: Bomb sent to New York City's main post office in 1937.

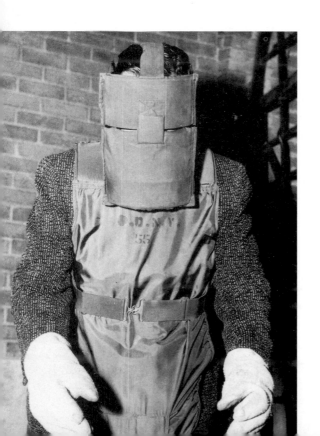

Left: An early bomb suit.

Opposite page: Memo concerning the "Mad Bomber" from the 1950s.

January 4, 1957

PIPE BOMB

The object illustrated below is a PIPE BOMB of a type that has been detonated in a number of places in the city in the past several years. IT IS EXTREMELY DANGEROUS AND MUST NOT BE DISTURBED UNDER ANY CIRCUMSTANCES.

When any such mechanism resembling this construction come to your attention, you should forthwith clear the surrounding area of people within a radius of 300 feet and you are to immediately notify the New York City Police Department at CAnal 6-2000 or SPring 7-3100.

MODUS OPERANDI: On prior occasions the perpetrator has inserted the pipe bomb in a man's sock, apparently to camouflage it. Bombs of this type have been found in various public places including telephone booths (attached to bell box or inserted in the fan casing), theatre seats, public lockers, men's lavatories, and subway cars and stations.

INCHES

STEPHEN P. KENNEDY,
Police Commissioner.

Left: Lt. James Pyke, Commander, Bomb Squad; 1936–1943.

Right: Det. Claude "Danny" Richards; killed in the attacks on the World Trade Center.

Below: Det. Raymond Clair and Winston, his NYPD Explosive Detection Canine at Rockefeller Center for the lighting of the Christmas tree, 2004.

Above and Below: Det. Billy Popper suits up to investigate a suspicious package in Times Square in 2004.

Below: Det. Brian Hearn and Tucker, his Explosive Detection Canine, in Times Square.

Below: Det. Brian Senft and Det. Jeff Oberdier at the 2004 edition of New York's Macy's Thanksgiving Day parade.

Above: Popper and Klippel suit up at the Squad's range in the Bronx.

Above: Lt. Mark Torre, the commanding officer of the Bomb Squad, in his office.

Left: Det. Joe Putkowski, senior man on the Bomb Squad.

Right: Det. Craig Callopy and Det. Thomas O'Riordan prepare for a sweep at Rockefeller Center.

Below: Brandy, one of the
first bomb-sniffing dogs to
join the Bomb Squad.

Above: Sgt. Joseph Hourihan.

Above: Robot training at the squad's command center at Rodman's Neck, the Bronx, 2004.

2

A Grueling Month

By April the jobs, sweeps, training runs, and planning sessions blurred: sign in, sign out, keys off the Peg-Board, keys back, gear in the trucks, gear onto the garage floor, dogs into their cages and back out again. The teams were on the run. The lieutenant wheeled from the squad to Police Headquarters to the Secret Service and back to the squad. From the gas pump in the forecourt outside the squad, to his desk, and back to the Secret Service and to Police Headquarters. The Republican National Convention was coming to New York City for the first time at the end of August. The security preparations were meticulous, the drilling intense. And the convention would be but one event on a Bomb Squad calendar that appeared to contain the entire New York City social diary.

Soon to take place would be a presidential visit, the arrival of tall ships and military vessels for Fleet Week, the Fourth of July celebratory fireworks, home games for two professional baseball teams, and the U.S. Tennis Open. The Republican convention would be followed within days by the September 11 anniversary celebration and the opening of the UN General Assembly the next morning.

Tens of thousands of spectators would come with Fleet Week. The nightmare of packed stadiums came with the home games; hundreds of thousands crowded into confined spaces for the fireworks; and about 160 heads of state and other dignitaries created a steady stream of high-security convoys during the UN opening. Each event required sweeps, security checks, suspicious package runs, negotiations with private security and other law enforcement agencies, and a visible presence of the Bomb Squad. As the city entered a season of celebrations, the squad members already longed for autumn. Nationally, the post–Madrid atmosphere remained tense.

On April 7 a suspicious device was found inside the luggage of a passenger at an Atlanta airline terminal. A robot was brought in to remotely disrupt the device. It was a flare. The owner had decided he would just leave it on the men's room floor rather than try to get it through security.

That same day an Orange County, California, man boarded a bus and announced he was carrying "an explosive device in a backpack." Several blocks south of downtown LA were locked down before the emotionally disturbed man was brought into custody. He had no bomb.

April 8 the Yankees played their home opener. It was as traditional as the tossing of the first pitch for the Bomb Squad in their khakis, shirts, ties, and Bomb Squad windbreakers to fan out across the stadium and walk their dogs through the clubhouse, the lockers, the below-the-stands corridors, and right out into the dugouts and onto the field. Two days later, on the tenth, at 11:15 A.M. a suspicious device was found in front of 205 East Sixty-ninth Street. It was logged as Case #924: "The package was deemed to contain nothing of an explosive nature but was constructed in such a manner as to cause public alarm and is therefore deemed to be a 'Hoax Device.'"

In Philadelphia that day a bomber who believed he was a religious figure was released from jail. He gave an FBI surveillance team the slip and planted a hoax device in a bathroom at the airport.

At the Pennsylvania–New Jersey border a suspicious package was discovered on the railroad tracks. This set of tracks ran through the New York–Philadelphia–Washington corridor, one of the densest commuter rail corridors in the nation. An initial investigation determined that traces of explosives were present.

But deciding who would conduct the investigation took five hours. The package sat there and commuters sat in their terminals and stations. It turned out to be fireworks. All agencies in Pennsylvania, New Jersey, and New York that studied the response agreed that a disaster would have occurred had the package instead contained a live bomb.

On April 13 there was a little more excitement. A federal bomb-sniffing dog indicated there were traces of explosives in a car parked illegally in front of FBI Headquarters in New York.

Sheets of rain poured down. The building was sealed off, and hundreds of immigrants endured the rain rather than give up their place in the long line for visa renewals, citizenship papers, and residency.

Jeff Oberdier got the job of crawling under the vehicle. When he was satisfied there was no bomb under the car or its hood, the interior or the trunk, he got up, walked away, and returned the hand tools he had borrowed.

Every bomb tech has his superstitions. Following the rules of his particular fetish is one way a tech keeps the numbing pace from wiping out his sense of humor—the first sign of tiredness. In Jeff's case, he never used any of his own equipment. He borrowed whatever he needed from the other guys.

"Sometimes I just like ta use the riggin' kit and a borrowed pair of pliers, ya know." Jeff spoke in a farmland drawl. "Pigman," as the other techs called him, had come to New York from Ohio, and moved with the pace of a quiet morning on the porch. It is a good pace for a man with a life-or-death job.

On the fifteenth of April a bomb threat forced New York City Police to cordon off Eighth Avenue between Thirty-fourth and Thirtieth Streets. Facing the stretch of roadway were the main post office, Pennsylvania Station, and Madison Square Garden—the site of the upcoming Republican convention. At least one hotel was evacuated before it was determined that the threat was unfounded.

3

The View from the COBS's Desk

"We are incident driven," Lieutenant Torre explained.
"But for the most part, when response is the focus of
national security, failure is the result," he said. Torre is a proponent of keeping specialty units small, highly trained, and flexible.
He is a proponent of integrating them with a highly aware larger
force of officers. He is a proponent of good information as the
best threat deterrent. To this end his squad conducted bomb
awareness seminars for police, firefighters, emergency medical technicians, and transit workers. Anyone of them could find themselves
in a situation where a suspicious package, improperly handled or
identified, could put lives at risk.

Torre also thought that virtually every dollar spent on
Homeland Security has been a dollar wasted. Most of that
money has been allocated for target-hardening, the beefing up
of physical security at buildings, roads, and terminals, and response equipment. Not nearly enough had been put into prevention, which simply speaking is the development of good
intelligence and the training of as many law enforcement and
public safety personnel as possible on bomb awareness. Good
intelligence, in the end, was all that could protect New York

City. Torre, for all his griping, loved the city, the Police Department, and the Bomb Squad.

"It's really all I care about. This job, this freaking department, the commissioner and his strategy."

Since becoming commissioner in January 2002, Raymond Kelly had devoted most of his energy, staked his formidable reputation, and spent a substantial proportion of his department's manpower and budget to build a large and creative intelligence collection and analysis section. As a result, New York had thousands of cops and informants working the streets, hunting for leads to a terrorist threat. The city stood a better chance that any other American city of knowing in advance of a terrorist plan to strike.

The work spread out before the lieutenant in the summer of 2004 was part of his familiar routine: a duty chart, a sheaf of vacation requests, overtime balances, and new equipment purchase orders.

This was the job of the commander: deployments, morale building, small team action training, and lending an ear to every problem under the sun. He was assigning heavy hours of overtime on a regular basis now, as the Republican convention drew nearer. The men liked the money. But the stress on him, and on them, grew by the day. At the same time as he was distributing overtime hours, he did a daily check to make sure that the teams were getting rest. And that no one officer was getting a lion's share of extra money that went unnoticed.

"Not in my Bomb Squad. Markie ain't like that," he explained.

Because of his rigorous attention to detail and relentless questioning on the little points of management, he had earned the sometimes affectionate nicknames the Little Dictator and Little Caesar. Drinking milk, eating soft-boiled eggs, and being tough—they were all parts of Torre's persona: the little tough guy.

Mark's weekend and evening fishing expeditions that spring had not been a great help in easing the stress of running the squad at full tilt. He had tossed his eels into the Atlantic time and again, and each time his hook came up empty. The striped bass would not cooperate.

"The ocean is like a wasteland to me. Its hopeless. Hopeless," he said. Still he kept casting, enjoying the company of Sergeant B or Ray Clair and the moonlight and the surf.

On April 20 the President had come to visit. The visit turned out fine, and the President certainly never noticed, but from a security standpoint it was a snafu from the start. The Port Authority Police and the Secret Service had decided that Port Authority dogs, not the NYPD dogs, should perform the olfactory search on the presidential convoy before it departed the airport for Manhattan. This was a drastic change from past practice, and it had implications for the continuity of protection for the President. The rest of the search would be performed by the Secret Service without the squad's assistance. During the trip into the city from the airport, the Bomb Squad would be relegated to a truck in the convoy. In other words they were put in a position that guaranteed to make them too late to do anything but help pick up the pieces if the dogs failed or a non–explosives specialist agent missed something at the start of the convoy.

For more than fifty years—stretching back to the opening of United Nations New York offices in 1951—New York City had prided itself in keeping every diplomat who entered its precincts safe. The model the city used was one of total control and total involvement in security. It had been drummed into the police mind-set. Altering a safety scheme for the worse was not something Torre gave in to easily. "Not on my watch. Not with my Bomb Squad. It's my city that gets the blame if anything goes wrong." He argued against the plan. He did not prevail. But this incessant attention to detail was part of the cult of police management that also had been bred into the NYPD. It was why Torre was always on the lookout for interference in security plans. It was why integrating the dozens of agencies that would work together at the Republican convention was Ray Kelly's job one.

Once in Manhattan, President George Bush's convoy finally came under the additional protection that only the Bomb Squad could offer. His hotel was swept by bomb dogs and secured room by room by Secret Service and detectives from the Intelligence Division. The convoy, as it motored to the hotel, drove down streets that had been secured by uniformed officers spaced at uniform intervals along barricades, by Emergency Service squads, by police and Secret Service sharpshooters and heavy weapons teams, and by two mysterious unmarked white vans.

For hours before the convoy neared its final approach to the hotel where the President would stay, each car or bus or truck that entered that street was forced to slow, be examined by Secret Service, military explosives experts using mirrors to look under hoods and chassis, and NYPD bomb dogs. Then the vehicle was ordered to move forward slowly. As it did, it passed between the two parked white vans. In Iraq the rebel forces call these vans the white devils. The police described them as "backscatter vans," after the name of the broad and deep X-ray field they set up.

With the equipment humming behind them and the sides of the van vibrating with unseen radiation, the van operators sat at laptops and examined pictures so clear and so detailed they could pick up guns, knives, pocket change, cell phones, and wiring— anything that looked suspicious.

One van peered deep into one side of a vehicle, the other van into the other side. The two fields of X-ray vision interlocked, and the vehicle was given a final bill of health. The $850,000-plus systems were the pride of the squad. The Secret Service had a couple, other squads had a couple, and the military had deployed dozens to Iraq, where they roamed at night with their X-rays, able to pierce thick walls in the hunt for explosive caches and weapons dumps. The success they had had was what earned them the nickname white devils.

. . .

April 28, 12:00 P.M., Bomb Squad Base: A Transit Bureau patrol officer decided he could open suspicious packages himself. Apparently he had confused watching experts on CNN with actually knowing how to successfully open a package so it didn't blow up in your face. The job was at a sensitive location—the subway at Wall and Broad Streets, the heart of the largest financial market in the world. By the time a team got in to their response vehicle, the Transit Bureau had called in again: "Don't bother. We opened it. It was nothing."

Sergeant Hourihan continued down to the package. Once the first call had come, the squad protocol dictated that a response was required.

"When I got there, the transit sergeant had opened it." Hourihan was describing a black Samsonite suitcase. "He opened it by unsnapping the locks. In other words, the exact way you do not open it if it was suspicious enough to think it might be a bomb.

"If there was a bomb inside, he would have been dead," Hourihan said. "People don't understand what a pound of C-4 can do. They don't understand we are never going to arrive and say 'You wasted our time.' If you thought it was suspicious enough to call us, *wait*. We'll check it out. If it's nothing, we will thank you for calling and go on our way."

4

A Grand Old Pain

"It's all going to work because I am going to shut up," Mark explained. "But, Rich, I tell you, I have been pulling my hair out."

The lieutenant was referring to deployment plans, command structure plans, and a relentless pace of meetings, presentations, PowerPoint shows, and 3-D Secret Service animations to cover every contingency from the use of new concrete and Plexiglas barricades for crowd control and to prevent car bombs, to the number of toilets in temporary jails and the details of arresting demonstrators, right down to what kind of camera would be used to take the mug shots.

For New York City, winning the bid to host the Republican convention was a major coup. The mayor of New York, Michael Bloomberg, who was in many ways visionary, was in a battle for the city's long-term economic prosperity. He wanted to use the convention as a leading edge for the wings of tourism that he knew would be an important part of future revenue streams that would keep the city's gross economic product aloft. The traditional businesses—Wall Street, publishing, law, and accounting—had found less and less need to employ masses of people on

Manhattan Island, shrinking payroll tax, corporate taxes, and money spent in town. Nothing, but nothing, was going to be allowed to go wrong with this convention.

The Police Department was the guarantor of his bet. The tension in the department became palpable. One source of relief was the squad room discussion of novel linguistic usages such as "paradigm shift," which threatened to alter a time-honored police vocabulary that tended toward the monosyllabic: "The perp was in the house," "The package turned out to be nothing," "10-85 forthwith," "Affirmative Loo." It was agreed in the squad that the term "paradigm shift" more fittingly belonged in the Style section of the newspapers, where if two persons wore a particular hat it was a trend, and if three wore it, well, that was a paradigm shift. The squad room was a tough place. Other new terms appeared:

There were intelligence skiffs and Classified Intelligence Centers (CICs), where the high priests who wore top secret clearance badges could send and receive sensitive raw intelligence. There were Joint Intelligence Commands, or JICs, where a larger group of analysts could view the data. There were forward tactical commands inside Madison Square Garden, FBI Hostage Rescue Teams (HRTs), Weapons of Mass Destruction Teams (WMDTs), and Joint Operational Commands (JOCs). And, of course, there was the "paradigm shift." The new piece of squad room language had arisen out of Torre's reflexive instinct to say no to everything new.

Fundamentally conservative, Torre did not like change. Any suggestion of sharing command in a "liaison" with one of the new multi-agency commands prompted a no. Any idea that came from an officer outside the Bomb Squad—or possibly outside the Police Department—that could affect the deployment of the squad prompted a no and a day of muttering, head scratching, phone calls, and finally at least one call from his car to a trusted aide on the car speaker phone—the "scream-a-phone"—where he could vent his anger before getting home to his family—his wonderful wife of thirteen years, Lisa; his son; and his two daughters. Finally the squad convinced him to imagine he had written the word "Yes" on the palm of his hand. Each time he went into a meeting with the chief of detectives, the police commissioner, the head of the Secret Service, the chief of Patrol, the FBI special agent in charge, or a Republican convention political planner, he was to begin his first sentence of any answer with the word "Yes."

"Mark, do you think deploying more dogs on the street would be effective?"

"No. [Are you insane?] The Bomb Squad doesn't work that way," the old Mark Torre would have replied.

"Yes. I am glad you mentioned that," the new Mark Torre said. "We have looked at that and we have a plan in the works. May I get back to you to see if we can do it with the manpower we have, or if we will need to ask help from the squads in neighboring jurisdictions?"

So far, the new approach was working.

"We had a paradigm shift today," Assistant Chief Phil Pulaski explained when he saw that the lieutenant had become a sophisticated manager. He and Mark could now see eye-to-eye on how to proceed in this strange new world.

In the past when they had to grapple with one of these deployment issues, Pulaski and Mark would often fight like two brothers who were rivals as to who was smartest. That Pulaski had tolerated the arguments was a tribute to his own new-age police management style. As long as the argument was on the merits, he would engage in it. The old-school chiefs would simply have issued Torre an order and they would have expected the lieutenant to follow it. Now Pulaski and Torre could go head-to-head before the meetings, come to a decision, and enter the meeting rooms calm and unified. Mark, for his part, would now say yes or say nothing, until Phil had cleared some of the ground for him.

In the squad room these concerns receded. The talk centered on the pressing day-to-day concerns of bomb technicians—new fuzing methods that terrorists were trying out; methods bomb makers used to convert garage door openers into explosives initiators; the techniques of using a newly acquired roto-cutting tool to slice through the skin of a vehicle that housed a bomb; and just what flavor ice cream would the squad be having after dinner. And there was that favorite pastime: gossip.

The senior men's and the sergeants' kitchen-table speculation on Torre's future as their commander had finally shifted from the mid-winter betting that he would be relieved of command before the convention to the mid-spring betting that he would be allowed to continue to command until after the convention. Then, definitely then, he would be relieved of command when the police brass breathed a sigh of relief over the success and said, "Okay, now, where is that little thorn in our side?" Torre didn't mind the gossip and from time to time sat down at the kitchen table with his squad and put the gossip out there with humor and aplomb. It immediately eased the tension. At least for the next shift or two.

5

The Squad Room

A police precinct at night has special warmth. The *hmmmm* of fluorescent lighting; the *bzzz* of the outside street lamps; the lowered, less urgent voices over the police radios; the hollow resonance of metal doors closing; and the soft tick of the hands on the clock. The night watch police precinct sounds become a blanket, just as the watchmen are the security blanket for their city.

As this night watch began, an episode of *Law & Order* was on. In it a passenger discovered a suspicious package on a city bus and a cop was sent to check it out.

The A Team was relaxing. Hearn, Popper, and Klippel were in the blue swivels, leaning back, enjoying the show. From 16:00 to 23:59 and 00:00 to 0:800 the posted roster for May 7 noted theirs would be the one team on duty, working a double shift.

"Get everyone back two hundred and fifty feet," the police officer on the screen said.

"That's my role," Steve Lanoce said. The producers had drawn their inspiration from one of Lanoce's first jobs on the Bomb Squad. But he didn't get the part.

"Get everyone back two hundred and fifty feet," the fictional police officer repeated.

"I could have said that," Hearn said. "And that could have been you, Steve. Come on. Can't you get your acting career moving?"

Steve took his acting career seriously. Every day, in between The Job and the family, he studied hard, and he had worked hard at trying to get on the air with a speaking part. He recently had tested to play a bomb technician for another episode of *Law & Order,* but he was rejected. He was not believable, the producers felt. He kept trying. Each time the show sent its attractive assistant producers over to obtain free information from the squad, someone said, "Hey, we'll help you, but when are you going to hire Steve and make us rich?"

When things were quiet, the double tour overnight could include some "soft overtime," meaning overtime not driven by the pressing nature of special events or a surge in suspicious packages but by the need to cover for officers on vacation, out sick, or on a military tour. A lot of catch-up reading, TV viewing, and conversation could take place. Tonight Brian was exhausted. He had been at work since eleven o'clock and was turning gray at the jowls. But teasing Lanoce had cheered him up. His eyes twinkled as he leaned back in his chair, put his hands behind his head, and looked into the middle distance, while a seascape of furrows folded and unfolded on his brow.

"We're gonna have trouble ahead," he finally stated, leaning forward, his hands fiddling across some papers on the table, "if they keep relegating us to the sidelines. It's no good and it's gonna be no good if something happens."

Brian and the lieutenant had been trying to keep the number of non-NYPD bomb squads assigned to the inner perimeter of the Republican convention to a minimum, or better still, to none. They did not want the risk of working side by side with less skilled or less well-trained technicians, or simply technicians they were not familiar with. Hearn was worried that Mark might not be able to carry the day presenting these arguments to the Secret Service. The Secret Service had the overall responsibility for security. Mark had to get them to agree that the best course was for them to use their own techs, Marine and Army explosive ordnance technicians, and the Bomb Squad as the primary line of defense. There was ample reason for the federal government's concern that there were enough techs on hand for a rapid response. During the 2000 Republican convention in Philadelphia the squad there recorded forty-eight "hoax" devices. These had been placed by activists attempting to disrupt the proceedings. The devices looked like bombs, were placed where bombs would have been placed, and had to be treated as such. Sometimes when one was opened up, a note that said "Boom!" would be found.

"Mark is fighting the fight. But some of these guys have tunnel vision and they are not looking at the bigger picture," he said. "We've been doing this a long time. When something comes down, we don't need a hundred guys. What are those hundred guys going to do? If something goes off, I don't need a guy from Oklahoma looking over the post-blast."

A patrol officer stuck his head into the kitchen. He had four bags of fireworks—rockets—to drop off. This gave Hearn something new to worry over. It was too much explosive power to leave in the precinct overnight. It would have to be driven up to the range at Rodman's Neck and put in the locker. More than twelve hundred full bags of illegal fireworks came in to the squad each year—tens of thousands of pounds—and as it came in, it grew into a mountain of discarded fun inside heavily walled explosives magazines. When there was enough for a "burn," as a controlled destruction of the fireworks was called, then the fireworks would be arranged carefully and would sizzle out in a large cloud of black smoke. But they would not explode. A fireworks burn is one of the most dangerous routine chores the squad engages in. The fireworks are completely unpredictable. So what starts as a burn can end with a boom, and an injured bomb tech.

Lanoce called home. His personal dog, Jaeger, had epilepsy, his wife had just given birth, and he was checking in because her previous night had been filled with too much drama. The dog had had a seizure; his wife, a police officer in Upstate Rockland County, and a neighbor who was a nurse had swaddled up the newborn, snapped up the dog, and rushed it to the vet for treatment. Each time this happened, it cost Lanoce's family at least $500. Between covering the income loss for his wife's pregnancy leave—her job suspended pay—and paying for the dog, Lanoce was only too happy for the night shift overtime—or any other overtime he could get.

Reassured that all was calm at home, he ended the call and went back to figuring out who would play the other guys in his coming movie featuring the Bomb Squad.

May 13, night watch, Bomb Squad Base: Tasti D-Lite was the iced treat of the moment, and everyone on duty was eating it. The squad gained weight as a group and tried to lose it as a group. Tasti D-Lite was the tightrope down the middle. When the squad was in the middle of a "Chunky Challenge" they would try to cut out desserts, exercise harder, and eat smaller portions. But at no time would they alter their diet of Italian home cooking, meat loaf, carb-laden take-out, or stuffed pork chops. The results were predictable. Sooner or later, the food won out over the desire to lose weight and larger portions and second helpings were back on the plates. The results in the weight-loss competitions were also predictable. During the course of the Chunky Challenge of the previous season, both Hearn and Lanoce started out at 215 pounds. As the challenge wore on, they found that neither of them was able to fend off a cookie. Lanoce gained eight pounds and Hearn put on five. Finally their weights leveled off and Lanoce was able to lose five pounds. Hearn broke even at 215.

Tonight, *Spartacus,* a favorite of underdogs everywhere, was on TV.

"We'll follow you anywhere, Spartacus." It was Lanoce speaking.

Over the six months we had spent with the squad, he seemed to have developed into the resident TV critic. As the squad watched the movie, he announced that Paul Perricone was Paulicus, Hearn was Hearnicus, and of course, Mark Torre was Spartacus.

"But really you are Hernicus, Steve," Torre said. He was working a night tour that overlapped with the A Team's. Everyone laughed. Lanoce faked hurt feelings. He had strained his groin muscles as he had lifted his bomb suit up out of its bag, and a hernia had been the result.

"Pound for pound, he is definitely the softest guy in the Bomb Squad," Hearn replied. Torre was amused. He donned a pair of thin latex crime scene gloves and offered to do the preop shave for Lanoce.

Then the lieutenant's eyes looked off into the distance. His rest was over. He rose, nodded, and walked to his desk, where he settled behind the pile of discarded machine gun shells and artillery rounds perched on its edge and a mountain of paperwork at its scarred center. Around the kitchen table a notice was shared. The Republican convention protestors intended to target the dogs.

The notice, an FBI "Leads Report" from May 4, stated that an Internet posting had surfaced suggesting tactics to defeat the dogs.

"It appears the purpose of this posting is to disrupt transit trains during the Republican Convention. . . .

" 'Get some nitrate fertilizer. Sprinkle small amounts of it [dogs can smell a few grains] into inaccessible spaces starting a couple of months before the convention.

" 'Try to ride each and every car on the line as you commute to work. . . . (and drop a little fertilizer in it). This will not constitute any sort of danger but as soon as the dogs enter the trains they will alert, the trains will be stopped, the people will be removed and subjected to humiliating searches. This will really improve the average New Yorker's opinion of the Republican Convention.'"

This cleverness was an earmark of the sophisticated modern protestor. The use of the Internet to spread the message was another. But the threat never materialized.

The city had some propaganda tricks of its own. They came up with a plan to offer discount shopping coupons to all demonstrators and a button welcoming demonstrators to New York and the Republican convention.

"Welcome Peaceful Political Activists," the button read. Such was the world in which the squad operated.

Torre was looking through columns of numbers, reviewing a multimillion-dollar shopping list of new trucks, X-rays, bomb-smothering devices, and cutting tools against anticipated delivery dates, to see what would be on hand, tested, and trained on in time for the convention.

Outside his office Perricone disclosed that he did not really like parts of *Spartacus*.

"I'd rather not watch," he said. Perricone explained that he became sick at the sight of blood. During his physicals, he preferred that his blood be drawn from his hand, not his arm, so he didn't have to imagine it flowing out. This same man calmly could describe investigating a crime scene where "the teeth were sitting like Chiclets on the floor" after a man had blown his own and his girlfriend's brains out. People who do dangerous jobs are often very sensitive to any form of violence in movies, at the doctor's, or anywhere else in their lives. They prefer quiet lives and quiet pastimes.

Just as Jeff Oberdier had spooned his chili into a bowl and started to sit down, the first job of the day tour on May 17 came in: a suspicious package at Police Headquarters.

"Stay, you're eating, I'll go," Tommy "Sack" Sullivan offered.

Jeff just put his chili down, shook his head quietly, picked his radio up, signed himself out, and walked through the squad room door. It was his turn. The suspicious package was in the auditorium at Headquarters.

A grenade run came in seconds later. Billy Popper and Mike Klippel picked up their radios, took their truck keys from the Peg-Board, signed out, and started on the long journey to the farthest reaches of the city, Staten Island. They would meet Sergeant Mike Walsh on the way; like Hearn, the sergeant made the island his home.

Staten Island has two eras, Before the Bridge and After the Bridge. Before the Bridge, meaning the Verrazano, one of the world's longest suspension bridges, no one came to the island. After the Bridge, people came and got lost. The island was remote from the rest of city life; even the Bomb Squad called its officers "The Staten Island Police."

Klippel was in the recorder seat. Popper was driving. They could pass for brothers. They had the same build. They smoked the same cigarettes, and they were together, so they often alternated buying packs. They had the same buzz haircuts, and they wore the same wraparound sunglasses.

"Just because they say it's a grenade, doesn't mean it is . . . ," Klippel said when asked how a tech approached a grenade.

"You don't want to focus on one thing only to have it turn out to be something else," Popper added.

"You have to be ready for anything," Klippel continued. With their minds open, their badges visible, and their tools in their hands, the pair would enter the scene.

Sergeant Walsh met them and took the lead at the off ramp from The Bridge. They followed him onto the military base where the grenade had been discovered.

It might have been May, but it was dark, cold, and rainy, and the island had the windswept feel of a Northeast harbor winter. The grenade was in Room #141, "Officer's Locker Room." The lock has been knocked from the locker room door. The bottom portion of the door had been booted in, and the entire place felt neglected, semi-abandoned, and distant from any command. No one was willing to admit how a grenade had managed to get put or left in a locker. The grenade was in locker #19. The X-rays showed that it was live. And they showed that it had been tampered with.

Klippel and Popper put down the pictures, approached the grenade, and gingerly checked that it was not booby-trapped with an anti-lift or other motion trigger. They made certain nothing had been rigged to hold the firing pin down until it was jiggled. Then the grenade was carefully lowered into a heavy containment box. That was placed in the total containment vehicle, which had been sent for once it was obvious the grenade was a live one. The 11,000-pound TCV and its cargo of a single one-pound hand grenade drove off.

It was impossible to keep up with Sergeant B. The Ford Explorer doors opened, closed, opened and closed again; the engine was turned on and off and on again, and he was in and out of the car in a breakneck sequence of suspicious package runs. The blue and white SUV slid rapidly from job to job, weaving through crowds and gliding slowly through interlocking security perimeters.

It was May 23, the day of the annual Salute to Israel Parade. A day in which it did not take a journalist's imagination to notice that the sky above Fifth Avenue was as porcelain blue as the clear sky blue of the Israeli flag.

Sergeant B's smile, his windbreaker, his chinos, and his excited stride were familiar and reassuring to dozens of cops along the way.

"Wonderful, wonderful, I worked with her in anti-crime. A great gal. Good cop," he said, flipping open his cellular phone after saying hi to an undercover officer who had switched into a uniform for the day from whatever she usually wore to work.

"Yeah. We are tasked pretty good," he told Lieutenant Torre and ticked off another job on a list he kept under the sun visor.

"The major, yeah, he's doing great, great," he said, referring to Detective Jimmy Schutta, a former Marine major just returned from Iraq and brand-new to the squad. Schutta was driving, Sergeant B was guiding. There was no way to teach experience. So Schutta watched. This was a training mission for him, and before the parade had kicked off, Sergeant B and Schutta had been to suspicious packages on Broadway between Sixty-second and Sixty-third Streets, and at Fifth Avenue and Fifty-seventh Street. They were now on the run again, to another package. This one was in front of the Mary Boone Gallery on Fifth, across from Bergdorf Goodman.

Every new guy in the squad was on duty for the parade and was working with an experienced bomb tech or supervisor. This parade was an excellent opportunity to get some on-the-street and some on-the-package experience—experience where the eyes and the hands would matter more than the robot and the remote entry teams. There never failed to be at least a half dozen packages reported at the Salute to Israel Parade. Israel had plenty of enemies, and the attitude of police on parade duty was better safe then sorry, so they called in anything the slightest bit suspicious and the squad responded.

In maroon Bomb Squad golf shirts, chinos, and wraparound glasses, Klippel and Popper were standing at the entranceway to the very exclusive gallery when Sergeant B and Schutta stepped through the blue police horses and walked over. It looked like mail. Possibly a FedEx delivery. Before they considered blowing apart the package, the techs called FedEx and tried to find the gallery owner. This was where judgment and experience came into play. They determined the time of the FedEx delivery. They confirmed it was a regular delivery, and then instead of using a powerful jet of water to blow the package open, they gently opened it with the tip of a knife and examined the contents.

Mail. They marked it as safe and pushed it to the door before moving on. When the gallery opened its doors, its business would go on uninterrupted by a missed correspondence.

"Look, you pay a high premium, especially for units like the Bomb Squad that may never be needed. It's like an insurance policy. If it's not going KABOOM, it's bullshit. But when it's not bullshit, well, then it's worth the price."

Sergeant B was on the move again, taking the carriage road through Central Park, pulling to a stop at Seventy-second and Fifth, and grabbing a bottle of iced tea. The crowd was celebratory and dense.

"All this standing. All this running back and forth, back and forth with the X-rays and the tools; we don't get paid for what we do. We get paid for what we *can* do."

When the next radio call came in, he moved like sprung steel. He and Schutta were pulling up to it in less than five minutes. The handheld portable radio crackled: "ESU has responded. There is a Proper ID at Seven Five and Five [meaning at 75th Street and 5th Avenue]. All units cancel." Schutta turned the car away, and he and Sergeant B waited for the next call.

By the time they ended their tour, they had recorded seventeen jobs. Sergeant B was still smiling, and Schutta, who understood discipline, was still silent as they headed back to base. He had listened, he had observed, he had occasionally asked or answered a question. On the radio they heard a city official describe the day to the media as "uneventful."

Night watch on Tuesday, May 25, was not a TV night. The fleet would arrive on the next morning's tide. A convoy of military might, the newest ships in the twelve-vessel flotilla were armed with the latest electronic devices to ward off attacks from swimmers, divers, and small-boat suicide bombers. The entire parade was guarded by a contingent of heavily armed and highly trained fleet protection sailors who knew their jobs cold. From the shore they would be protected by the NYPD. They welcomed the help. The blowing up of the USS *Cole* had been a clear example of what a small boat full of explosives could do to a mighty cruiser.

Lieutenant Torre was in his office. The teams on duty were reviewing security plans, considering roster adjustments, and finalizing liaison arrangements with Naval Intelligence and the Navy Criminal Investigation Service officers. The sergeants were in touch with the ferry managers, making sure their boats—which had already been swept by the squad and its dogs—stayed secure until the fleet had moved through the harbor and to their berths. There were updates to the lieutenant and calls to and from the Joint Terrorism Task Force. There was also the last-minute rereading of papers designed to help the squad understand new Navy fleet protection measures, which included invisible fields around the ships that when penetrated would kill whatever came into their grasp. There was a Bomb Squad detail assigned to be in place by 3:00 A.M. at every boarding and landing site. With the arrival of the fleet, the season of spectaculars had begun.

"Now I'm getting one of those headaches," Hearn said. It visibly clenched his head. In turn he clenched a small bottle of white aspirin. It would get him through the night. Sergeant Duke dropped a roster on the table, and the group reviewed deployments for each shift of the week ahead. Torre came in. He took his chair at the head of the table and summed up the meetings he had had that day. He had most recently met with Chief Pulaski, who was the NYPD senior representative on the FBI-NYPD Joint Terrorism Task Force. There were no credible imminent threats to the fleet or to the spectators. It was a time to reminisce. Protecting the Navy was no new thing to Schutta, or to many of the other members of the squad, they liked to remind John Scomillio. The young tech was ex–Navy EOD, had about zero body fat, and was high-strung and wiry; for all that, he was Navy on land, unable to escape the burden of being identified as someone who needed a real soldier to hold his hand. Schutta and Scomillio had come to the squad within weeks of each other, and soon they would head to Hazardous Devices School together to complete their basic training.

May 26, 6:20 A.M., under-vehicle surveillance, Fifty-fifth Street at the Hudson pier: Sergeant Coughlan, Jimmy Carrano, Jimmy Schutta, John Scomillio, and Bobby Schnell, the squad dog trainer, were huddled beside their blue surveillance van. The rain had blown in with the fleet, and slashed across what were now the battleship gray green waters of the Hudson.

WARNING RESTRICTED AREA KEEP OUT
USE OF DEADLY FORCE AUTHORIZED
In accordance with
DOD Directive
5216.56

This was a federal issue valet parking sign. It greeted each car that approached the checkpoint.

The Bomb Squad team manned the checkpoint's under-vehicle surveillance system. It was a simple system. There were two cameras. One, mounted to face an approaching car, recorded the license plate. A second array of video lens and lights was mounted in a thick rubber speed bump that lay across the road. This lens conveyed images of the car underside to a monitor inside the van.

Fleet Week was a test run for the use of the system at the Republican convention. The team watched as cars refused to slow down, unless the driver was threatened by a sailor with an M16. It watched cars knock the rubber mounted cameras out of line because they drove over the bump too fast, and it watched water collect on the lens. By the time of the convention, there would be metal barricades that popped up in front of the car, holding it in place until the search was completed. The lens array built into the speed bump would be embedded in the road, and the lens of the camera mounted to face an approaching car would have a proper rain shroud.

The other Bomb Squad teams on duty had spotted, properly identified, and disposed of three suspicious packages that morning, before the fleet had even docked.

Patrolling between the Bomb Squad and the vessels was a dog handler, Benjamin Woods, United States Navy, E-5. He was standing in his poncho in the rain. His dog was trained to bite, to hunt explosives, and to work well in a gunfight. This was not the way the PD preferred dogs to be trained—one dog, one mission, was the preference there; certainly no mix of aggressive response-attack and passive response-sitting, when a bomb was found.

The Navy fleet protection teams had a different mission and therefore a different doctrine. Their dogs needed to serve a small force in various combat situations that required every member, including the dog, to have multiple skills. But the fleet protection detail and the Bomb Squad detail had one thing in common: The members were a team, and a calm one at that.

"To do this work, you've got to be laid back; you've got to be willing to be part of a team and to not stand out. But there is no point in playing a percentage," said Woods. It is the same reason the bomb techs wear their heavy suits, try to disrupt bombs from a distance, and walk instead of run toward danger. Benjamin Woods, United States Navy, E-5, took his dog, his automatic pistol, and his long gun and continued his patrol.

BOOK SEVEN

Bomb 101

1

Greetings from Baton Rouge

Welcome to the International Association of Bomb Technicians and Investigators' annual convention, the Louisiana Edition, 2004. Pickled pig lips, boudin sausage, low country barbecue, alligator étouffée, hard liquor, and looking-up-at-sea-level humidity were on the menu. Hundreds of bomb technicians forced their way in and out of a small, hot hospitality suite, and their sweat poured out into the hotel corridors. The IABTI conference was hosted by Jerry Denny: madman; Alcohol, Tobacco and Firearms explosives expert; and outgoing international director of the bomb technicians' association. He had built the Baton Rouge conference with a determination to have himself the finest farewell bash the IABTI had ever seen. He succeeded.

If there was ever a time and a place for pointillism in description, the International Association of Bomb Technicians and Investigators' 32nd Annual International In-Service Training Conference and Trade Exhibition was it. A blur of handshakes, cards, hats, and badges, it was a conclave of the brotherhood of the bomb, the masters of the black art of snipping wires, the students of the science of defusing explosive devices. It was a chance to eyeball your brethren who one day, if the crisis was big enough, you might find yourself working with as squads from around a region or across the country were called to respond. The IABTI was a hub in a spidery network that spanned the globe.

"We maybe do it because we have a loose screw; we maybe do it for love of our country, and I don't just mean the United States of America," Denny said in his valediction. He said it at a podium before more than seven hundred collected bomb technicians and demolition experts who had come from police departments; fire departments; FBI divisions; Alcohol, Tobacco and Firearms field offices; and military units across the United States and the world. The applause was raucous.

There are many kinds of law enforcement get-togethers. Chiefs gather at large convention halls when the International Association of Chiefs of Police convenes its annual policy initiative and networking event. They host panels on use of force, bias crime, speeding, ethnic profiling, and crimes against juveniles. They browse equipment vendor stalls, collect telephone numbers, and attend cocktail parties and formal dinners. These useful events are paid for by the taxpayer. Then there are "rackets" held in church basements, Polish halls, Bohemian halls, Irish bars, Russo's on the Bay–type catering halls, and other for-the-night venues. These raise money for wounded officers, celebrate retirements, and gather fraternal organizations—the Hibernians, the Columbus Society, the Asian Jade Society, and all the other ethnic and religious police groups. These sentimental events are paid for by the individual ticket. Next, there are police union annual picnics and conventions, which have become sedate things of late and no longer feature the shooting up of hotels and lodges or tossing of all of a resort's furniture and loose fixtures into a swimming pool. The mountainside and seaside resort hotels had begun having second thoughts about getting the police in their beds. These events are paid for by the union members' dues. (The insurance companies in the past covered the outcomes.) And finally, there are the charitable fund-raisers—very fancy luncheons and dinners put on by law enforcement foundations and graciously underwritten by corporations who value municipal services, and by wealthy supporters of police. Some are altruistic supporters; others want to play cop and are willing to pay good money to ride in a police car, carry an honorary shield, and possess some form of get-out-of-jail-free card endorsed by a local big shot and good for showing to an occasional traffic cop.

And then there is the IABTI. The lectures are serious, but the convention is definitely alcohol-fueled. Normally the attendees eschew alcohol even when off duty, during the days or nights before it is their turn to stand over suspicious packages. The IABTI is an opportunity to unwind without a risk to the well-being of—or an affront to the naive eyes of—too many civilians.

"A lot of nurses and not a lot of doctors in there," said ex–British Navy Petty Officer Ian Barker during a break in the dinner. Barker was referring to the attendees who hadn't defused anything except the point of a conversation.

"Yeah, well whatta ya gonna do," said Jeff Oberdier, who headed the New York City contingent.

The vendor aisles and meeting rooms—the business end of the convention—were down at the end of a long entrance hall behind him.

The aisles glittered. There were stalls selling bomb suits and total containment vessels—pressure cookers for the controlled release of explosive gasses.

There were carpeted walls and felt-covered tables hung and lined with hats, belts, thick work gloves, dull metal- or thick-black-plastic-cased tool kits that cost $15,000 apiece, and rope rigging kits used to tip and turn suspicious packages from several dozen feet away. The merchandise was oiled and shined and polished and pretty as a pig at a 4-H show. The rigging kits in particular were a salesman's dream of a high markup on various lengths of braided line and rope made of stretchable or non-stretchable stuff, clips, carabiners, and pulleys. All of this was gear that a prior generation of bomb technicians had accumulated a piece at a time in order to put together their squads' kits. It was more efficient and standardized this way. The manufacturers were sure to put the latest and best bits in their kits, and a tech from any jurisdiction could now enjoy the benefits of a standardized set of tools. There were tables filled with electronic wizardry—geek dream boxes ablaze with digital readouts. They had become increasingly sophisticated at electronically jamming the signals from cell phones, pagers, personal digital assistants—anything using radio waves—which bombers used to create carnage from a safe distance. These boxes contained software that could search for specific signals to jam, barrage entire ranges of frequencies with an electronic rain, and home in on specific, narrow frequency ranges, blocking any signal in that spectrum.

But every carnival has a main attraction, something beyond the two-headed babies, the sheep with six legs, the bearded ladies—the one tent that has them stepping right up without the outside barker having to do very much at all except hold out his hand to collect the money. At the IABTI, that tent holds the Med-Eng bomb suit exhibit.

The Med-Eng suit is de rigueur; the only proper suit for the occasion. With the ardor of a French couturier, the manufacturer refines the suit each year—improving the armor, the cooling fans, the face mask lens, and the flexibility the suit has to resist various nuances of blast and shock and compression from front, back, sides, and top. The exhibit this year featured Richard L'Abbe, the company founder. After an introduction, the meaty part began with L'Abbe standing on a green lawn clad in the ninety-pound khaki fruits of his engineering efforts. He put his helmet on, set down a block of plastic explosive, and detonated it while standing over it. Knocked back, he slowly got up and then walked away. Sold! I'll take six for my squad. The armored product with the ergonomic helmet had prevented the fatal effect of being knocked on one's back by a blast wave. The demonstration was not a one-time thing. D'Abbe pointed out in his testimonial that he had performed the demonstration nineteen times. He stopped, he explained, only on doctor's orders.

At night, as the heat sank below ninety-five and the humidity leveled off somewhere nearby, members of the squad from New York drifted apart. Retired Lieutenant Sheehan went off with his older cronies. Oberdier and a couple of other guys headed to the casino. Others stayed out by the pool. The black curl running down the forehead of Sergeant Mike "Dino" DeMarfio had caught the attention of one of the women at the convention. The forty-three-year-old bachelor settled in at the hotel, sipping a scotch and soda while he waited for the group to get lost. DeMarfio had made one mistake in his life, he reflected—joining a bomb squad. When the day came when he had to defuse his first bomb and had to cash the check with his ass that he had written with his mouth, his first words were "Jesus Christ! Am I doing this?"

2

The Big Casino

While bomb squad members are risk-averse by profession, casinos do play an important part in U.S. bomb technician lore. It was in a casino that the first "undefeatable bomb" exploded in 1980, despite attempts to defuse it.

The 1980 casino bomb was devised and planted by John Birges, Sr. When he died in prison in August 1996, his obituary in the *Washington Post* bore the headline CRIMINAL MASTERMIND; although as the circumstances of his death would indicate, it was a very generous headline.

Birges, a Hungarian immigrant, a successful businessman, a man prone to boasts of having been a Luftwaffe pilot, a World War II prisoner of war, and a Hungarian freedom fighter before emigrating to America in 1957, was also a degenerate gambler. By August 1980 he had been banned from many casinos on the Lake Tahoe strip and was in debt to Harvey's Resort Casino Hotel for $15,000, according to published reports.

His solution was to build an unbeatable bomb—a large, complex bomb containing high explosives that equaled one thousand sticks of dynamite in power. He encased it in steel, having armed it with an array of toggle switches, relays, and motion and water sensors designed to make the device unde-featable.

On August 25, 1980, at 5:00 A.M., a white Econoline van pulled up to the loading ramp at Harvey's, on the Nevada state line. The letters IBM were crudely stenciled on the truck, and the device wheeled out of it and into the casino was encased in a wooden crate as if it were a piece of office equipment. Three men and a woman assisted in delivering the crate. They wheeled the cart to the deserted second-floor executive offices of the casino and removed the crate and a set of blankets stenciled with IBM. (Later the newspapers would note that the stencil was not the computer giant's proper logotype.) They adjusted four spirit bubble levels epoxied to the four top corners of the box. To an onlooker, it would have appeared they were leveling the large machine. But they had begun arming the bomb. They then slipped strips of electrical tape into an opening between the top and bottom parts of the box. Doing this closed various switches in the electrical circuit, completing the arming of the device. All of this was contained in a never-before-disclosed post-blast re-port filed by NYPD Bomb Squad Detective Bill Schmidt. Schmidt had been sent to Nevada to develop a "lessons learned" brief in the aftermath of the incident. Upon leaving the execu-tive offices, Schmidt explained, the team stuck toothpicks into the locks and epoxied the knobs on the doors to the complex, sealing the area. But before the glue set, one hotel employee entered the area and saw and read the three-page extortion note stuck into a handle of the box. This was Birges's demand for the cash he felt the casinos owed him:

STERN WARNING TO THE MANAGEMENT
AND BOMB SQUAD:

Do not move or tilt this bomb, because the mechanism con-trolling the detonators in it will set it off at a movement of less than .01 on the open end Richter scale. Don't try to

flood or gas the bomb. There is a float switch and an atmos-
pheric pressure switch. . . . Do not attempt to take it apart.
The flathead screws are also attached to triggers and as much
as ¼ to ¾ of a turn will cause an explosion. . . . This bomb
can never be dismantled or disarmed . . . even by the cre-
ator. . . . There are three automatic timers, each set for three
different explosion times. . . . Only if you comply will you
be given instructions on how to disconnect the first two automatic timers and how to move the bomb to a place where
it can be exploded safely. . . . I repeat do not try to move,
disarm or enter this bomb. It will explode. . . . It is full of
TNT. . . . We demand three million dollars in [unreadable
word] hundred dollar bills. We don't want any trouble but
we won't run away if you bring it. Happy Landing.

Within minutes a nearby Army EOD unit was en route. A
Federal Department of Energy Nuclear Emergency Search Team
and a team from the Lawrence Livermore National Laboratory
were close behind. Birges's Trojan Horse—a metal box about four
feet long, two feet wide, and two feet high, with twenty-eight toggle switches and at least twelve flat-topped screws attached to triggers, withstood thirty-four hours of investigation into possible
methods of rendering it safe. None were found. During that time,
three thousand tourists and gamblers were evacuated, a highway
was shut down, and according to *Newsweek* magazine, 260,000
sandbags were brought up to surround the device. The Livermore
Lab meanwhile used a computer in an effort to create a shaped
copper-cased charge—similar to an artillery round—that contained
four pounds of plastic explosive and if successful would disrupt the
bomb's firing chain before the bomb could detonate. This was the
method that was finally used.

As word of the impending controlled blast spread, "a carnival
atmosphere prevailed" according to *Newsweek*.

As authorities tried to cope with the device, the hotel owner,

Harvey Grossman, tried to comply with the demand. But Birges's proposed helicopter delivery arrangement went awry. The hotel owner waited, but Birges never made a second request for the money.

At 6:30 P.M., on August 27, Douglas County Sheriff John Maple was heard on his police radio, warning that the disarming attempt was about to begin.

"This," he said, "is a fifteen-minute notification," the Associated Press reported.

Ten minutes later Maple came on the radio again:

"In approximately five minutes we will have an explosion in the Stateline area, coming from Harvey's."

Silence. Then the siren. And the blast. It was 6:43 P.M.

The blast was a bit larger than expected. The engineers and scientists miscalculated. The shaped charge wasn't properly formed and the controlled detonation had failed. Five stories of the ten-story hotel were destroyed.

"Almost immediately, T-shirts appeared, declaring: 'I Survived the Bomb Scare at Stateline' and 'I Had a Blast at Harvey's,'" *Newsweek* reported.

A witness, Tracey Heaton, twenty-five, told the *Washington Post* she wasn't even fazed when a hotel worker burst into her room early Wednesday to warn her a bomb was about to go off.

"I'm originally from New York, and this happens all the time in New York." At the time she said it—1980—explosions were occurring in New York, if not all the time, with great regularity, thanks to the ongoing efforts of the FALN and others.

Detective Schmidt's eight-page memo and a seventeen-page appendix became the basis for revising evacuation distances and for establishing new practices for safe transport of such a device. The most troubling element of Schmidt's report: A determined man had proved that a bomber could make a device that could defeat many if not all of the available techniques for rendering it safe.

It took a year to catch Birges, and a few more to put him behind bars. He may not have been a criminal mastermind—he did get caught and he never got his money—but he was an exceptionally clever bomb builder, who created a large, vehicle-delivered bomb well before any modern terrorist.

In 2004 the threat to casinos remained significant. Five of the September 11 hijackers transited through Nevada casinos, and the day after Christmas in 2003 the *Washington Post* reported: "US government officials said yesterday they believe some of the passengers boarding one of the three Air France flights from Paris to Los Angeles that were canceled this week because of security concerns might have intended to hijack it and crash land in Las Vegas or another city along its flight path."

In 2002 the Justice Department had seized videotape that showed two separate surveillance operations by al Qaeda operatives at three Las Vegas hotels. A witness at a Detroit terrorism trial told authorities that al Qaeda viewed Las Vegas as the "City of Satan" and boasted "the brothers are going to destroy it." The threat to Las Vegas remains very real in 2006.

3

Bomb 101

"I'm here to tell you I am not an expert. I have been doing this for twenty-seven years and I am not an expert."

With that sincere sentence, U.S. Army Master Sergeant Paul Carter began the first class of the first day of Hazardous Devices School's basic training course for bomb technicians. For the occasion, Paul wore an American flag tie. It was the last time he would be seen in a tie for the next five weeks.

"We take safety seriously. Everything was learned the hard way. Meaning someone was hurt or killed." He ticked off the basics for the intent audience.

It was July 2004, the IABTI was over, and now the business of learning to become a bomb tech had begun. Two New York squad members, John Scomillio and Jimmy Schutta, were attending. The class was held in a quonset hut inside the HDS compound on the Redstone Arsenal Army Base in Huntsville, Alabama. A set of manikins clad in biohazard suits, blast-resistant rescue suits, and full-on bomb suits stood in a row against a wall.

"Keep shop talk in the shop. Be aware of your conversations. Be aware of your surroundings. Talking in bars is a great way to give away our secrets." "Loose Lips Sink Ships" was the way the old World War II posters stated his message.

Paul was plainspoken. His simple words were based on decades of experience. He did not feel a need to embellish.

"Is there someone from the Navy here?"

John Scomillio, the wiry, tightly wound former Navy explosive ordnance technician from the NYPD, raised his hand.

"Sorry, I didn't recognize you. I'm used to people from the Navy walking into the room backwards." Paul Carter kept the pace up and kept mixing it up, from joke to point to joke.

"This is a great place. I'm not from Alabama. Best part of Alabama is every week blowin' a part of it up."

Paul Carter, master sergeant, U.S. Army, retired, was the chief supervisory training instructor of the Hazardous Devices School. He *was* Bomb 101.

"The training you get here is approved by the Department of the Army based on requirements we get from the FBI," he said, then introduced the instructors for the course work ahead. A sampling from one day in the first week:

0840–0930 Pretest
0940–1030 FBI presentation
1040–1130 Bomb Squad Responsibilities WMD
1230–1320 Protective Equipment
1235–1415 Bomb Suit Components
1425–1515 Protective Equipment (Bomb Suit)
1520–1610 Protective Equipment (Search and Rescue)

On the afternoon of that first day the class was divided into two groups of twelve to begin a rotation through the three practical exercises noted on the schedule. Each lasted fifty minutes. A reporter took his turn. These are his notes, taken as soon as he could breathe again:

Putting on the suit for the very first time, the heart begins to pound. The ice vest placed on the occupant first in an attempt to keep the body's core temperature from rising to match the heat of July in Alabama felt like it was freezing up the chest. The heavy suit at the same time starts to heat up the extremities. The air tank strapped onto the back of the suit threatens to pull the occupant backwards to the floor. Then the helmet is locked on, and the face plate pulled down, and the respirator is the only link to the outside world. The claustrophobia, isolation and inability to understand why he had tried this exercise came into play. Now the only sound was his own heart and the scratchy noise of the respirator as he tried to breathe. He knew he was breathing too fast. He could barely hear the shouts from outside: "Are you all right in there?" He nodded. He felt dizzy. He was certain he would run out of air. Are they crazy? Who could carry this suit, an X-ray, a bag of tools and maybe haul a person out of a building where one bomb has already gone off. The next 12 minutes were to acclimate to the suit. The time was spent leaning back against a table and listening to the heart rate go down and the breathing slow down. Then came the walk through the obstacle course. A walk on a nice Alabama day with the temperature hovering near the low 100s. Inside the suit, sweat. The walk through the yard, up some steps, over a door frame and back into the training area took another 11 or 12 minutes. Then the suit came off and there was a great gasp for air.

"That's the long walk." It was after class when Paul Carter explained the walk in the suit. He was seated at a gunmetal desk in his office just off the classroom.

"I believe it is a British term; it is where you put a bomb suit on, and you're walking downrange toward an IED. I tell my students the day ... the first day they arrive, I think this is one of the few jobs where everybody is moving away from the area. And you're by yourself. You don't have a partner behind you. You don't have a SWAT team behind you. You're walking downrange, in a suit, carrying tools and equipment, to look at an IED. And that's the long walk. Whether it's a mile, three hundred feet, or a hundred feet. It's a very long walk.

"The first thing I tell them is get rid of their bad habits. A lot of them have been waiting two years. And during that time they've been out working with their bomb squad. And there are some bad habits out there. Some of the students are former military EOD. I tell them all, 'Get rid of your habits; we're going to teach you the safest, the most efficient way to do it.'

"Because when we have a man or a woman inside a bomb suit, they're thinking about procedures, they're thinking about their training. They're not thinking about being hurt. They're not thinking 'I may get killed' or 'I may get injured'; they're thinking about doing their job. They've got their tools, their techniques, their procedures in their mind. And they're a machine, they're moving downrange, and they're trying to take care of this incident. We want them to do it in a safe and efficient manner, without getting anybody hurt and if possible any property destroyed."

To that end HDS also teaches its students that whenever they can, they should avoid hand entry to a package, unless a human life is at stake and the hand entry is unavoidable. "Start remote. Stay remote" is practically a school motto. There are the robots that can see, talk, and wield tools, and there are percussion disrupters for the robot to carry, and there are X-rays and roto-tools for it to use; there are plenty of means at the tip of a joystick, when time and risk to life permit, to avoid walking up to a package and cutting it open with a prayer and a pocketknife.

Paul Carter had a staff of fifty-two instructors whom he had handpicked, hired, and now oversaw. He came to EOD work in 1974, having seen a jeep with red fenders and a siren flash by and, being pretty tired of the signal corps, deciding that wherever that jeep was going was where he wanted to be. That took him to the

EOD training school at Indian Head in Charles County, Maryland. It is on the crab of the Charles County estuaries that the EOD Crab is based.

"I cannot think of any other job I'd rather have than being a bomb tech. I would still be in the Army today if I could; I would still be an instructor if I could. I believe I would put on a bomb suit today and go down and work on the device. It's the best job in the world.

"Actually, it's a lifestyle, I believe, more than a technical career. I say it's a lifestyle because I've done things and had more experiences and met some great people and I . . . Where I come from I never would have thought I'd do the things I've done being a bomb tech. Things some people, most people, don't want to do, and I'd gladly do it. I'd rather do then teach, and I'd rather teach than run the school. I've had an opportunity to see the world. I've been down in tunnels, I've been through minefields, I've been in some munitions areas, I . . . Unfortunately, I've been in areas where children have been hurt and people have been killed, and I've had to clean up the aftermath. I met some really good people. I've met some bad people. But . . . uh, across the board, it's been an experience I wouldn't give up for anything." Paul had colleagues equally devoted to their profession, or lifestyle. Until his retirement, Ray Funderberg was one.

Ray Funderberg has a face as scoured by weather as driftwood. His eyes are as clear as a western sky. His hands remain still, as a first-rate mind glissades through the forest of challenges posed by the growth in sophistication of improvised explosive devices. Funderberg came to the Hazardous Devices School at the Redstone Arsenal in Huntsville, Alabama, as an instructor in 1981. When he left in 1999, he was the chief instructor. He too is Bomb 101. He was considered by graduates to be one of the finest instructors and chief instructors they had ever seen. His explanation of the development of bomb-making and bomb-defusing technology was eloquent, especially his explanation of the difference between X-raying the known and X-raying the unknown.

"The technology of bombs has increased manyfold. Comparing today's devices with the devices that existed when I first started, it's like talking about a piece of paper and a computer.

"So to go out and do blind hand entry in this day and age— it wouldn't be suicide, but you would be contemplating suicide.

"Since nobody really wants to contemplate suicide, you use the new techniques and technology—because in addition to new fuzing techniques, you also face a much greater possibility of facing a weapon of mass destruction.

"Today, if you had no [advanced] tools, it would be a bad job, and I wouldn't want it."

Ray Funderberg describes the work of the bomb technician through a simple device—it is, he says, the exploration of the unknown on life-and-death terms.

"You go to the doctor's office. There's been a jillion pictures made of human beings and we know exactly what the density is of everything. We know what's supposed to be here, what's supposed to be there. The settings on the X-ray have been refined for different outputs. Literally, an X-ray tech can look in a book and say you're six foot and you weigh so much and take a picture and it's gonna be almost perfect, because everything's been refined for that.

"When a bomb technician looks at a package, the only thing he has to go on is whatever the exterior material appears to be. If it's wrapped in paper, all he sees is paper. He has no idea if it's a steel ball wrapped in paper.

"Then when you get to the interior components, you have absolutely no idea. It could be anything. So what you do is you make a best guess based on the size of the package, what you see on the outside as far as material."

That is why the portable X-ray is such a valuable tool. It provides clues to the unknown. Although New York had primitive X-ray devices for the lab beginning in the late 1930s and for the field beginning in the mid–1950s, there were none that came into widespread use among bomb squads into the 1980s.

"We do a great job of X-raying an unknown. Nobody X-rays unknowns, basically. Bomb techs are the rare few that do that. I think most of us are a little similar in that we agree it's a really complicated thing to approach a total unknown. Almost nobody knows the answer to that. Total unknowns are very difficult. You have no knowns. None. It's a difficult problem.

"To work on a package with absolutely nothing is almost impossible. You say, well, you don't know what it is. That's true. I don't. But there are things that I can gather that give me some knowns. It might only be the size. Well, that tells me something. It might be the exterior material. That tells me something. These are things that I now can start formulating. If I can get more knowns, that's very useful. One item is a giant leap. When you are walking up on one of these items, you better be observing. 'Is there a booby trap? Is there a problem of approach?' You're trying to get other little knowns—little bitty ones. Most of the time, what you're really going to attain out of that approach is little bitty bits of information. Obtaining this information and so forth occupies 98 percent of your approach. 'What am I going to do? Am I getting something? Is there something here?' So you don't think so much about other things. You don't have the mental capability to do all these things and be scared at the same time. It's not heroics. It's not bravery. It's just that you're doing something and you're intent and you're focused on these other things. You can't be focused on 'I wonder if it's gonna blow up.' Of course it could possibly blow up. That's a given."

This is the course work of Bomb 101. Not merely the drills in techniques, the practice in using them, but a set of lessons in coming to terms with the uselessness of bravery, and with the extreme importance of developing any clue as to what is inside a suspicious package.

The Hazardous Devices School compound is three hundred acres of courses, houses, booby traps, swamps, and forest. It has been the training site for bomb technicians in the United States since January 1971, when it first opened its doors on very short notice.

"I was one of three guys from EOD Division who were assigned under a major to get it started," explained Bobby Nye, one of the first instructors and now the senior man at the school. "They sent the four of us down from Indian Head [Maryland]. We had ninety days—lesson plans, workbooks, the range—they all had to be ready."

Since that first course, 7500 students have taken the basic course, and 16,000 students in all have attended HDS—attending basic, recertifying every three years, and participating in week-long robot, weapons of mass destruction, and bomb squad management courses. A total of 450 bomb squads have been accredited, and every working bomb technician in the United States now shares the common experience and discipline of this standardized training.

Nye was now putting the finishing touches on a new $25 million complex of classrooms and training villages. It would open in September 2004. He would then retire.

Until meeting these men, you could be forgiven for thinking that you could not find a droller, drier, wryer, softer-spoken group than the NYPD Bomb Squad. Now you have. If buttoned down and relaxed can exist simultaneously, in the same person, at the same time, then here it was in Paul Carter, Ray Funderberg, and Bobby Nye.

Finally there is Floyd Pirtle. He has every quality of these other men, save one. He will never be buttoned down. He was a narc, an undercover, and he wears the distinctive, if graying, ponytail of a man who worked alone inside crime, looking out. He began as a cop in Huntsville, the town outside the Redstone Arsenal gates. There he did his stint in Narcotics and then wrapped his hands around a few live devices and never looked back. Gruff, tough, someone who had been there, done that, got the pin, the hat, the T-shirt, and still had all his limbs and fingers, Floyd was a pretty good bomb technician. No bomb tech is great, he would say, until, like Funderberg, they retire. Until then, they are a mistake away from dead or maimed.

"Working on a suspect package or a bomb, whether you know it's a bomb or a hoax, you know, that is a very irrational thing for most people to do. If you can just step back and make a rational judgment of what is the best, safest way to handle that device, then you're good to go," Pirtle explained.

"The movies, I think, do a lot of discredit to real-life bomb techs. The students that I see come through here are very professional, very dedicated. They're not the Rambo or Mel Gibson type. They're levelheaded. They can make a rational decision in an irrational situation, and that's what we're looking for."

The selection process that guaranteed the candidates are level-headed was overseen by FBI Supervisory Special Agent Dave Jernigan, a twenty-year FBI veteran. He fell in love with bomb work in his first year in the FBI. He was stationed in Idaho, when his office was bombed by one of the Aryan Nation groups. Assigned to the Crime Scene Unit that worked in the shards of glass, scattered files, and destroyed furniture of his new office, Jernigan looked into himself and said, "Man, it doesn't get any better than this." Within four years he was attending HDS.

"I'm a firm believer of, you're going to play like you practice. If we can instill in them some basic safety tenets, I feel that that's going to follow them through their career. It's very easy to slip. It's very easy to get complacent. It's very easy to get lax."

That was why bomb technicians had to return to Huntsville every three years for a refresher course in order to stay accredited.

If the tech passed the course, he or she stayed in the fraternity. If the tech failed, then he or she was a former bomb tech.

Jernigan was the man in charge of administering the "National Guidelines for Bomb Technicians." The nineteen pages of guidelines were enshrined in the "FBI Bomb Data Center Special Technicians Bulletin 87-4." This "law enforcement sensitive" booklet outlined everything from HDS candidate selection procedures—including background checks—to training methods, to three double-spaced pages of equipment required by each accredited bomb squad, to the rules for formation of a new squad. The guidelines were first drafted in 1996 at an FBI-hosted Bomb Squad Commanders Conference. Ninety-one commanders from thirty-seven states and the District of Columbia attended. They reviewed and revised the guidelines, and following the conference the FBI surveyed every bomb squad in the nation and also incorporated their responses. In 1998 the National Bomb Squad Commanders Advisory Board was formed, and the guidelines were revised again into their current form.

The standardizing of training methods, modernization of training facilities, and improvements to the tools at the bomb technician's command have occurred only relatively recently—in the decade from the late 1980s through the late 1990s. Despite the lessons of Viet Nam and despite domestic terrorism, the nation's bomb squads had until very recently been underfunded and undertrained. Until the fundamentalist and secular Middle Eastern bombing campaigns captured the political imagination, money was very scarce. The HDS budget first hit a million dollars in 1996; in 1997 the school operating budget quadrupled to $4.3 million.

"Since 9/11 it seems like everybody wants a bomb squad. I think there is some kind of security blanket feeling that they've got somebody who they can call to take care of things right away. If you have them in every town and every city, all over the United States, the experience level would be very low."

Detective Jimmy Schutta, former major, United States Marines, surfed into Jernigan and Carter's HDS for his basic course one summer evening, and he did it with a New Yorker's aplomb. He is the kind of student HDS looks for. A combat-hardened Marine major, Schutta had volunteered to again become a junior man. When he graduated HDS, he would once again cross a line of departure, one every bit as significant as the one he crossed when he served as a chief of police for the Dhi Qar Province in Iraq, where he and thirty-three Marines attempted to organize fifteen hundred Iraqis into the first local police squads.

"When they leave, we have done everything we can do in five weeks. Statistics tell us somebody will answer a call this weekend," Jernigan said. "You have to ask yourself, are you ready? There will not be an instructor looking over your shoulder."

Schutta's first call came the day he returned to New York. The city was in a heightened state of alert because of the looming Republican National Convention. A suspicious package had been called in near the Long Island Rail Road yard in Jamaica, Queens.

"I suited up. I went down. I took some X-rays. Sometimes it's not what you can see, but what you don't see. I didn't see anything. I didn't see any of the four components of an IED—an explosive device. So I was pretty confident by the time I went for my second trip down, when I cut it open, that it was going to be an empty suitcase.

"But you definitely have an adrenaline rush, because you're thinking, 'It's my first job. I can finally sort of legitimize my being here.' But for me—I guess it goes back to the military—also going through my head is what I learned: 'Take it from Step 1.' I know what I was trained to do."

LVB-61 (Large Vehicle Blast-61), Lompoc, California: The training never stops. Ask Special Agent Bomb Technician Kevin

Miles. Kevin, the senior man of the FBI's 146 SABTs, Special Agent Bomb Technicians, teaches Large Vehicle Post Blast Investigations sixteen times a year, a week-long course. It is one more step in the training; it is graduate school.

At the start of each course, as the students are inside classrooms being lectured, Kevin takes several hundred or a couple of thousand pounds of explosives and blows up a school bus, a commuter rail car, or in today's case, a Winnebago.

Blown apart, the Winnebago became four acres of gleaming shredded aluminum shards, some as small as a fingertip. When hurtling through the air they could slice through flesh and bone before being heard or even felt. Also scattered by the blast were lengths of fake wood trim and contact paper, and bits of blue plastic from the burst fifty-gallon drums that would have held the ammonium nitrate explosive.

The task of Miles's class was to put the parts of that Winnebago back together. The class had to do it without trampling the crime scene, and do it in a fashion that a U.S. attorney or district attorney could then use to put a bomb maker into jail. In order to build that case, they were instructed to find any pieces of the initiator to the device, any key to the Winnebago, and any partial of a license plate; on the intact chassis they were to look for the Vehicle Identification Number.

Kevin, with his bowl-cut blond hair, acerbic humor, and complete dedication to his job, was teaching what it takes to make a case in court: how to gather the evidence that says to a jury—*this bomb was on a timer; this bomb was a suicide; this bomb was on a trip wire; here are the pieces, here is the video of the crime scene; here are the logbooks from the search and the global positioning system coordinates for each piece of evidence, flesh, metal, or bone.* Identifying evidence was an important part of the NYPD Bomb Squad mission if a blast occurred. They were the experts on hand to guide the Crime Scene Unit in collecting evidence that was critical, but might not look so to the untrained eye.

You certainly have not lived until Kevin has ordered you to walk fingertip to fingertip through the hot, high desert of Lompoc, California, picking up and piling up the debris from the Winnebago as your protective clothing causes a thick froth of sweat all down your body.

"And, gentlemen and ladies, remember, drink lots of fluid, lots of fluid, and keep your lines tight. And remember, you go onto paper right away," he said.

Because if it isn't recorded on paper, it isn't evidence. And if it is recorded later than it is found, it may not count. While much of the class is practical work in the field, the other portion of it comes from a series of lectures and presentations on preserving crime scenes, evidence recovery, the specifics of forensics in post-blast crime scenes, and a lessons-learned segment.

The other LVB-61 class members are from Texas, New York, the Air Force, Baton Rouge, and New Orleans. The class includes auditors from England and Germany—these are seasoned, senior bomb technicians, and Kevin has brought them in to critique his course. The German tech has a well-fitted color-coordinated outfit and the most gleaming, purposeful gear.

The reason for the course is deadly serious: Bad forensic post-blast work, clowning around on a crime scene, and just plain carelessness almost cost the government the case against the Oklahoma City Bomber, Timothy McVeigh. And sloppy crime scene work certainly cost the government the case against O. J. Simpson.

"They did not find O. J.'s blood for three weeks, gentlemen and ladies, so do we have a guilty double murderer walking the streets today because they did not do a final survey of the crime scene? You will do a final survey. You will have two supervisors for the overall scene. One for the inner scene, right around the blast crater, and one for the outer scene. This is the Crime Scene Command. There will be one entrance to the scene and one exit. Why? Because it is the right way. The only way. And we want our cases to stand up in federal court. We don't need a terrorist playing golf with the O. J.," Kevin explained.

"And let's face it. That scene is always pretty nasty. Your mouth will taste of iron. But when you step outside, remember, yes, it's still abhorrent, and yes, the world is still beautiful."

The class reviewed the details of a blast in Italy that killed an anti-mafia judge—a crime scene a half mile long with trees knocked down a quarter mile from the epicenter of the blast. The lead car in the convoy was traveling at a hundred miles an hour; the blast knocked it back two hundred yards. The evidence collectors and forensic investigators looked and looked for the spot where the bomber triggered the blast. Finally, by the side of the road two miles away, overlooking the crime scene, they found cigarette butts and footprints. Enough butts and enough footprints had been scuffed over one another to indicate someone had been waiting. Bagged, tagged, and sampled for DNA, the cigarette butts entered the evidence train. Coupled with what was not found inside the crime scene, it was determined that a remote control from the roadside spot had triggered the blast. To complete the forensics for their court case, the Italians had duplicated the entire blast.

Jim Norman, the FBI special agent bomb technician from Oklahoma City who was the case agent on the Alfred P. Murrah Federal Office Building, gave the most chilling presentation of all. It was 9:02 A.M. that morning in March 1995 when the blast that killed nineteen children and sixty-one pensioners and credit union employees went off. Within minutes too many people were inside the crime scene. Within hours souvenir hunters had tampered with the evidence. Within twenty-four hours any hope of a solid case had been almost irredeemably lost.

"They don't have me do the presentation to tell you I was doing a fabulous job. Things were going wrong all the time." The presentation is a painful object case study. "I was standing by my desk when the entire building shook violently, and we were almost five miles away."

Norman got there quickly, but by the time he did, things were already out of control. At first the closest he could get was two blocks away. It took hours to secure the crime scene. Even then, the perimeter was placed too close to the center of the blast, and damage from the blast—and possibly evidence—was on the outside of it. But during a major disaster it is almost impossible to get these things right. Rescue and victim recovery always come first.

"When I arrived, there were a lot of people curled up in the fetal position bleeding . . . ," Norman said. "Although I had trained for years, I stood in front of that building and I was in shock. In the debris there were lots of kids' things in there—plastic furniture, tricycles. You could not look at that building without seeing an arm or a leg or a body sticking out."

Norman became the case agent on the bombing. It was an odyssey that would consume years of his life. Videotape surveillance from the building had captured a Ryder truck. It also captured "a young woman who was a car thief on probation—in a car, not her own. She had gone back to her old ways." Early on these became parts of the evidence chain.

"During one of these investigations," he explained, "you always have to be thinking, 'What do I want to show the jury?'" This is the other part of the bomb tech's job, assisting at the post-blast crime scene. It is where the tech's expertise is married with that of attorneys, forensics technicians, and medical examiners in the effort to re-create the crime so that it will stick in a jury's mind.

There were, Norman said, huge egos in play almost immediately—a doctor who said his triage work made him feel like god, politicians, misguided supervisors. One police officer was ordered home after two months. He did not want to go. He wasn't ready to be alone. Ordered home, he drove to a field and killed himself. He was one of seven suicides that resulted from the case, including the assistant U.S. attorney assigned to prosecute it.

"When you work on cases like this, you're going to have a lot of memories. Don't take it for granted other people are looking out for your well-being," Norman warned. He described the little handprints on the walls of the crushed day care center. He described some people wandering into the scene just so they could say they were there. These were all part of his memories, his grief, and his anger.

"Are we going to document people who are there with their own agenda, or are you just going to get them out?" Think of the jury. Think of the case. Think of the jury. Don't let anger carry you away. "Get them out. Or they are discoverable." Norman was attempting to illustrate all of the things a smart defense attorney could use to cast doubt in a jury's mind, and all the things cops at the scene could do to prevent it, by keeping their chain of evidence as uncontaminated as possible. People walking through the evidence were the perfect vehicle for a defense attorney to use to suggest that perhaps, just maybe, they had a motive for altering the evidence. People became myopic. The first "law enforcement" photos were taken by an off-duty officer in his agency helicopter. He sold those to a magazine. They were never entered into evidence.

Eight thousand investigative hours went into that crime scene. All the while Norman had to contend with people who wanted to sneak in and take ghoulish "happy snaps," posing at the scene. Those "happy snaps," if discovered, would look very bad before a jury. They would prove that the scene was not secure—they could destroy the carefully made links of evidence to a perpetrator. Who was to say one of these people did not just drop a piece of evidence? a defense attorney could ask.

In the first twenty-four hours the case was virtually lost. The evidence collection team had failed to collect residue from the bomb itself. That night it rained. The next day, it looked like there would be no residue to collect. Fortunately one piece of metal that could be linked to the vehicle, its underside shielded from the night's rain, held residue that could be linked to the bomb and to Timothy McVeigh.

This course, which he teaches over and over again, is Kevin Miles's contribution to the education of the bomb technician, and his labor of love. Because, to the mind of the FBI and the mind of the policeman, overseas we have a war on terror, but at home we have battles that ultimately will be decided in the arena of a court of law.

BOOK EIGHT

Pride and Remembrance

Case Sheets and Conversations

Det. Sqd. BOMB SQ
Day/Date of Original Report: June 2-04 / Wednesday
Time: 1725
Place of Occurrence: C/O Valentine Ave & Fordham Rd
  MTA Bus
Crime/Condition: Hoax Device
BS Case #: 1209

   This item was found by the bus driver at the end of
a run. . . . The item was examined . . . and found not to
contain any explosives. This item consisted of 2 9-volt
batteries, wires and an electric audible type device. These
were all taped together with black electric tape. Due to
its construction this item was deemed a Hoax Device.

Det. Sqd. BOMB SQ
Day/Date of Original Report: 6/3/04/Thursday
Time: 0830

*Place of Occurrence and Type of Premise: S/E c/o East
    60th and Lexington Ave.*
*Crime/Condition: Investigate Suspicious Package
    (Small Smoke Bomb Investigation)*
BS Case #: 1214

The services of the Bomb Squad were requested . . .
in regards to a report of a grenade inside a newspaper
box. . . . Squad members were informed that a passerby
attempting to get a free AM New York Newspaper from
an AM New York Newspaper box observed what he
believed to be a hand grenade. . . . Examination revealed an
approximately 3 inch plastic grenade shaped commercially
manufactured smoke bomb, a common class "C" firework.

It was June 3. The caseload numbers had kept pace with those
of the prior year. Twelve hundred and fourteen had been
recorded by eight-thirty. It was the last sheet on the pile that soon
turned the squad room cranky. It was just a smoke bomb. But because this smoke bomb had been discovered inside the "golden"
upper East Side zip code—10021—there was a gridlock of TV
trucks and a pack of newspaper and radio reporters just outside
the crime scene. The golden zip code contained the most presti-
gious of New York's Park and Fifth Avenue addresses. It was one
of the wealthiest neighborhoods in the world.

The plastic mock hand grenade had been found in a newspaper
box that happened to be diagonally across from Bloomingdale's, a
shopper's mecca or a terrorist's soft target. It was two blocks away
from the most significant synagogue in Manhattan—a high-
profile symbolic target. And it was not far from a handful of con-
sulates, the General Motors Building, and the Revlon Building.
But Brian Hearn grumbled over his newspaper, "Why is it such a
big deal? It's another smoke grenade, for crying out loud."

The reporters didn't see it that way. They wanted a briefing and they would get it. Torre was annoyed. It was a smoke bomb. He asked Sergeant Brian Coughlan to handle it. Coughlan was annoyed. It was a smoke bomb. Coughlan sent Detective Second Grade Joe Putkowski in front of the cameras. If Joe was annoyed, he didn't say so or show it. He handled it with the drollness of a middleweight champ leaning against his locker room door for a post-fight briefing. "Yeah, it was no big thing. We do what we got to do."

The reporters were not the only ones who wanted a briefing. The chief of detectives wanted one. The Joint Terrorism Task Force wanted one. The Intelligence Division wanted one. The police commissioner wanted one and the mayor wanted one. They wanted their information now, and they wanted every detail. The incident report that Sergeant Coughlan had begun typing even as the telephones started ringing was detailed. It included notations that the squad had followed the procedures to "check for secondary devices," a careful description of the "examination of suspicious package," and a summary of the "forensic recovery of evidence," and of the "conferral with the 19th Squad, Arson & Explosion Squad, and Crime Scene Unit."

This was all part of the standard operating procedure, but usually on a smoke bomb or firecracker accident or other minor incident, it was shorthanded in an Unusual Occurrence Report. Sergeant Coughlan had a full day of paperwork ahead of him. At the bottom of his completed "Unusual" there were fourteen names in the notifications box, more than twice the norm. The rule in New York, self-appointed media capital of the world, is that the closer to Central Park a crime occurs, the more time or space will be devoted to the crime on the evening news and in the morning papers. And the more time will be spent on the paperwork. Sixtieth Street and Lexington Avenue was three blocks from the park.

As the report was typed, a grumbling group of working class heroes would pause from time to time to express their bemusement at the ways of the world. "If the same smoke bomb had gone off in another neighborhood—in my neighborhood on Staten Island—who would care?" Hearn said.

2

Disrupters and Disruptions

It had become evening as Coughlan typed his report. Watching him work at his clean desk, in his neat clothes, was a window on the professionalism and pride of a supervisor of detectives. As he typed, he also kept an ear on the crackling radios, the sometimes powerful music of the squad room. Other members of the squad got ready to sign out on their assignments.

The weather was perfect for an evening Mets game, with a cooling breeze off Flushing Bay. Ray Butkiewicz and Craig Collopy headed to Shea Stadium for a pregame sweep of the dugouts, bullpens, and corridors.

They had barely made it over the bridge to Queens when a report of a suspicious package came into Bomb Squad Base and Coughlan picked up a cell phone and turned them around and back to Manhattan. The package, at 106th and Park Avenue, turned out to be a letter to Univision, the Spanish-language television network. Inside was a "2001 Dollar Bill" with a "Commander Bush" face on it, Colin Powell and Dick Cheney on the signature lines, and a dedication to September 11 on the reverse. More tumult. More grumbling from Brian. Another mountain of paperwork for Sergeant Coughlan. Every fifteen minutes or so

Coughlan queried Joe Putkowski about a facet of the computerized filing system. Each time the senior man had an answer. Not that Joe was a computer wiz. He had learned the answers to the questions from Claude "Danny" Richards, who had organized and computerized all of the squad's various files, and even some of its shelves and lockers, before he died on September 11. Danny was the heart and soul of the Bomb Squad, and when he died, the squad did not lose only Danny, it lost a piece of every other man. He was that important to the group personality.

At eleven o'clock, Joe spoke. "I had that dream again. I was at my son's school, and there was one of those beautiful carved cabinets sitting in the office, we were looking at it. Right then, Danny comes walking into the room. He walks up to the cabinet. Opens one of the drawers and looks in. 'Everything looks good in here.' And that was it."

In the long rows of green lockers, Danny's stood out. It was cleaner than the rest. Inside, it had the neat carpeting and spotless clean walls he left behind. It was kept empty. There was no need for any other memorial. There was enough room inside the locker to hold the dreams, memories, and keystrokes that reminded each member of the squad of Danny.

Det. Sqd. BOMB SQ
Day/Date of Original Report: June 9, 2004/Wednesday
Time: 2015
Place of Occurrence and Type of Premise: Waterbury Ave &
    Baisley Ave.
Crime/Condition: Post Blast Investigation Chemical Reaction
    Bomb
BS Case #: 1268

Investigation at the scene reveals that the below listed victim was injured as a result of a "soda bottle bomb" exploding. The victim suffered chemical burns to his face. According to the complainant/victim and witnesses . . . the victim picked up a soda bottle that had been thrown from a passing vehicle. When the victim picked up the bottle that he believed to be trash the bottle exploded causing his injuries.

The victim in this instance was an eighty-one-year-old good citizen attempting to pick up after what he thought were teenaged slobs. He became the latest victim of the plastic soda bottle bomb trend.

These crude bombs were increasingly earning mentions in police reports around the nation. For the most part mischief was the motive. The trend was Internet-driven. These chemical bombs had existed in the past, but Internet message boards and Web sites now provided recipes and videos, and with these it seemed the number of incidents had increased. Soda bottle bombs had recently been found in mailboxes, school lockers, and now on a quiet Bronx sidewalk.

From: Fahy, Ursula
Sent: Tues 6/15/2004 4:29 PM
To: #ABCTV Breaking News
Subject: Situation Cleared on Suspicious Package (at LaGuardia
Airport)

About 3p TSA (Transportation Safety Administration) contacted PAPD (Port Authority Police) about a suspicious piece of luggage at Term 1. The police evacuated the entire terminal . . . NYC Bomb Squad secured the bag and properly identified it. Non-event. . . . There are 15 airlines flying out of Term 1. . . . Most are international.

About 500–800 passengers were in the terminal. . . . The terminal has now been reopened . . . was closed about an hour.

Unlike the smoke bomb in the golden zip code, this time there was no barrage of calls from reporters to the squad. But there was an interesting story there; one that went unnoticed by the public, but that for the cops opened a window onto the limits of airline security precautions, even when they worked as intended. A man from Cleveland—a man who had already been stopped and searched in Cleveland—was traveling with a small mining tool used to trigger a blasting cap. The tool was a "blaster," according to Detective Mike Oldmixon. He said it was covered with explosive residue and had been packed in a suitcase with clothing, also covered with explosive residue. TSA dogs and TSA sniffing devices at both airports sensed the residue, triggered alarms, and TSA agents stopped the man. He had broken no law. He was on his way to France and was allowed to continue there, where it was expected he would also cause delays and inconvenience to others when he was stopped and searched again.

Det. Sqd. BOMB SQ
Day/Date of Original Report: 06/24/04 Thursday
Time: 0800
Place of Occurrence and Type of Premise: Brooklyn, NY
  Residence.
Crime/Condition: Recovery of Two Improvised Explosive
  Devices (IED)
BS Case #: 1409

The services of the Bomb Squad were requested . . . in regards to (2) Improvised Explosive Devices (IEDs) and

(2) Hand Grenades (Military Ordnance). . . . Utilizing
Bomb Squad procedures, the Improvised Explosive
Devices were examined and determined to be live.
Examination of the (2) Hand Grenades revealed that they
were inert and contained no explosives. The Improvised
Explosive Devices, Hand Grenades, Explosives Powders, and
numerous components used in the making of IEDs were
removed to the Rodman's Neck Bomb Squad Demolition
Range. . . . Bomb Squad members will conduct Render
Safe Procedures on the IEDs on Friday 06/24/04/.—
Supervisor Signature Sergeant Michael Walsh.

The items had been discovered during a narcotics raid. The
narcs had stopped their search and called the squad after arresting
two occupants. This pair also had a human skull and Nazi memorabilia. A detailed search would determine whether or not Joe
Putkowski's rule held true. The rule: Wherever there are bombs
and Nazi memorabilia, there will be dildos and other sex toys. The
dildos were found. As the search went on in Brooklyn, other jobs
kept coming in. By 10:35 A.M. there was a report of a bomb on a
bus that the A–Team ran on and there was an investigation into a
suspicious package on Third Avenue at Sixty-sixth Street that took
the attention of Joe Hourihan, Ray Clair, and Andy Rea.

When a bomb technician wearing an armored suit leans over
a package as five lanes of traffic are diverted into a one-lane side
street, it is not a bad idea to back up as far as possible. But there
are always otherwise logical citizens who don't.

"SIR, WHAT PART OF THE SENTENCE 'GET BACK
INSIDE AND AWAY FROM YOUR WINDOW' DO YOU
NOT UN-DER-*STAND*?' " Sergeant Joseph Hourihan was not
showing his normal toothy grin. He was biting his words again.
"MA'AM, GET BACK INSIDE AND CLOSE THE DOOR
TO YOUR TERRACE BEHIND YOU!"

He was beyond frustration. "This is a really bad situation. Then, if it blows up in their faces, who gets to do the explaining? Argch." He was at the scene of a suspicious package that sat in the middle of the sidewalk on Third Avenue, in front of a large, sparkling clean plate glass window. The window and the package were just north of Sixty-sixth Street in Manhattan. Hourihan plunged his hands into the pockets of his blue windbreaker, stubbing out his anger. Until he had shouted, what seemed like half the neighborhood had thought leaning out over their high-rise balconies to get a better view of the suspicious package and all the attendant preparations was an excellent afternoon's entertainment.

Had you heard Hourihan, you could not have been faulted for wondering what kind of teenager he was while attending his Roman Catholic high school or how he had thought he would fit in afterward among the forty-two boys in his junior seminary class. The answer was simple: You have not met the tough priests of the Bronx, New York, in whose ethos an order was an order, and if it had to be shouted, then a boxing match with the priest was a surer way to forgiveness than confession. Joe had left the junior seminary, became a superintendent and then a doorman before he became a cop and rose to command a homicide squad in the Bronx. He had tried a psychological approach in explaining to his wife how the Bomb Squad was not nearly as dangerous as Homicide. She understandably failed to see how investigating the already dead was more dangerous than fiddling with live explosives. But Joe could have a very persuasive smile.

By 10:35 A.M., as the squad and their response partners from the Emergency Service Unit responded to these incidents, another team of ESU guys had to take a run over to the Triborough Bridge, where they talked and walked down a suicide whose actions had brought the tail of the morning rush to a standstill. And as this police activity unfolded in New York, a large explosion aboard a parked airplane in Istanbul had captured the attention of bomb techs everywhere. The blast occurred near the runway where the President of the United States would land within forty-eight hours. The device was simple and difficult to detect. It was a wallet filled with malleable plastic explosive, possibly slipped in by a maintenance man. One of the characteristics of plastic explosives that made them so worrisome was the plasticity itself: statuary, shoes, belts—the stuff could be molded to fit any container and it packed an enormous punch.

June 25, 7:00 A.M., Rodman's Neck: Mike Walsh and his team had arrived early to pop the tops off of the two small explosive devices found in Joe P's search of the drug dealer's home a day earlier. The procedure was one of many "render safe" procedures in the techs' playbook. It was stifling hot and humid, and the tall grasses didn't sway one bit.

Sergeant Walsh wore a flak vest, a heavy military helmet, and his blue utilities. Ray Butkiewicz came in his chinos and black boots. The new guys, Jimmy Schutta and John Scomillio, were unloading the night's seized fireworks into the fireworks magazine. The heavy steel magazine contained a mountain of cherry bombs, M-80s, long strings of firecrackers, rockets, and Roman candles, all in their colorful wrappers. It was getting nice and full. Soon the techs would empty it and burn the contents. Schutta, the former Marine, cinched his blue utilities with a web belt that held his Glock nine and his tools. Scomillio wore his green work pants. It was humid. Summer had come to New York City.

The two IEDs were small bomblets called "crickets." They were made by packing a CO_2 cartridge with explosive powders. A simple twist of explosive-soaked hobby fuse lit by a match was all it took to detonate them; just like the fireworks in the magazine.

Before the team got started, an ambulance pulled up. It was routine to have one at the range, just in case there was an accident during a render safe. Walsh thought the ambulance might be a little too close to the blast, so he walked over to the emergency medical technician behind the wheel, explained the day's procedure, and asked him to back up a bit. The EMT did; stopping about a quarter mile up the dirt road, where he was still just seconds away.

The team set the crickets on a railroad tie embedded in packed sand. A wall of stacked railroad ties boxed in the area on three sides. Behind them were high bunker walls of packed dirt. Behind the dirt was another wall of cinder block. Behind that, the trigger would be pulled that set off the firing train leading to the disruption device, which would fire a jet of water, hard as a steel hammer, right at the tops of the devices.

The slender aluminum tubes of the percussion-actuated non-electric disrupter—the PAN, the device that fires the water jet— were arranged a few yards back. The barrel of the disrupter in its most basic form was a length of pipe aimed to shoot the nippled tops from the crickets, disabling them while preserving some of the powder inside for the Crime Scene Unit. The CSU would send the powder to the lab to compare with loose explosive powder found during the search. This would most likely yield another piece of the evidence puzzle needed for a tight court case. The PAN allowed for surgically precise disruptions, which was one of the reasons it was so useful. The other was that it created distance between the device and the bomb technician. A shotgun shell was inserted to propel the water jet on its way. Twenty-five feet of yellow shock tube was paid out from the disrupter back to the concrete-block safety area, where it was attached to the handheld trigger. The safety that held the bolt in check had been marked in green for SAFE and red for READY. With a snap, the bolt rammed home and sent a charge down the thin line of high explosive inside the shock tube. A nice "pop" and a puff of smoke, and it was over and the ambulance driver waved good-bye.

For the reporter who had been allowed to observe the setup and then pull the trigger, what was rammed home with that bolt was the precision and care put into safety before the bolt ever moved. The pop that took the place of a loud blast was simply the signal of a job well done.

By the time the pop was heard and the EMT was on his way, the suspects in the case had made their statements to detectives. Oh, and the dildo found was silver, causing one detective to muse, "I wonder who got the gold one for first place?"

3

At What Price Freedom?

It should be no surprise that the Fourth of July is a day of celebration that surpasses New Year's Eve in terms of excitement and importance to the Bomb Squad. The squad members really enjoy loud, bright, lively explosions. Many of their best childhood memories are of blowing up fireworks, building rockets, rattling a few windows, and running from the scene. The Fourth in New York features barge loads of explosions. It is also a day of pain and remembrance.

Lieutenant Torre picked up a bouquet and checked in with the squad from his Crown Vic to let the boys know he was on his way in from Long Island to the memorial site in Flushing Meadows Park—the site of the 1940 World's Fair blast that killed Detectives Ferdinand Socha and Joseph Lynch.

At 4:45 P.M. on July 4, Socha and Lynch, protected by nothing thicker than their suit coats and ties, were attempting to dismantle a dynamite time bomb found outside the British Pavilion. The bomb went off, killing them. It was suspected to have been an IRA attack, but nothing was ever proven and the case had never been closed. According to NYPD pension records and historical reports, their widows, Genevieve G. Socha and Easter C. Lynch, were each awarded $3200—a year's salary plus $1600 a year from the police pension fund. Each widow also received another $5000 from the New York City Relief Fund, payable in $50-a-month installments. Five hundred dollars was paid to each to cover funeral expenses. Both widows were honored by the British government. Viscount Halifax, on behalf of the British government, presented each with a memorial "silver plate."

Later that morning of July 4, 2004, another squad member stopped at Flushing Meadows to polish the brass memorial plaque to Socha and Lynch. This was the way the Bomb Squad's Fourth of July had begun every year since that fatal blast.

Since September 11, 2001, there had been another annual Independence Day ceremony of pain and remembrance. It took place inside the deep pit at Ground Zero.

By 10:00 A.M. the concrete retaining walls and the concrete slab floor of the pit were bleached by sunlight and a shimmering heat. There was no shade except against the walls studded with the bitter ends of the thick cables—tiebacks—that helped keep this bathtub from collapsing under the pressure of the river outside; no shade anywhere but by the walls or the overhang of the ripped floors of the garage. Fluorescent Xs and DANGER ASBESTOS signs still dotted the cavernous spaces. The Port Authority Trans-Hudson commuter trains—running again—slid in and out of their sleek aluminum-and-steel temporary station until service paused as the ceremonies began.

An elegiac procession of survivors, construction workers, politicians, police, and firefighters came down the five-hundred-foot-long ramp to the bottom of the seventy-foot-deep hole. It was up this ramp that the dead had been borne and over which nearly a million tons of steel and rubble were carried away.

It was three Independence Days after September 11, 2001, and by now the thousands of rescue workers, hundreds of police officers assigned to pit duty, the Red Cross workers, the reporters, the public officials, survivors, and relatives had become a large family of familiar faces.

At the head of the ramp, in helmet and dark glasses, was Sergeant John Flynn of the Port Authority Police Department, which had lost thirty-seven members. He had ridden a rubber raft two hundred feet underneath the Hudson River, through the riverbed itself, from New Jersey into the depths of the burning rubble. No one was found alive inside the crushed train coaches. At the edge of the growing crowd, in white gloves and dress uniform, was Lieutenant John Ryan of the PA Police. He had spent nine months supervising the pit; keeping peace, managing visiting dignitaries, and ensuring dignity. Ryan said the nine months aged him twenty years. "It was hard coming here today."

Under a single white awning was an angelic youth choir. Its hymnals floated over a map of GPS coordinates that marked every shard of bone, bit of flesh, arm, or leg found in the pit. It seemed no sunlight, no amount of power washing, no accretion of time would remove the yellow smell of death.

Lee Ielpi, John Vigiano, and Dennis Oberg—firemen whose sons became firemen and who were among the 330 firefighters whose lives were lost—stood side by side. For eight and a half months they had been the Zen monks of the rubble pit. In silence they slowly raked through the garden of ashes for any sign of a human's life. They did not quit raking until there was nothing left to sift.

Lieutenant Torre, Detective Roger Mack, Digon the bomb dog, and Detective Barry Nagelberg looked down into the pit. They were there for the squad, to remember what Socha and Lynch had given for liberty and what Claude "Danny" Richards had given when he left the squad room, went into the rubble, and never came out. They quietly reflected on the largest bombing in American history, one that no tech could stop.

"On this day . . . on this day . . . on this day . . ." The words echoed off the walls. "We reclaim this ground in the name of those we lost . . . we lost . . . we lost."

Mark Torre paid his public respects, wearily climbed back into his black Crown Vic, and returned to the squad, where he was more comfortable sharing his grief. He had his coffee and made sure the deployments were in good shape for the evening. The mood in the squad was ruminative.

Joe Putkowski, Roger Mack, Bobby Schnell, Jimmy Carrano, Glen Ostermann, and Barry Nagelberg were meditating on progress: They measured it in lives. So much progress came from the death or injury of Socha and Lynch; those deaths earned the squad its first bomb disposal truck—the LaGuardia/Pyke truck— and its first bomb disposal baskets. So much more had come from the maiming of Senft, Pastorella, and Pascarella on New Year's Eve 1982. Those injuries earned the squad its first robots and bet- ter bomb suits. An avalanche of money crashed down on them after the 2749 deaths at the World Trade Center, enough for every conceivable bit of equipment the squad would need.

None of it would bring back Danny. This was what the Fourth of July meant to them. This was the price of freedom.

The phones began ringing. The spell was broken. The radio chatter picked up. A dog sweep in a garage raised a hint of explo- sives. The dog had sat, and a full search had to be done. A kid in the Bronx blew his hand off lighting fireworks. Sergeant B threatened to cut a reporter's socks off because they did not fit his sense of style. Mark's voice grew louder from behind his closed office door. The celebratory part of the day had begun.

Soon the squad's teams were in place in Brooklyn, where a viewing area for the Macy's fireworks display had been set up on the promenade that looked across the East River toward Manhattan and out toward the harbor and the Statue of Liberty. In Manhattan other teams were in place along the riverside drive that would provide a viewing area for 250,000 other spectators.

Brian Hearn and Mike Klippel were in Brooklyn, where first they checked in with the mobile police command post parked at the base of the Brooklyn Bridge. The post was there to coordinate police on that side of the river. They performed a quick security sweep of Pier 11. Later the mayor would arrive at the pier to view the fireworks. Sweep done. Area secured. A call came in for a sweep of the Brooklyn Promenade. After the sweep, 100,000 people would crowd the Promenade. It was a wise precaution.

Next Hearn piloted toward the Verrazano Bridge. The graceful span would take him home to Staten Island for a stop at the family barbecue. It was 6:00 P.M. Lieutenant Torre was now in position on the promenade on the Manhattan side. Three barges of fireworks floated in mid-river. With Torre were the commander of the Crime Scene Unit, the commander of the Arson and Explosion Unit, and the chief in charge of all three. A call came in that brought everyone to alert. The caller reported that the Police Department had received a "credible" report that five "Arab men" armed with explosives planned to mingle into the crowd and then blow themselves up. The report had come so close to sunset that the crowd was already too dense to search. If it turned out to be real, there might be little else to do except pick up the pieces. It was unlikely that any dog or man or surveillance camera was going to find the bombers in time.

But five minutes later the situation changed. This is the fluid way of intelligence. Another call came in. There was new information: The terrorist plan was to strap the explosives to a dog. The dog would walk the bomb into the crowd and then the bombers would detonate their canine-borne explosives. It was as absurd a plan in its own way as the threat to put poison in the New Year's Eve fireworks. A bomber recently had tried to use canine-borne explosives in Palestine, but could anyone think they would get a dog wearing explosives into this crowd—through all the checkpoints, past all the barricades, past the emergency cops, past the counterterror detectives and the rules prohibiting any luggage backpacks or large purses, and finally past the suspicious eyes of several hundred thousand New Yorkers? Not one spectator had brought their precious pet to stand in this heat, in this crowd, so that when the first fireworks exploded and every car alarm in lower Manhattan went off in sympathy, the dog could panic in the cacophony of sound and light. A dog with a bomb would not have gone unnoticed—it would have been the only dog in sight.

By dusk the intelligence had been reviewed, analyzed, and dismissed. This is how the process of collection, dissemination, and analysis works in a real world, in real time: Intelligence comes in, a response is ramped up, and stress comes down hard on the intelligence gatherers, the disseminators, and the responders. Then all of these forces stand down. They ramp up again as the next bit of data flits onto someone's screen. Millions of bits of intelligence come in each day, culled from billions of conversations, surveillances, phone calls, data transfers, and pictures. With that in mind, the possibility that something could easily be overlooked becomes a little more understandable; like missing a weed in a national park.

The backyard to Hearn's house was packed when he arrived. The guests had kept the driveway clear for his response vehicle. They knew he might have to get in and out fast. By seven-thirty the barbecue had wound down, and Brian prepared to head back into the field. Before he did, his wife, Kathy, turned to her husband and his brother: "Would one of you heroes get up and get me a beer? Thank you. You're my heroes." At home Brian must share the spotlight with a brother who is a firefighter. The knee-jerk jibes that cops and firefighters make at each other's departments aside, the arrangement is more common than not in civil service families, where brothers and cousins and sisters are spread out across city agencies.

The sky had turned smoky blue and held flickers of neon, dots of aviation warning lights, and a necklace of light spanning the waters along the cables of the bridges. The dinner cruisers made their way into position for the display.

Atop the roof of a five-story reinforced-concrete municipal parking garage with a perfect view, Lieutenant Torre, Jeff Oberdier, Tom Sullivan, Glen Ostermann, Joe Hourihan, and a few dozen other police officers and police family members stood looking out toward the barges. The red, white, and blue of the Empire State Building stood behind them. At 9:20 the first of 35,000 shells erupted into a starburst of light.

Within seconds the concrete beneath their feet rebelled as 40,000 pounds of explosives launched into a dance across the sky. Aboard the barges, the fireworks technicians' fingers flew across their keyboards. The firing rate was one thousand rounds per minute. Mark Torre gave an excited running commentary of the switches, the feast balls, the cylindrical charges, the preparation, and the perfection of the display. It was a little like trying to explain magic to a child. "About 65 percent of the product goes up in the finale," he explained. In the instant it did, the bright flashes and the smoke swirling below them were transformed into the "bombs bursting in air" that are imagined when Francis Scott Key's anthem is sung. For the first July 4 since September 11 a barge had been stationed off of the Statue of Liberty. Guests gathered at the monument's base were bathed in lights as the 120,000 bursts "gave proof through the night" that their flag was still there. The bomb techs on Liberty Island were there to make sure they would come to no harm. But on a night like this it took no imagination at all to understand why New York, as newspaper writer John Leonard said, was the "Imperial City." On a night like this, it was easy to see why the private lives of that city were a public trust.

4

Case Sheets and Conversations

Det. Sqd. BOMB SQ
Day/Date of Original Report: 07/04/04/Sunday
Time: 1255
Place of Occurrence and Type of Premise: Randall Avenue
  (The Bronx)
Crime/Condition: Post Blast Investigation/1 Serious Injury
BS Case #: 1564

The victim suffered an injury to his right hand after lighting a firework that exploded in his hand. . . . The victim's injury . . . is consistent with that of an M–Series Forbidden Explosive.

The victim was a twelve-year-old boy, Detective Andy Rea noted in his report.

Det. Sqd. BOMB SQ
Day/Date of Original Report: 7/12/04

Time: 1400
Place of Occurrence and Type of Premise: Queens, N.Y.
Crime/Condition: . . . Chemical Reaction Bomb
BS Case #: 1655

Bomb Squad members examined the bottle which was inside of a dumpster and determined it had not exploded. The Bottle was a plastic 2 liter Schweppes Ginger Ale bottle with an unknown liquid inside. . . . A further search . . . revealed two (2) additional 2 liter bottles that had previously functioned . . .

"They were filled with acid," Detective Billy Popper said; it was a chemical bomb that had not exploded. It was carefully removed. Later that afternoon, "Someone left a radio with a nine-volt battery dangling from it aboard a train," Brian Hearn said. The job came in as a suspicious package, and as a result, the tracks into and out of Pennsylvania Station were shut down and Hearn went in to investigate. The scene was cleared. All in a day's work, Hearn said.

In the squad room a new flat-screen monitor had arrived. The boys were under strict orders not to call it a television. It was a monitor, for training purposes. Hearn had hung it on the wall. Sergeant Bobby Duke connected the wires and Billy Popper assembled the cabinet that would house the DVD, VCR, and cable box. For training purposes Fox would be programmed into the favorite channels queue.

Det. Sqd. BOMB SQ
Day/Date of Original Report: 07/19/04/Monday
Time: 2004
Place of Occurrence and Type of Premise: West 43rd St–8th
   Ave. Confines of MTS Pct. Subway Station Stairwell

Crime/Condition: Post Blast Investigation
BS Case #: 1712

Upon arrival Bomb Squad members were informed
that an MOS [Member Of Service] was injured as a result
of a knapsack that exploded. At this time a search for
secondary devise was conducted . . . with negative results.
A preliminary post blast investigation of the scene and
debris revealed that an Improvised Explosive Device that
consisted of a small PVC pipe bomb of unknown length
filled with low explosive powder and fragmentation
materials in the form of BB size spheres, initiated by a
pyrotechnic fuse, had exploded. This device was enclosed in
a cardboard box inside of a black nylon backpack type bag.

While Detective Andy Rea's report of the 1712th incident of
the year was explicit in its detail, it did not offer an opinion as to
who planted the bomb. But by the time he had finished typing it,
there was little doubt. Times Square was the subway station
where the bomb had gone off. It was the top subway target for
terrorists. It was a device that had been delivered in the same kind
of nylon bag that had been used in recent terrorist attacks. It was
all somehow too perfect.

An attack on a subway or rail system cannot be ruled out.
An attack on a subway or rail system could cause substantial loss of life and would have an adverse impact on public confidence resulting in massive economic loss.

This excerpt from a Department of Homeland Security bulletin was the scene against which the explosion was set. It was the
context for the massive police response and for a massive media
turnout. The station was shut down for two hours. All possible

reasons for an attack were explored, and one by one were rejected. There was no rush to quickly home in on a suspect based on common sense and a detective's instinct. The case was being worked quickly but methodically. From the outset several things did not fit. The location where the bomb went off, a deserted stairwell, did not seem right for a terrorist target. The explanation by the injured officer as to how he came upon the device did not seem to fit with the time line the detectives were building. The bomb had gone off long after the rush hour was over and theatergoers were already in their seats, which made no clear sense. The nature of the wounds to the officer and their location seemed consistent with self-inflicted wounds. The small size of the bomb suggested it was built to have low impact. Finally there was the officer's personnel file. It was spotty. The Police Department began to investigate one of their own.

The device had been found by a transit cop—Police Officer Joseph Rodriguez. The officer had performed heroically on September 11, assisting in the rescue of several people. But he had been a wreck since then and his career had fallen apart.

When his performance became an issue, the Police Department had considered firing Rodriguez as mentally unfit for duty—but a deal was struck with the police union, who noted that his disability resulted from 9/11. This would allow him to retire on a disability pension. The retirement was set to be finalized within three days of the blast. For his last days on the job, Rodriguez had been placed on modified duty and assigned to man the Times Square transit police switchboard. A few minutes before the end of his shift, he left that post, telling other officers on duty that he wanted to grab a last cup of coffee. The blast occurred soon after he stepped out. When he was found wounded, Rodriguez told responding officers that he had spotted the knapsack burning and was trying to extinguish it when it exploded. His response lacked the ring of truth.

A bomb dog was sent to Rodriguez's car. It sat three times,

indicating repeatedly the presence of explosives. A search of Rodriguez's apartment was ordered. It uncovered a brush coated with black powder, shotgun shells, and BB-sized pellets. His police locker was searched, but it held nothing more ominous than comic books.

Rodriguez's motive was simple: He had not wanted to retire. He had put off signing the necessary papers. Rodriguez, detectives theorized, just wanted to remain a cop at any cost. Failing that he wanted to retire as a hero. Instead his faked heroics were a sad marker at the end of a career that had become another casualty of 9/11.

5

The MacGuffin

No sooner had a 450-pound, seven-year-old white tiger named Apollo been returned to his cage on July 31 (after he finished his calm Saturday stroll through a church picnic, and his visit to the Jackie Robinson Parkway that caused a multiple car accident) than hopes for an August filled with lighthearted summer capers were dashed.

August was normally the silly season, when New York's oppressive heat, brutal humidity, and absent politicians aligned to create a dearth of news. Reporters had learned to rely on miracles, tragedies, shark sightings, and the tender quarrels of lovers that often resulted in a halfway interesting homicide to fill out their columns. This year it was not to be.

The first inkling had come the night before Apollo's stroll. At 5:37 P.M. Friday, July 30, an NLETS (National Law Enforcement Telecommunications System) alert was issued. It did not specify the nature of the threat but was headlined HIGH PRIORITY MESSAGE REQUEST NATIONAL BROADCAST. It warned police to be on the alert for a serious threat to the country.

The NLETS alert was a cover-your-ass document. It warned against everything and specified nothing. But by 8:00 P.M., in response to demands from regional intelligence and law enforcement officials, the Department of Homeland Security and the FBI had issued a joint advisory spelling out the threat a little more clearly. The threat information was credible, the advisory said, and it specified the use of heavy transport vehicles to deliver large bombs.

By Saturday afternoon, July 31, the first tremors of this massive terrorist threat to New York and New Jersey were on the verge of becoming public. Reporters had learned the exact nature of the targets and the specific types of bomb delivery systems that would be used. The targets were the New York Stock Exchange and Citigroup in New York, Prudential Insurance in New Jersey, and the World Bank and International Monetary Fund in Washington, D.C.

Authorities learned of the threat barely a month before the Republican National Convention and smack in the middle of the final security preparations. An arrest in Pakistan earlier in July had yielded a hard drive and discs filled with detailed security plans as well as detailed means of attack. By the beginning of August British officials had charged at least eight men with planning the attack—their preparations went back almost four years. But no one in the intelligence community knew if the attack—planned to occur before the presidential election—was already in progress. Cops and federal agents went door to door, informants were pressed to deliver more reports, and undercover agents took risks to their cover in order to get more information. As the days wore on, so did the angst for the security forces. In the end, eight days of public attention, the British arrests, and other forces that still are unknown all came together and no attack materialized.

For the Bomb Squad the threat was one more very big headache tossed onto the pile; one more topic to discuss in the Wednesday convention security planning meetings with the United States Secret Service; one more set of targets to review, enemy tactics to consider, and one more reason to produce dogs for security sweeps. The details that emerged of the terrorists' operational plan showed they had intended to attack using bombs hidden inside limousines and attached to the struts of suicide helicopters. Torre viewed this information with his cool technician's eye:

"There are different delivery systems. There are different motivations. There are a lot of different parameters involved in a bombing attack. But in the end, there is the bomb itself. If you remain focused on the bomb, and you don't get complacent, and you take all the steps you need to take, you have a great chance of success."

The terrorists' base of operation for surveillance had been in the same northern New Jersey area they had used since 1990. It had been the base for the 1990 murder of radical rabbi Meir Kahane, for the 1993 bombing of the World Trade Center, and for the run-up to the 2001 World Trade Center attack. In each case, the terrorists had operated undetected.

During the height of the threat, bomb squad teams in New York and New Jersey were prepositioned in the field should the worst occur and a device be discovered. Additional techs from nearby areas were on standby. Teams of dogs from several agencies began sniffing containers and cars in the hundreds of acres that comprised the Port of New York and New Jersey storage areas. Teams of technicians began running radiation monitors over fleets of freshly imported cars and self-storage lockers—in case the planned attack included "dirty" radiation bombs and the radioactive material had been stashed in advance.

In the end, the threat either evaporated or was diffused. The intelligence community settled into months of reading seized computer hard drives and discs. The material fell into two loose categories: One was a clear set of operational plans, the other was a terrorist wish list—a sort of jihad-by-dream list of attacks that the hopeful terrorists would launch, if only they had the means.

For the Bomb Squad, the event was in the past. Torre was much more concerned with the fact that he felt as though he was betting his command during each intense and often heated Republican convention planning meeting. During these meetings he continually had to explain a tactic, reject a solution to a problem—and to be right, in his mind, 100 percent of the time. He was constantly alert to being so meticulous in his presentation that no one else in the meeting could find a point he'd overlooked and use it to raise a question about his expertise. So far he was winning, but he felt he had only to lose once to exhaust his political capital. The stress was taking its toll. There were arguments at the squad over little things. There were heated multiagency discussions of prepositioning assets, a tug-of-war over turf between agencies and over who would control the interaction his squad would have with these other agencies. Every agency was eager to participate in defusing bombs.

Occasionally there was a little time to reflect that in its own way the Republican convention was the silly season this year, a plastic version of the once heartily sweaty, delightfully smoky, and nationally important feast for the political cognoscenti, the pre-election convention. It still demanded the full attention of every police officer in town, even though it had become so devoid of meaning that TV networks increasingly limited their coverage. To observers, they could have considered charging for airtime. But the show was good for New York City's $21-billion-plus tourist industry, an industry badly damaged in the post-9/11 years, and one needed to keep the city thriving.

In the midst of this security storm and the overseas terror threat, the first "chemical reaction bomb" call of the month came in on August 2: Two devices, each built around a common drain cleaner, had exploded at the Brooklyn Public Library. A security patrolman was injured. A search disclosed two additional bombs. The motive behind the attempted book burning was criminal mischief, according to the Bomb Squad report on Case #1794. There would be at least one other chemical reaction bomb incident in August, the second coming in right on the eve of the convention.

On August 4 an off-duty MOS, while walking his dog, found a pipe bomb in front of his neighbor's house. According to Sergeant Walsh, who wrote the incident report, the off-duty officer, in keeping with the department's ethos for self-sacrifice, picked up the device so that neighborhood children would not stumble on it while he called for help. While perhaps not what a trained bomb technician would suggest, it was certainly heroic. He placed it in a grassy area between the two houses. Then he went into his home to call 911. Coming on the heels of the officer who faked the discovery of an IED in the subway, this officer got nothing but headaches for his trouble. Although he volunteered to have his home searched by the Bomb Squad's dogs, and it came up clean, he was subjected to a thorough investigation before he was ruled out as a suspect. The device was taken to the Bomb Squad range, where it was determined to be a live device and held as possible evidence.

On August 10 three inert hand grenades, twelve rifles, four handguns, and four improvised smoke grenades, as well as flares and black powder, were recovered from a house in the Bronx by the Joint Firearms Task Force, a multi-agency unit that takes guns off the street.

With this case load, the Republican convention, and the U.S. Open, all regular days off were canceled at the squad. The squad records show that it had settled into a steady month of seven-day-a-week twelve-hour tours. For Sergeant Mike Walsh, it was what he drolly called "another busy patch."

"We get those sometimes," he said. When he said it, he was holding a case folder in his lap. That folder summed up an August 19 incident in which military explosive ordnance was brought into John F. Kennedy International Airport, in Queens.

The case was testimony to the profound ignorance of consequences or lack of regard for the safety of oneself or others that many people seem to develop when intent on a private mission. At 9:30 P.M. on that Thursday evening, the Bomb Squad had been called to investigate explosives seized several hours earlier when an EMT employed for $169,000 a year in Afghanistan by a major defense contractor—basically about four times what an EMT would be paid in a major U.S. city—was stopped by Transportation Safety Administration airport security at Terminal Seven, Gate Ten, John F. Kennedy International Airport. You would think the call would have come in sooner.

At his pay grade, you also would think the EMT, who was a military veteran and a reservist, would have known better. He did not. He had flown on a military charter from Afghanistan to the United Arab Emirates, boarded a commercial flight there to Switzerland, and another flight from Switzerland to New York. Problem one was that no security screener right up until Kennedy Airport had detected the contents of the man's luggage. Problem two: He had with him a live three-inch-long, three-inch-diameter device called a "point detonator fuse." Basically this was the explosive tip to a large Soviet-manufactured artillery round—the kind used by the Taliban. He also had a live six-inch-long, one-inch-diameter incendiary antiaircraft round—a tracer that burns white hot—also of Soviet manufacture. And he carried nine small-arms cartridges and bullets. A nice, deadly collection of war zone debris destined for his souvenir collection.

The TSA acted as it should have: It notified the Port Authority Police. The man told those officers he was a highly trained explosives ordnance technician, and produced a letter from his employer—which clearly stated he was not a bomb technician but an EMT. To a sharp cop this could have indicated that he was lying, and not very well. But after several hours of questioning, even though he had violated several laws, he was allowed to board a flight to Los Angeles, although his cargo was left behind.

"He had totally bamboozled them," said Walsh. The sergeant had worked the Cold Case Squad, solving thirty-year-old mob murders. He was a man who had seen the most bizarre of human creations, excuses, and rationales, and who was not given to criticizing the Port Authority Police, an agency where one of his closest friends worked. But in this case, he was baffled by the stupidity of all involved.

Upon the examination of the devices by Detective Second Grade Thomas Sullivan—Lieutenant Torre's right-hand man— and a review of his findings by Sergeant Biondolilo and Sergeant Walsh, the FBI in LA was notified and Mr. Marshall Shaun, a misguided, lying souvenir collector of Bardstown, Kentucky, was arrested for violating a statute against possessing explosives on an aircraft.

"It certainly would have been easier if he just bought his war souvenirs in Chinatown," Walsh said.

The real fun was about to begin.

The six Bomb Squad new response trucks had been delivered, the new "white devil" backscatter X-ray vans were in the car park, the new robots were tested and ready, and the handlers had been trained on their new capabilities. All the goodies received under federal grant were in New York, either at the range or at Bomb Squad Base, and ready to be joined in the fight to keep the Grand Old Party partying, no matter how many firecrackers demonstrators tossed into hotels, how many hoax devices they planted around the city, how many false threats were phoned into the Police Department, or how much intelligence from around the world came in indicating that something more substantial than slightly uncivil disobedience might be in the offing. Good, early intelligence meant that any plans by protestors or extremists could be countered by a strong defense in depth. The Bomb Squad, of course, was a last resort.

The new response trucks had been outfitted with the "super woo woo" packages—new lights, new sirens, and all the bells and whistles integrated into one control panel. A nice, new kennel sat in the back of each. There was a control chair for the robot operator and a neat compartment to stow the robot in. And there was room for six bomb suits in another compartment.

The trucks looked beautiful compared to the old ones, but Brian Hearn had made a list of every possible flaw. For example, the overhead compartments where hundreds of yards of fiber-optic cable were meant to be stored. He thought the weight could shift as the truck raced to a job, and when the compartment was opened a mountain of cable could land on the tech. At this point in August, it seemed that if Hearn couldn't say something critical, then he saw no point in saying anything at all. There was a special space on the squad chalkboard to log comments on the new vehicles and a reminder to not use them on Greenwich Village's narrowest streets until the operator had become familiar with their massive bulk. The space was full.

The trucks weighed 11,840 pounds and could carry a payload of 7,160 including men and dogs. The bodywork was custom built onto Ford heavy truck frames. They would now roam the streets outside the sealed area of the convention, circling like fighters on patrol, ready to move in and lend support if needed. Despite Hearn's criticisms, they were a big improvement over the vehicles the squad had been making due with until they arrived.

Other teams of NYPD techs and U.S. Marines under Secret Service command were to be stationed on foot inside the target. The target—Madison Square Garden—by now was fully hardened and surrounded by a ring of vehicle traps, thick concrete car-stopping "Jersey" barriers, and heavy "French" barriers, similar to concrete barriers but topped with tall, thick Plexiglas shields, to keep projectiles from being tossed by protestors at conventioneers. If the NYPD was going to fight a pitched battle on flat terrain, it would give its troops a multiple obstacle perimeter to wait behind.

The best outcome of all occurred. Nothing happened. Nothing at all: about twelve hundred arrests of demonstrators, a couple

of evictions from the convention site, some unruly crowds—
pretty much a run-of-the-mill New York City mass event.

For the squad, after twelve months of preparation, there was
not even an increase in number of runs, and there was only one
dumb move by an outside agency, whose tech unzipped a bag inside the perimeter. Zippers are often the trigger on a bomb in a
zippered bag. "Anything but the zipper" was how techs were
taught to open them. This tech, like New York, got lucky. The
President of the United States, Arnold Schwarzenegger, Rudy
Giuliani, and pockets full of new money for the Republican
Party came to town on August 28 for a weekend of fun, and left
on Thursday, September 2, without incident. Then it was Labor
Day and the silly season was officially over.

6

Good Night, Danny

On September 10, 2001, Sergeant Tony Biondolilo said, "Good night, Danny," and watched Detective Claude "Danny" Richards walk out through the squad room door.

It was Danny's first day back from bereavement leave. His older brother, a crippled airborne ranger, had died a week earlier.

Sergeant B turned to another sergeant sitting across from him in the bullpen, and they began talking about what it would take to have enough overtime figured into their final year of retirement for them to consider retiring before they were forced off The Job at age sixty-two.

"It would have to be bigger than that," Sergeant B said, and he pointed at a picture of the destruction of the Alfred P. Murrah Federal Building in Oklahoma City.

"Dad, wake up. You'd better get up." It was Sergeant B's daughter who shook him. "A plane just hit the World Trade Center." There would be no more dreams.

He turned on the TV, saw the smoke and flames, called the

squad, and then called Mike Walsh, who lived around the corner from him on Staten Island.

"Mike, we better get in."

He began to pack his gear, and then:

"Bang. That is when the second plane hit."

Walsh showed up soon after, and Sergeant B hopped into Walsh's pickup. They sped to the Staten Island Borough Command, where another neighbor, Highway Sergeant Jim Lavelle, loaded them and their gear into his powerful blue and white highway unit, stepped on the gas, and pegged the speedometer at 140 miles an hour all the way to the Battery Tunnel entrance in Brooklyn.

"We were turned back at the Brooklyn Battery Tunnel; it was shut down. We raced to the Manhattan Bridge and came in that way. When we got there, we didn't know anything had come down," Walsh said. All across New York rescue workers were racing toward the flames, fighting roadblocks and closed roads in a race to risk their lives.

Lieutenant Torre was commander of the Arson and Explosion Squad at the time, having left the Bomb Squad nine months earlier upon his promotion from sergeant. He had planned to go to work early that Tuesday morning. He did not. The night before he had gone fishing with Detective Tommy Sullivan after work but had neglected to tell his wife. Not only did the big-shouldered Atlantic once again reject his baits, but when he came home, his wife rejected his excuse and gave him the cold shoulder.

"I was sent to the basement."

He lay awake and brooded until he heard Lisa's footsteps come down the stairs. She told him to come up to bed. By then it was very late. He fell into a sound sleep.

"I think you'd better come and look at this, Mark. I think you had better get to work," is how he recalled being awakened by Lisa. This is the police officer's wife, a woman brave enough to send her husband into danger each morning even if the world is in flames outside her door and death seems imminent.

He stumbled out of bed, saw the smoke and flames from the first tower, jumped under the shower and right out again. "In time to see the second plane hit."

He called Nassau County Highway—his own department car was in the shop and his Honda beater would never get through the roadblocks without an escort. The Nassau officers raced him in from Long Island to the Highway Three headquarters—a barracks in Queens just over the city line—where he met Chief Phil Pulaski. He rode in with his chief.

"We could hear it blow by blow as the towers came down; we heard it from Aviation and we heard it over the SOD frequency." By the time they arrived at Police Headquarters the Special Operations broadcasts and reports from the squad had put them in a bleak mood.

"We already knew by then that Danny was lost. We couldn't imagine who else was lost."

Fortunately for the police officers who first responded, the police bosses had somehow gotten an order out: All officers stand back from the site and await commands. After the initial wave of losses, many were saved from themselves by the solid chain of command.

"If I hadn't slept late, I probably would have died," Torre said. "Not because I am brave. But because I would have been an idiot running in there in my shirt and tie."

Detective Jimmy Schutta had also been monitoring the Special Operations Division frequency. He had been at the Barrier Unit, where he had collected and deposited barricades at polling places for a September 11 primary election that now would have to be redone in another two weeks. The voice that haunts him today is that of Police Officer Moira Smith. The last pictures of her show her standing outside the rubble, guiding citizens to safety. The last time her voice was heard she stood tall in the darkness beneath the rubble of the fallen towers guiding one after another person along a human chain to safety until finally her flashlight died. Her last words were a simple call for help over her radio.

Name: Smith, Moira   Rank: P.O.
Shield #: 10467   Command: 013 Pct.
Date of Death: 2001-09-11   Cause of Death: World Trade
                                      Center Attack

Moira Smith received the Police Department Medal of Honor posthumously. On December 11, her two-year-old daughter, Patricia, wearing a beautiful red dress, stepped up onto the police auditorium stage and accepted her mother's posthumous medal, holding her head steady as the thick emerald green ribbon was draped over her neck. Her father, Officer James Smith, then gently took her hand to accompany her from the stage.

Brian Hearn had been working his off-duty job, sitting in a security trailer at the New York Stock Exchange, when he heard the first plane hit. He called the squad and was told that a small plane had hit the Trade Center.

"OK, let us know if you need anything, I'm down at the trailer." He was with two other off-duty officers.

"When the second plane hit, the trailer moved," Brian said. "It moved. It moved two feet off the street. What the hell is that?

"I look out and see papers flying. And there were people that were going to work and now they're running out. People are running up Exchange Place. They're running down Broadway." By the time Hearn dialed the squad again, Detective Kevin Barry and Detective Mike Oldmixon were already at the intersection of Church and Vesey Streets, on the edge of the sixteen-acre World Trade Center complex.

"All you see is shoes. All up and down the street, shoes, just empty shoes. Empty shoes," Oldmixon recalled. Parts of the planes were coming down around them. A turbine blade struck the response truck. An engine block landed a few feet from Kevin Barry. They were standing near that engine block, Hearn remembers, when he found them.

"We're going to go in and get the people outside," Barry said.

"With that, Danny comes down the street," Hearn said. "He's in his jumpsuit. He has his helmet on."

"What are you doing here?" Barry asked. Danny was the squad intelligence officer, and an intelligence officer's battle station would more naturally have been at the telephone.

"It's a loony bin in the office. I had to get out," Danny said. The former Army Ranger had gone from home to the squad, where he met two other bomb squad detectives who lived in Manhattan—his partner that day, Danny McNally, and Steve "Ziggy" Berberich. They joined the group of bomb technicians that now included Oldmixon, Barry, Hearn, and Phil Goldwin. Four of the seven are now retired.

"The drive from the Bomb Squad office to the location of the World Trade Center was a short one, and we arrived just after the South Tower had collapsed," Danny McNally later wrote in his personal account of the event. "Smoke and dust was everywhere but you could still see plainly. We parked our vehicle at the staging area at Vesey and Church. Other members of the Bomb Squad were there waiting for direction. The North Tower is in flames but still standing."

FBI Special Agent Bomb Technician Lenny Haten ran up and told them that another plane had hit the Pentagon and yet another had crashed into a field in Pennsylvania. It was all word of mouth. The telephone lines were down at the FBI Headquarters in New York; part of the police command structure was in place at One Police Plaza, but the rest of it was commanding on the run. Cell phone service was out, and the circuits that carried regular telephone service were overloaded with calls in and out of New York. Rumors swirled. Haten went in. He was never seen again.

"Looking west on Vesey Street I see a lone NYPD sergeant trying to direct victims down from the elevated plaza area of the World Trade Center. He is alone and in a very dangerous location," McNally wrote. "Debris is coming off the tower from as high as a quarter mile up. He looked scared but determined not to abandon the remaining victims. I decide to join him and Detectives Claude Richards, Steve Berberich, and Officers Mike Oldmixon and Joe Dolan join me. This is no longer an investigation but a rescue mission.

"Berberich and Oldmixon started to clear debris from the broken escalator that goes from Vesey Street to the plaza area between WTC #5 and 6. It is littered with sheet metal that has peeled off from the remaining North Tower. Once they cleared the escalator they posted on the plaza near the escalator to direct victims to Vesey Street. Myself, Richards and Dolan respond onto the Plaza area to direct victims to Berberich and Oldmixon and on to safety.

"I wish I could describe what was happening on the plaza in great detail, but I can't. Years of experience in police work has taught me to maintain my focus on my job and not be distracted by sirens, blaring radios, smoke, dust, and the carnage that I have no control over. I was up on that plaza to get the living to safety.

"Myself, Richards and Dolan met up with members of the New York City Police Department's Emergency Services Unit [ESU]. While conferring with them as to how we could best help with the evacuation, a piece of sheet steel came down and cut the upraised arm of their lieutenant to the bone from the thumb to the mid-forearm. He was still standing and refused to leave the scene. Joe Dolan convinced him to seek medical attention and guided him to one of the many ambulances staged on Vesey and Broadway. That left Richards and me.

"Richards and I were physically fresh, having just arrived. . . . We raced to the ambulances and retrieved a backboard. When we got back to the plaza area the ESU members that had requested the backboard were gone. Richards and myself posted under the overhang of WTC #6, which held the US Customs offices. This building was directly north of the North Tower and its overhang afforded us some protection from falling debris. It was from this location that we would dash out and pull people to safety and direct them to Berberich and Oldmixon and the escalators.

"While directing victims to safety I see two uniformed NYPD cops assisting this very large woman across the plaza. She had lost one of her shoes and was having great difficulty walking across the debris-filled plaza. She was about to give up and the two cops struggled to keep her on her feet. She was certain to die if she sat down and quit while still on the plaza. I ran up to her and yelled, 'Lady, if you don't walk off this plaza we're all going to die because we're not going to leave you.' She found her strength and with the help of those two young officers she made it to safety."

Soon after, McNally and Richards entered the Customs House, and within a few minutes, the North Tower came down.

"Some survivors say it sounded like a freight train going through your head. To me, it sounded like a mine collapse. We could hear it coming down, powerful, unstoppable. I knew what it was and followed the lead of the man in front of me. I crouched down against the north wall of the lobby and tried my best to become very small. I held onto the frame of the SCBA [self-contained breathing apparatus] of the man in front of me. I held on so hard that I bent the frame. I held on because I did not want to be alone. The man behind me held on to me so hard that his fingers bruised my sides just under my arms. The next day I had perfect purple handprints on my sides.

"The sound and vibration of the tower coming down was frightening. It sounded so powerful and large that I believed

I was going to die. I didn't have the gall to ask God to spare me. I asked only that if He was going to take me, take me fast. I waited for a piece of steel to spear my back and come out my chest because I thought that might be a fast way to go. Seconds became all that was left of life and they hung in the air as I waited. I was terrified. When parts of the overhead ductwork and ceiling collapsed, I thought it was the end and waited for the big blow or sharp object that would crush or pierce me. I was pushed, by the overpressure from the collapse, into the wall I was bracing against, breaking the heavy Sheetrock with my right shoulder. I started to rise to my feet when everything went black. Thick heavy choking dust that defies description stormed into the lobby. I couldn't see, and within seconds, the respirator I had on clogged. I couldn't breathe. I thought about how strange it would be to survive the collapse, only to suffocate. After a minute I started to panic, my lungs were burning. I couldn't breathe and for one brief moment I considered pulling the gun from the officer in front of me and ending this painful nightmare for myself. (I had rushed out of the Bomb Squad Office without my own gun.) Then I felt ashamed, because I really felt that God had heard my prayers and that I had doubted him. Soon I could take short painful breaths that reminded me that I had to find some clean air.

"In the blackness that defies description we felt our way along the wall. . . . After a few minutes the dust began to settle. I could start to make out shapes. It was at this time I noticed Claude [was] missing. . . . I started to call for Danny (Claude's nickname). While searching for him I found a civilian survivor with a very powerful flashlight. I took his flashlight and headed back to where I thought . . . Danny might be. . . . Enough dust had settled to breathe life into the fires that surrounded us and filled the abyss before me. I knew if Dan . . . were behind me when the building came down, [he was] buried under all that burning steel."

. . .

Jeff Oberdier had dropped his daughter at day care in Rockland County. He turned on the radio. Normally he would have tuned to music, but he was running late, so he turned on the news to make sure he knew what was going on in New York before he entered the city. The news was not good. But what had happened was not yet clear. He dialed the office. All the lines were busy. He tried the range. It was the same. He drove home and tried from a hardwire phone line. The same. Something was badly wrong.

He hit the Palisades Parkway entrance ramp already at full speed. The parkway was devoid of cars.

"It was already shut down."

He swept onto the George Washington Bridge.

"There was not a car on the bridge, like *Independence Day*.

"By the time I hit Manhattan there were agents everywhere. Teams were out with heavy weapons. I kept showing my badge and my gun, which is what I had with me. When I got to the office it must have been ten-ten, ten-twenty, right around when the first building comes down. It was mass chaos. Dust was everywhere. White dust. Thick.

"Calls are coming in, bomb job after bomb job after bomb job." People were seeing suspicious packages everywhere.

At the point in the day when Jeff arrived at the squad, there was only a semblance of government in New York; the mayor and police commissioner had ducked for cover, narrowly escaping the tower as it pancaked down—they had gone to the scene of the attack to command in person. Much of the top Fire Department command had done the same. They now lay dead or dying.

"Nobody knows where the police commissioner is. Nobody knows where Giuliani is. There are reports that the Fire Department lost everybody. At the same time there are reports that the Police Department is losing everybody," Hearn recalled.

"An officer named Manny Lopez says he has the boss nearby and he's got to get him out of there." Hearn was reliving a moment. He was standing at the same spot on Vesey Street where he met with Barry and Oldmixon. He grabbed Kevin Barry; they jogged to the response truck and pulled it up next to First Deputy Commissioner Joe Dunn.

"OK, Commissioner, get in."

"No. I've got to direct the troops."

"No, you've got to get in the truck."

Joe Dunn is a big man. They pushed him in. But as Kevin Barry spun the wheel into a U-turn, Dunn jumped out.

"So I get out, go to him, and say, 'Commissioner, get in.' He says he has to give leadership.

"I punched him in the chest and threw him back in the truck. As I did, you could hear the second building going down. We whipped around, ran him to Police Headquarters, and he was in charge of the Police Department at that point."

This ethos of bravery, the rigors of training, the devotion to their oaths and their city caused thousands and thousands of officers and firefighters to dig into the rubble, to crawl into it, and to dig out, carry out, and lead out those they could. Their love of their families did not cause men and women to run home to them. It led them to walk into the danger that was beyond any all but a few combat veterans had ever seen.

Bravery and duty did not stop at the city line; teams of bomb technicians drove in from New Jersey, from Nassau and Suffolk Counties on Long Island, and from Philadelphia. A commander in Miami had already selected ten of his officers and begun the drive to New York. Some of the ironworkers who had put the towers up were racing with their sons and nephews and younger union brethren to start cutting through the same steel they once had riveted together. Already engineers were bringing in cranes. Weekend warriors of the National Guard had put on their uniforms, raced to their armories, and were already on their way in with convoys of supplies and with weapons at the ready. The heat, at the center of the inferno, was still hovering near 16,000 degrees.

This was all occurring in seconds and minutes. Suddenly a girder sliced the ground in half. Mike Oldmixon was trapped, even as inside the building Danny Richards was separated from his partner and plunged six stories down into a pit of rubble where his body was later recovered. This was when a white cloud of bone fragment and building materials covered all of New York; when everyone in New York inhaled a little bit of those who'd died. This was when the yellow smell of death began to blanket New York. It would lie there over the city, thick as the dust, for months, as the fires burned and burned and burned, before they finally burned themselves out.

Oldmixon had rescued several people and was in the process of rescuing more when the world collapsed around him. Now he began crawling toward a pinhole of light, along the way leading several more people out of the rubble.

"A few minutes after Tony B and I had arrived at the office, Mike Oldmixon came in," Mike Walsh recalled.

"All you could see were his eyes. He had on a nice tweed sport coat, and he was completely covered in white dust and debris.

" 'I'm fine,' " he said when he was asked. But he wasn't.

"You could see the bruises and the cuts on his back."

"We took him into the garage, stripped him down, and began to clean him up." He had been trapped for an hour or more. Then he put on a jumpsuit, went to the lockers, took a shower, put the jumpsuit back on, and came upstairs.

Sergeant Mike DeMarfio and Detective Jerry Fitzpatrick were at an Alcohol, Tobacco and Firearms training course in Fredericksburg, Virginia. They were about to begin their first day of classes when the first plane hit.

"Everything was grounded."

DeMarfio said that they loaded their gear into their rental car and convoyed back at top speed behind a New Jersey State Police trooper. The trooper had come down in his official SUV, which had a flashing strobe light in the grill and a siren package. They made it as far as the Delaware River. The Philadelphia–New Jersey bridges were shut down. Riflemen were on patrol. The NJSP packed the two bomb techs onto a helicopter and flew them the final eighty or so miles.

"It was just us, the NYPD helicopters, and the Air Force jets— you could hear them talking," DeMarfio recalled.

"About the time the second World Trade Center collapsed, I am looking out the window. I said to Jerry, 'This can't be.' We landed at the heliport. I commandeered a radio car. We get back to the office and I'll never forget. Mike Oldmixon is there. He's got the garden hose on, outside the garage. He's washing his eyes out. The building had collapsed on him."

At this point Hearn, Barry, Ziggy Berberich, and other members of the squad had regrouped at Bomb Squad Base.

"Ziggy is in the corner; sitting in the chair over there. He's bawling. He's sitting here saying, 'I lost Dan. Danny's gone. No, he's not gone. He'll be in. He'll come back in.' "

A year later Claude "Danny" Richards's picture and plaque were placed on the wall of Bomb Squad Base, alongside the pictures of the other squad members lost in action through the squad's history.

A year later Danny McNally was still recovering from the trauma he suffered when the man who everyone remembers as a partner, and who along with Berberich rode with him to the disaster, slipped away from them both.

"I still have the occasional nightmare and I still cry in my sleep, I guess when I need to. But I am alive and serving my country the best I can. . . . In time, if all goes well, my patience will return and maybe someday I will be able to attend a Manhattan cocktail party without throwing a punch at some fool who wants to blame America for everything."

7

Nuclear Aftermath

The surgeon from New Year's Eve 1982, Sergeant Charlie Wells had become Inspector Charlie Wells by September 11, 2001, and he was NYPD head of the Joint Terrorism Task Force in New York. In the aftermath of 9/11, he was at the nerve center of a deluge of intelligence. None of it was good. It seemed the nation was under assault from all sides.

It was early October, and the fires at Ground Zero were still burning underground. The steel girders and beams were as white hot as a grill. They were fueled by every bit of combustible material that the towering offices had contained. The dust, the smoke, and the stink hung over the site of the declaration of war, when Wells first received the terrifying warning of a terrorist nuclear bomb being smuggled into New York.

There had already been one rumor of a nuclear device. In that case, Wells informed the mayor of New York, Rudy Giuliani, and his staff. That rumor soon became public. It was quickly dismissed as unfounded and the city deftly reassured. Teams of experts had been quietly afoot in the city, reporters were told, and they had found no evidence of a hidden radioactive device. In the climate of the day, the reports were not sensationalized as they might have been at a time when national security had less resonance to the newspaper editors and TV and radio news directors.

What neither the mayor nor the public knew was that a truly terrifying new threat was already present. A CIA source believed to be very reliable had brought the information to his handlers. Although it remains highly classified, this information has since been made public in at least two accounts. They differ in some details, but have a common thread: The CIA source appeared to have firsthand knowledge that al Qaeda had procured or made a nuclear weapon or weapons, and those either were being smuggled or were already in place in either New York, Washington, or both. At this point in time even the lowest probability event was not beyond the perception of al Qaeda's operational capacity; especially if it had such high consequences.

Extremely secretive meetings got under way. Military commanders, NSA wizards, Department of Energy officials charged with managing such a catastrophe, CIA analysts, and Wells shuttled back and forth between Washington and New York. Meanwhile, Special Operations teams, nuclear bomb hunters from the Department of Energy Nuclear Emergency Search Teams (NEST), cops, soldiers, and FBI agents armed with radiation wands and pagers patrolled day and night. Few of them knew the specific threat behind their patrols. None of the foot soldiers knew that overhead, unmarked intelligence community aircraft with sensitive radiation detection equipment flew low and slow across the skies of New York and the capital.

"We had a whole plan to deal with it," Wells recalled. "Military people were tasked. Timetables were made—what was the ETA for the team if the device was in D.C., if the device was in New York." Wells was willing to discuss how he arrived at his very sober decisions on dealing with the threat, but not the information itself.

On his office wall there was a plaque from the United States

Army Special Operations Command honoring his participation in this operation. There was no date and no reason on the plaque. He pointed to it to sum up just how seriously the secrecy was taken, even afterward.

"After a couple of weeks of back and forth, the bottom line was 99.9 percent the federal team wasn't going to make it here even if we were lucky enough to intercept the device. They had one team, and one cutter," he said, using "cutter" as his personal shorthand for the technician who would try to defuse the bomb. "At best that team would be several hours away and well, hey, if they had to choose between Washington and New York . . .

"So after a couple of weeks, I decided to bring in the Bomb Squad," Wells said. Wells and the others involved have not publicly acknowledged what happened next. The commander of the Bomb Squad at the time, Lieutenant Jerry "Pappy" Sheehan, would not even entertain a conversation about it. But those there recall him appearing in the office with a briefcase cuffed to his wrist. At Wells's behest, a series of quiet conversations were held with the most senior members of the Bomb Squad and a few recently retired members with extensive experience.

"We had no confidence that al Qaeda was going to properly shield a device. I mean we figured we would know we found it when we found a van with the driver fried and a bomb in the back," Wells recalled.

A handful of men, all with families, children, and some with grandchildren, were asked to volunteer to take the long walk up to the device.

"I mean, you couldn't really order a guy. . . . We figured someone might say no," Wells says. But no one did.

Dennis Mulchahy, Sheehan himself, Kevin Barry, and Joe Putkowski all agreed to disarm a device knowing full well they would almost certainly die, even if they succeeded in saving the city of New York. Not one of them asked whether it was possible to defuse the device. They knew the answer; it was a bomb, more dangerous than other bombs, but with enough time and a set of hand tools they could take it apart. To this day, not one of them has even acknowledged that the event happened, or that they had been willing to walk down a street to an almost certain death.

8

September 11, 1976

It seemed to come out of nowhere.

On September 10, 1976, Croatian terrorists hijacked a TWA airliner as it lifted off from New York's LaGuardia Airport, with ninety-three passengers and seven crew members on board. As proof of their seriousness the hijackers left behind a note that directed authorities to a locker in Grand Central Terminal. Bomb Squad police officer Brian Murray and his partner, Henry Dworkin, were sent to investigate.

When they opened the locker, they found a large, heavy Dutch oven that contained ten sticks of dynamite.

Murray, Dworkin, and a sergeant, Terry McTigue, were instructed to take the device to the range and leave it there overnight. On September 11, 1976, Sergeant McTigue and Brian Murray were back at the range squatting over the cast iron–covered bomb in an attempt to defuse it.

"It was just Brian and me. So we went over, and I think I was front. We started to squat down. . . . Everything seemed OK. And then, it blew. Just like that. Hadn't even touched it. . . . I was blinded instantly. . . . I felt the blood rushing down my throat. I remember being just thrown back, tumbled back. I couldn't hear much. I was trying to say, 'Take care of my boys, take care of my boys. I'm OK.' But the words weren't coming out. . . . My mouth wasn't hinged on [one] side at all. This was just flapped open," McTigue recalled. "I heard a guy say, 'How is he?' 'No pulse.' I knew I had a pulse, so I knew it was Brian.

"The Croatians killed Murray, of course. The bomb maker that killed Murray was Zvonko Busic, and he was convicted," Inspector Charlie Wells recalled. Busic today remains the chief suspect in another lethal bombing.

During the peak holiday travel day of December 29, 1975, a bomb exploded in a coin-operated locker at LaGuardia Airport's TWA terminal. It killed eleven people, wounded seventy-five, and left the floors ankle-deep in bloody water after the blazes were extinguished. Why attack the United States when the war they were fighting was with Yugoslavia? The logic was in a manifesto they later issued: "For the multitudes who are suffering innocently, you, the responsible gentlemen, you in the United peoples [sic] nation and outside will be held responsible in the court of history."

The letter became a part of BS incident reports #2712 and #2713 of 1978 and was signed "Croatian Liberation Forces." It was delivered after Busic's imprisonment began.

9

September 11, 2004

"**S**quad—fall in!" At 0843 hours that command was given at each of the seventy-six police precincts in the City of New York.

At the 6th Precinct the precinct officers and the members of the Bomb Squad gathered in front of a podium set outside the precinct doors on West Tenth Street in the morning latte quiet of Greenwich Village.

"Squad—attention!" At 0845 this command was given. The uniformed officers and detectives stood straighter.

0846 Hours: "At this very moment, three years ago, on September 11, 2001, New York City came under terrorist attack. Almost three thousand people died. The NYPD responded to the World Trade Center buildings in a show of strength and courage that earned us the respect of the world. Twenty-three brave members did not return from Ground Zero. We honor them daily by protecting the American way of life, for which they died on that day."

The Friday night before the ceremony, two detectives answering a mother's plea for help were shot and killed by her son on a

Brooklyn street. As he lay dying, one of the detectives talked dispatchers to the scene, telling them a picture of the suspect was on the seat of the detectives' car, directing them patiently to the correct address, and finally, his breath exhausted, but with no fear or panic ever rising in his voice, he said, "I'm going out." Then he died. His death and that of his partner were as aptly described in the department directive as the deaths of their colleagues on September 11.

"They and each one of you personify what is best about this city, this country and our ideals. . . . Take pride in knowing that history will remember that the New York City Police Department demonstrated the highest principles of service and humanity in our response that day. We will now call the roll of our members killed in the line of duty on September 11, 2001."

"Squad: Present. Arms. We will now call the roll of our members killed in the line of duty on September 11, 2001.

"Sergeant John Coughlin. Sergeant Michael Curtin. Sergeant Rodney Gillis. Sergeant Timothy Roy. Detective Claude Richards . . . Police Officer Moira Smith . . . Police Officer Walter Weaver."

There were twenty-three names in all. Heads were bowed. Silence was observed. The precinct ceremony was over.

The Bomb Squad regrouped. In full dress it walked the two blocks to West Street, a street by the Hudson River and from which you once had a clear view down to the World Trade Center. A new street sign was unveiled renaming this stretch of Manhattan "Detective Claude 'Danny' Richards Way."

In their published tribute to him, the *New York Times* said:

If ever a man was to the Bomb Squad born, it was Detective Claude Richards of the New York Police Department. Fearless, meticulous and disciplined nearly to a fault, Detective Richards, 46, the Bomb Squad's intelligence coordinator, spent his off-duty hours working, working out and planning his next workday. When he took some time off, it was to defuse land mines in Bosnia with a United Nations peacekeeping force. All the way from boyhood, Dan, as Detective Richards was known, "always wanted to charge up to the front," said his brother, Jim, "just to prove himself."

BOOK NINE

The American Spirit

A Real Good Salute

There was no rest and there would be little chance of any until New Year's Day. As the Secret Service team coordinating security for the Republican Convention stood down another team preparing for the opening of the United Nations General Assembly had simply stood up operations in its place.

Inside the Police Department the controlled chaos of the Republican Convention security package was replaced by security planning for the September opening of the UN Security Council, for the Thanksgiving parade, for the lighting of the Christmas tree in Rockefeller Center, for Christmas Eve midnight mass at St. Patrick's Cathedral, and for New Year's Eve in Times Square. All of these events would occur within three months. All of them would require the Bomb Squad. All of them were events that New York City policed and protected. Since the UN first opened its doors in Manhattan in 1951 not a single dignitary's life had been lost. But each of the plans would be reviewed, rolling road closures would adjusted, the locations and size of units would be changed, barricades would be repositioned, new commanders would learn their jobs.

With each year of its existence the Bomb Squad's responsibilities at these events grew. They were at the first Times Square ball drop. They were at St. Patrick's every holiday since the first bomb attack cracked the floor there. They were at Macy's Thanksgiving parade since the first FALN bomb attacks at Macy's. They have been to the UN each time it convened and notably during the threatening period in 1964 when an anti-Castro bazooka attack in December was launched across the East River at the Secretariat from Queens. The round fell short.

Inside his office Lieutenant Torre pored over duty charts. He considered the positioning of teams in relationship to targets and one another at each event. He considered the positioning of the total containment vehicle. He considered the overtime cost associated with each event. He tried to arrange a few days off around each holiday for as many squad members as he could. He had other concerns. He needed a new explosives storage locker. He needed refinements to the exhaust system of the vans that carried the large, mobile backscatter radar units—the operators were breathing fumes from the generator when the vehicle was stationary at a location. His senior man, Joe Putkowski, was eligible to receive a first-grade detective shield, and the prestige and extra money that went along with it.

"How do I do it? I want Joe to get it before the year is out." The Bomb Squad had not had a promotion to first grade in the entire time Torre had been in command. He wanted one. He wanted it on the merits. He wanted it for the morale. He wanted it to demonstrate the strength of his leadership. He presented Joe's case to his superiors in the Detective Division, making sure it was seen by the chief of detectives himself.

On September 9, as the date of the General Assembly drew closer, the squad once again went on alert. A series of letter bombs had begun showing up in the mail rooms of governor's offices across the nation. The letters contained incendiary devices made from the sulfur of match heads and an aluminum accelerant.

When the envelope was opened, a striker ignited the sulfur. At least one was successful. Others failed. They had been cleverly designed to scare the person who received the letter. One showed up in the Albany office of the governor of New York. None, it would turn out, arrived at his Manhattan office. But the squad knew what to look for if they had. Frank Tabert, the IABTI regional director, and the bomb expert assigned to New York State's regional homeland security system, had e-mailed them pictures of the devices as soon as the bomb techs in Albany and other jurisdictions had put them in his hands.

On September 14 the UN opened its gates to heads of state and prime ministers or foreign ministers of at least 164 out of the 191 countries that belonged, and New York City shut down row after row of its streets and line upon line of its avenues to accommodate the streams of flag-flying motorcades heading into the UN grounds for the 59th General Assembly.

At the squad, everyone got into his groove, inside his bubble, into his zone. By this time of the year everyone had seen and run on almost everything explosive at least twice. But each time could be the last time. So it was best to treat each time like it was the first time and the only time.

The jobs kept coming: a hoax device, a piece of military ordnance, an improvised explosive device, another IED, a KKK hoax, a chemical reaction bomb, an inert land mine, a grenade, another hoax, an envelope with "bomb" written on it inside a UPS drop box, a 60-millimeter mortar round in a Manhattan basement, a military smoke grenade and an IED inside a mini-storage facility, a small "cricket" IED inside a Queens apartment, fingers lost to the blast from a large firework, a hoax with swastikas and a preprinted cut-out signature of Vice President Dick Cheney, a soda bottle bomb exploding in a high school classroom, a Bomb Squad automobile windshield shattered by a small explosion, an IED made from a can of WD-40 and a large M-80 firework, a fake bomb used in a bank robbery, and a really clever hoax sent to the Museum of Modern Art—the MOMA Bomb as it was called, a piece of white PVC tube that lit up from inside when it was jarred. "Very artistic," said Sergeant B, as he typed up the case.

On September 21 the General Assembly began with a dog fight. The UN is a sovereignty. It is not patrolled by any of the city's seventy-six police precincts. It is not on the Fire Department dispatcher maps. It seems to take pride in the fact that although its buildings were built taking city building and fire codes into account, they don't necessarily adhere to them. That fact is noted in UN files. The day the President of the United States was to speak to the General Assembly, the UN security people were determined to use their own dogs to sweep the Security Council chambers. Even as Coast Guard cutters and NYPD harbor launches and scuba teams patrolled its back doors, even as three thousand cops protected its perimeter, even as the Secret Service provided body protection for each ranking government official, behind its wrought iron gates, the UN was sure it knew best.

"Fine, have it your way, and when something blows up, you can explain it," one of the sergeants said to a UN security official. The official started to buckle and wanted to negotiate a compromise. The sergeant had had enough. He turned his back and walked out. There was no compromise on this issue.

Raymond Cornmesser, the United States Secret Service Special Technician Security Division man, and the agency's liaison with the squad, lent federal muscle to the discussion. On this point the UN was going to relent and the NYPD and Secret Service would prevail: The President of the United States was not setting foot in the UN without his own dogs and his own dog handlers sweeping the rooms. Those were the dogs and handlers of the Secret Service and the NYPD.

While he waited for the dogfight to be settled, Sergeant B decided he would conduct his own in-your-face test of UN security. The UN had banned all law enforcement from inside the building itself unless they had special passes with a unique security clearance. Without showing a single pass, Sergeant B and a full team of technicians along with Cornmesser breezed through security. The team sat down to the bargain-priced gourmet food of the Delegates Dining Room, looked out through the large glass wall at the East River, and enjoyed their breakfast, taking time to laugh in between each bite.

Outside of the United Nations complex a matter of some actual urgency had developed over the weekend before the General Assembly. Sergeant B, along with other members of the Bomb Squad, had investigated it.

At LaGuardia Airport, inside a rear lavatory of Spirit Airlines aircraft number N808NK, which had arrived in New York via Florida and was in the process of being cleaned, four two-inch-long, one-inch-diameter forbidden M-Class explosives were found stuffed inside a tissue box. A mechanic on the overnight shift who discovered the box notified the airport. Port Authority Police called the Bomb Squad to explain the worker's discovery of what individually amounted to large fireworks. Together, however, the four sticks could possibly blow a hole in the airliner's hull.

Detective Andy Rea was assigned to the case and Sergeant Tony Biondolilo had driven out with him at one o'clock Saturday morning to investigate. They were met by FBI Special Agents from the Joint Terrorism Task Force. Bomb Squad Case #1287 was anything but routine. Just three weeks earlier two jetliners had been simultaneously blown out of the sky in Russia. Now New York had a case with too many similarities to ignore.

In the case of the Russian attack it appeared that the explosives had been placed in the restrooms by female suicide bombers boarding the jet, entering the restrooms, and pressing the explosives against the hulls—using their bodies to tamp the explosives down and direct the blast outward. The NYPD Intelligence Division and the Joint Terrorism Task Force had that information at their fingertips, and like the frontline techs, they were taking this discovery aboard the American Spirit airline seriously. It fit the pattern too neatly. None of these agents or officers believed in coincidence.

Officials downplayed the finding of the "fireworks" to the media, but federal agents and detectives repeatedly interrogated the mechanic who'd found the explosives. A person who reports a crime often becomes a prime suspect, at least for a time. In this case the mechanic was willing to take a polygraph, and after days of questioning he could not be shaken from his story. Nonetheless, there was no other suspect to be found, and he remained a "person of interest," although no one could explain why, if the man was seeking attention and praise as a hero, he would have made his discovery in the middle of the night at a virtually empty airport.

Lieutenant Torre and the squad took the explosives into evidence. On the day of the dogfight at the UN, Torre and a team from the Crime Scene Unit went up to the range. There they took apart the explosives and measured the quantity of powder in each. Then they tested a sample of each and bagged and tagged the evidence. Should it be needed in court, the examination and testing under Torre's direction would allow him to present expert testimony. As a next step, rather than speculate on whether the devices could have blown apart a plane, Torre and the Bomb Squad team on hand created four sets of four similar devices, attached them to four panels of an automobile, covered two sets with heavy plastic bags filled with an amount of water to give them some of the characteristics of a human torso—a suicide bomber's torso—pressing the explosives against the wall of a plane. The two sets without any water-filled bags tamping them down barely creased the sheet metal. The two sets with the bags affixed to them blew deep holes into the metal and separated body panels. From the perspective of the bomb techs, there was every reason to be suspicious of the airport discovery. The case, which was classified, remained under investigation at the end of 2004. Sometimes there are no clear answers in a war on terror, just new questions.

To Brian Hearn these were interesting questions, but more important, by September 26, 2004, he was back to living in his parents' home with his wife, Kathy, and his two daughters.

"Kathy and I started out in the backseat of a car, and right now I feel like that is where we are going to end up," he said.

Hearn and his wife had hired contractors to tear their house down to its foundations before completely rebuilding and modernizing it. He would have something new to grumble about. While Hearn grumbled, Steve Lanoce spent his night shifts wondering if ABC would consider him for any of the sitcoms that he had read would replace *Nightline*.

On October 29 Osama bin Laden released a video through the Al Jazeera television network. He directly addressed the American people and the upcoming election. In short, Osama suggested that the security of America was in the voters' hands: "Your security is not in the hands of [Democratic candidate John Kerry] [George] Bush or al Qaeda your security is in your own hands."

Polling-place security, already tight, was redoubled overnight. Past messages from bin Laden had often led to attacks, and what better date for a new strike than the presidential election?

In Austin, Texas, where Bush had watched the 2000 returns, Detective Jim Nielson and his bomb squad trained election judges on how to identify suspicious packages.

In New Orleans a full-blown antiterror plan was in effect and State Police bomb technicians were on alert. In New York City stepped-up vehicle checkpoints and an increase in roving police teams would be employed.

In Boston, Philadelphia, and Los Angeles, in New Jersey, Texas, and every other state and large city, officials had developed novel security plans that respected the sanctity of the polling places and the predisposition to keep police far enough away, to blunt any suggestion that their presence might influence an outcome. The election came and went. Bush won. Osama did not attack.

The night before Thanksgiving, under gloomy, wet skies, 16.6 miles of barriers—2468 wooden barriers and 7685 metal ones—were in place from Central Park West down to Macy's in Herald Square. The famed floats were inflated and the Bomb Squad teams tried as best they could to keep the rain outside their slickers and hoods.

The morning broke clear and blue. For Detective Roger Mack and his dog, Digon, it was their first Thanksgiving Parade together. By 7:00 A.M. Digon had bounded under the aluminum bleachers, around the flowerpots and ledges of the massive department store building, and over and under any objects in his path. Roger used a flashlight to check various bits left behind by workmen, who were still finishing up when the Bomb Squad arrived at Herald Square. Some discarded carpenter aprons filled with bolts and nuts bore a suspicious resemblance to suicide belts. They were examined and discounted. By the time the parade kicked off, Roger and Digon were walking along the lines of excited children. Digon was being petted and cheered by each group of children as he moved on, "Bye-bye, Puppy. Bye-bye, Doggie."

At a special spot set aside for the widows and orphans of police officers slain in the line of duty, Digon, Mack, Sergeant Hourihan, Sergeant Coughlan, and Jimmy Carrano stopped to chat and let the teams dogs be petted. Seven hundred and eight police officers' names were inscribed on the bronze memorial plaques in the auditorium of Police Headquarters, along with the names of five auxiliary police officers and seven crossing guards—all killed in the line of duty. Visiting the widows, widowers, and their children was important for the squad. Although they went out each day on a job that could mean life and death, it was the traffic cops, detectives, crossing guards, school safety agents, highway patrol officers—their brothers and sisters in blue—who most often died in encounters with strangers. As Sergeant Hourihan had said

in explaining his career decision to his wife, dealing with the unknowns of human beings was far more dangerous than an occasional encounter with a high explosive.

Ats 10:10 A.M. on Saturday, November 26, UN Inspector
Frank Bobbish informed the squad that mailroom personnel at
the UN had discovered a suspicious letter addressed to the secretary general, so the egos were back in check. The squad came.
The letter was examined, and an unmodified holiday electronic
greeting card was discovered. No threats or dangerous materials
were attached to it. The tiny battery and switch in this instance
had not been used to initiate the detonation of a thin-sheet explosive capable of taking off a person's hands and head. But similar batteries and switches had been employed that way in the
past. A good call by Frank Bobbish. Case closed.

The Christmas promotion list came in and Joe Putkowski was
on it. Mark lit a cigar in celebration.

On December 23 Joe Putkowski stood before Police Commissioner Raymond Kelly, wearing his sharply creased full dress
uniform and his white dress gloves, with his brass buttons and
black shoes buffed to a regulation gleam—the way he had been
taught in the Marine Corps—on the gleaming boards of the auditorium in One Police Plaza.

He saluted, shook Police Commissioner Kelly's offered hand,
stepped off the stage, and said:

"I snapped him off a real good one, a real good salute."

The next evening the vastness of St. Patrick's Cathedral was still
empty, dark, and quiet at 11:36 P.M. on Christmas Eve. All the ma-
sonry, pageantry, and tapestry of the Roman Catholic Cathedral,
towered over by an organ as tall itself as a village steeple, was in
readiness for Edward Cardinal Egan and his Midnight Mass. Ray
Clair slipped the leash off Winston's collar and the senior bomb
dog bounded over and leapt the velvet ropes to the Lady Chapel.
He sniffed and came to Ray Clair and was released again to run
down the steps of the crypt where cardinals past were entombed:

O'Connor, Spellman, and Hayes; Winston scampered over them all.

The sweep took half an hour. Then Winston and the team exited for a break. Fifth Avenue was a sea of pedestrians and traffic on an otherwise calm island. Winston lapped water. The team assisted a tourist from Russia who had experienced trouble breathing. Then it was back inside, where the gloom was replaced by stunning light. The pews filled with bright faces. A final sweep was performed on the coatracks, the aisles, and then, as the archbishop of the Catholic Diocese of New York intoned his prayers, at 12:25 Christmas morning, Clair, Winston, and the rest of the team slipped out the side door, wishing all a Merry Christmas and good night.

Bomb Squad case #2629 came in at 8:00 P.M. on New Year's Eve. It would be the last case of the year. A can of paint thinner, a propane tank, and an M-80 firework placed beneath a BMW partially exploded, scorching its gas tank but causing no other injuries. By now Brian Hearn and his A-team were walking through Times Square once again. Lieutenant Torre was high above the revels, looking down at the confetti, the scene bathed in noise and light. Mayor Michael Bloomberg, Police Commissioner Kelly, and former Secretary of State Colin Powell had kicked off the festivities with a brief press conference. Powell, a graduate of a city high school and City College of New York, said that it was great to be home. He recalled watching the celebration as a child on a black and white television set in his West Indian parents' bungalow in Queens, where they called it "Old Year's Night." "We always had to be a little different," Powell said. In that he also summed up his city.

Looking down from the balcony of the Viacom building, Mark Torre was as close to at peace as he could ever be. The night was going smoothly, his teams were moving effectively. He was able to report to his superiors that the explosion under the BMW was definitely not terrorist-related, and he kept pulling the cigar out of his pocket and putting it back in. No sense rushing.

It was the end of another year; another year in which nothing at all had happened; another year in which all of the members of his unit had gone home to their families. Another event-filled but uneventful year. High above Times Square at 11:48 P.M. everyone who could step to the edge of the balcony and feel the cool breeze of the larger than life night did so; and then there was a blinding snowstorm: confetti—bright, thick, and as magical as snow.

"It ain't half bad," said Detective Louie Alvarez afterward. Louie was seated on a black bench along the back wall of the command center. He had come out of deep undercover work— years of it—for this. Now he was the newest member of the Bomb Squad.

Appendices

EOD Wings Heraldry of the Bomb Technician Device:
The wreath is a symbol of the achievements of explosive ordinance disposal
technicians. The lightning rods symbolize the explosive power of the bomb.
In this case, the image is copied from a World War II bomb.

—Hazardous Device School, Huntsville, Alabama

APPENDIX I

NYPD Bomb Squad Time Line
1903–2004

Black Hand . . .
The Black Hand, a shadowy group, consisting of underworld members of
the Italian immigrant community, emerges. It begins to prey on the growing number of Italian immigrants in New York City. The Black Hand's
tools are simple: extortion letters backed by dynamite, left in their victims'
mailboxes when money is not forthcoming.

APRIL, 1903:
Italian Squad Formed   **1906-12-20 NYT***
Lt. Giuseppe Petrosino heads the newly formed squad. Newspaper accounts
describe it as operating out of a "little room in a saloon over Centre Street."
Their goal: to protect the Italian immigrant population in New York City
from extortion by the Black Hand.

* *The New York Times* newspaper archives. The notation is given as year,
month, day throughout.

JULY, 1908:

Leaders of the Black Hand Arrested   1908-7-06 NYT

The Italian Squad arrests a number of suspected Black Hand members, including "the master bomb-maker for the Black Handers."

MARCH 12, 1909:

Petrosino Killed in Palermo   1909-03-04 NYT

Lt. Giuseppe Petrosino is shot to death under the shadow of the trees of Marina Square in the city of Palermo. When his body was returned to New York more than 250,000 people jammed the streets of Little Italy hoping to catch a glimpse of the funeral procession.

German Spies . . .

From the outset of World War I, New York City becomes a prime area of operation for German espionage efforts.

AUGUST 1, 1914:

Bomb Squad Created/Italian Squad Severed
from Bomb Duty   *Throttled**

Police Commissioner Arthur Woods creates the Bomb Squad and puts about thirty-one men under the command of acting Captain Thomas J. Tunney. Their job is to pursue all bomb-related events in New York City. Much of the squad's work centers on stopping German spies.

1915:

Neutral Ships Are Targeted for Espionage   *Throttled*

Neutral ships, filled with supplies for France and England, mysteriously catch fire and explode at sea. Between January and April 1915 a half dozen ships leaving New York go up in flames.

1915:

Bomb and Neutrality Squad Formed   *Throttled*

"The trend of events in early 1915 made it apparent that the bomb squad would be called upon to handle more and more cases of attempted violation of neutrality. It is renamed to reflect that threat."

---

* *Throttled*. Thomas J. Tunney. Small, Maynard & Co., 1919.

OCTOBER, 1915:
Robert Fay Arrested   **1915-10-25 NYT/** *Throttled*
The Bomb Squad arrests Robert Fay, a German national, in Weehawken, New Jersey. He confesses to conspiring to blow up U.S. and neutral ships bound for Europe. Fay says he was paid about $4,000 by "a district head of the German Secret Agents."

JULY 30, 1916:
Black Tom Island
A massive explosion destroys this Jersey City, New Jersey, pier. German spies are suspected.

DECEMBER, 1917:
Bomb and Neutrality Militarized   **1917-12-13 NYT**
The Bomb Squad is put under the direct control of the War Department.

JULY, 1918:
Bomb and Neutrality Squad Is Abolished   **1918-07-10 NYT**
The bomb and neutrality squad is abolished. Some accounts rename the squad the "Alien Squad." Its targets are immigrants suspected of anarchist, criminal, or radical activities.

Radicals . . .
Communists and Anarchists become a national obsession. Left-wing groups spring up across the country.

JUNE 2, 1919:
Radical Bombs Explode Across
the United States   **1919-06-02 NYT**
Bombs explode in eight cities, one at the house of the U.S. Attorney General. It is close enough to the windows of Franklin Delano Roosevelt's residence that the Assistant Secretary of the Navy tells reporters afterward he is "standing on glass." In an attempt to discover the attackers, the Bomb Squad begins working closely with the U.S. Secret Service.

SEPTEMBER 16, 1920:
Wall Street—First Vehicle Bomb in U.S. History
Shortly after noon, a large bomb inside a horse-drawn wagon explodes in front of the Morgan Bank on Wall Street; forty are killed. It is the first large vehicle bomb in the U.S. Radicals are suspected.

OCTOBER, 1920:
Bomb Squad Seizes 5,000 "Red Circulars"   1920-10-10 NYT

OCTOBER, 1920:
Bomb Squad Finds 354 Sticks of Dynamite   1920-10-15 NYT

1921:
Squad Violates Civil Rights
The head of the bomb squad, Sgt. James J. Gegan, is accused by the ACLU of violating the civil rights of a number of immigrants in his ongoing search for radicals. During this period, the squad's mission is often used as a pretext for rumbling radicals without the niceties of due process.

FEBRUARY, 1922:
Bomb and Italian Squad Merged;
Bomb and Radical Squad Formed   1922-08-22 NYT
Headquartered at Centre Street, the squad now hunts the radicals and anarchists who increasingly have taken to using explosives as a means of dissent.

1931:
Bomb and Radical Squads Separated   1931-04-19 NYT

Forgeries . . .
OCTOBER, 1935:
Bomb and Forgery Squad Merged   1936-04-09 NY Daily Star
Because their work overlaps, especially in the investigation of "anonymous or threatening letters," the squads are merged.

X-Rays . . .
1936:
Use of X-rays in Bomb Detection Introduced
The X-ray becomes an integral tool for the examination of suspect devices
   "Experiments with the ordinary x-ray have proved that no package can be constructed, so that the police cannot clearly see at least how to open the package without setting off the explosive material inside. Today, every suspicious package the bomb squad works with is first examined with the unfailing eye of the x-ray."

Theatre Bombers . . .

OCTOBER, 1936:

Gas Bomb Attacks in Eight New York Movie Theaters

FEBRUARY, 1937:

Gas Bomb Attacks in Six NYC Movie Theaters

Members of the projectionist unions (*The Motion Picture Machine Operators Union, Allied Motion Picture Machine Operators Union, and the Empire State Motion Pictures Operations Union*★) in a labor dispute with the Independent Theatre Owners Association, begin to toss a series of "stink bombs" into crowded movie theaters. The situation becomes so serious that nearly 225 police officers are assigned to hunt down the bombers.

1st Bomb Squad Members Killed . . .

JULY 4, 1940:

Two Members of NYPD Bomb Squad Killed at World's Fair

A bomb is discovered at 3:30 p.m. near the British Pavilion of the World's Fair in Flushing Meadows, New York. After being moved to the edge of the fairgrounds for examination, it explodes in the faces of four detectives. Two detectives, Joseph Lynch and Ferdinand Socha, are killed and the two other police officers are critically wounded.

1940:

Bomb and Forgery Squads Separated

Following the death of Lynch and Socha, the Bomb Squad is detached from the Forgery Unit. This is viewed as the birth of the "modern" bomb squad.

JULY, 1940:

Early Use of X-rays

The fluoroscope is one of several new technologies adopted by the squad following the World's Fair bombing. Early on it is used to identify a number of suspicious packages found at the New York Stock Exchange building.

Containment Vehicle Introduced . . .

SEPTEMBER, 1940:

First Bomb Transporter Put into Service

The first "total containment vehicle" was a flatbed truck carrying a hut woven from 5/8-inch-thick cable that had been left over from the completion

★ *New York Times,* November 12, 1936.

of the Brooklyn Bridge in 1883. It was designed to safely transport a live bomb through the streets of New York and was named the Pyke–LaGuardia Carrier. Lt. James Pyke conceived the vehicle. Fiorello La-Guardia was the mayor of New York at the time.

> "The purpose of this is to take a bomb from a congested area to a remote or suburban district and to do so in a manner that will protect the public and the police. In this way it will eliminate the risk that occurred at the World's Fair where an attempt was made to defuse the bomb in place when it may have been safer to remove it to a police range and destroy it with a counter charge."★

1943:
Arrest of an Unsuccessful Suicide Bomber[†]

At 2:00 a.m., on March 31, Det. Harold Keichlin of the Bomb Squad and a U.S. Secret Service agent arrested Clarence Cull on charges of threatening to kill President Roosevelt by "means of strapping a bomb to his body, getting close to the president, exploding the bomb, and killing himself and the President." Cull blamed Roosevelt for lost convoys of merchant ships.

War Souvenirs . . .
1945:
World War II Ends

The squad is on the run, tracking down and rendering safe thousands of "souvenir" mines, hand grenades, and bazookas brought home by servicemen as the war ends.

Lone Bombers. . . .
MARCH 1951:
Mad Bomber

Dubbed the "Mad Bomber" by the City's media, a lone bomber quietly renews a relentless bombing campaign against New York City's power company, Con Edison. His campaign had begun before the outbreak of war. During the war his bombings stop. When later caught, he would explain he had suspended the bombings for patriotic reasons.

★ *Spring 3100*, March, 1944
[†] Bomb Squad files

APPENDICES

NOVEMBER 28, 1951:

Bomb Explodes in a 14th Street Subway Locker

While none are hurt, news clippings from the *New York Herald Tribune* and a letter containing threats against Con Ed are found wrapped around the debris from the pipe bomb.

DECEMBER 8, 1952:

Bomb Explodes in Lexington Theatre

A bomb explodes at the Lexington Theatre, Lexington Ave. and 50th Street, injuring one. This is the first time that anyone is injured by a device set by the "Mad Bomber."

APRIL, 1952:

Squad Moves from Manhattan to Brooklyn

The bomb squad and the Police Crime Lab move to the 84th precinct in Brooklyn because the subway running under Police HQ on Centre Street upsets their delicate lab instruments.★

MID-1950s:

An early version of the bomb suit, made by the Spooner Armor of New York City, is introduced. These suits are uncomfortable and hard to maneuver in. They were rarely used. Wes Somerville, a bomb tech present at the time, recalls that he would wear one only for press events.

NOVEMBER 7, 1954:

Bomb Explodes at Radio City Music Hall

Four patrons are injured. Mad Bomber is suspected.

DECEMBER 2, 1956:

Mad Bomber Injures Six in Movie Theatre Explosion

The Paramount Theater in Brooklyn, filled with holiday shoppers, becomes the bomber's most public target. At around 8 p.m. that night, an explosion rips through the theater, injuring six—three seriously. The police produce a profile of the man they believe is the bomber: male, unmarried, Catholic, in his fifties and living in Connecticut. He is also self-educated and a neat freak.

JANUARY 11, 1957:

Mad Bomber Captured

"George, do you know who I am?"
 "You're Detective Schmidt."

★ 1952-06-28, *Cue Magazine*

"Yes . . . didn't you read I was taking apart bombs, didn't you have any thoughts about me?"

"Oh yes, I worried about you. [But] I had to have people cry out against the monsters of 4 Irving Place [Consolidated Edison's headquarters]."★

George Metesky, age fifty-four, the "Mad Bomber," was quietly captured at the home he shared with his two sisters in Connecticut. He confessed that he was angry with Con Edison for causing his tuberculosis, firing him, and leaving him with no workers' compensation. Metesky was deemed a paranoid schizophrenic and sent to a hospital for the criminally insane. In 1973, after seventeen years, he was ruled no longer dangerous and was set free. He lived quietly, and died in Waterbury, Connecticut, in 1994. He was as suspected: male, unmarried, Catholic, in his fifties, a neat freak and lived in Connecticut.

OCTOBER, 1960:
The Sunday Bomber Strikes
The "Sunday Bomber" begins a series of subway and ferry bombings. Within a month, nearly 600 police officers (almost 1/4 of the police force) were assigned to track down this new bomber. Breathless press accounts kept the hunt, the hunters, and the Bomber on the front pages.

OCTOBER 2, 1960:
Times Square Blast Injures Six and Panic Ensues
A device attributed to the Sunday Bomber explodes in Times Square, wounding six and sending hundreds fleeing.

OCTOBER 9, 1960:
A Sunday Bomb Set Off at the Public Library
A bomb explodes outside the Public Library at 40th Street and Fifth Avenue, eight blocks from the scene of a similar blast the previous Sunday.

OCTOBER 23, 1960:
Third Sunday Bomb Rips Staten Island Ferry Deck
A bomb explodes on the Staten Island Ferry on its trip from Manhattan across the Upper Bay.

★ From a conversation between Det. William Schmidt (Rtd. NYPD Bomb Squad) and George Metesky, the night Metesky was captured.

NOVEMBER 27, 1960:

Sunday Bomber Suspect Held for Questioning

A dynamite and blasting-powder watchman for a construction company is questioned about the series of Sunday and holiday bombings. Detectives described him as "a red-hot suspect."

FEBRUARY 7, 1967:

Bomb Squad Acquires Outdoor Range

The outdoor range at Rodman's Neck, the Bronx, remains the squad's training, testing, and bomb-disposal facility.

Domestic Terror . . . Radical Terror . . .

The United States is swept by a wave of bombings by antiwar activists protesting the war in Vietnam. A second wave of bombings—by Puerto Rican nationalists—soon overlaps. Interspersed are bombings by foreign terrorists who target the United States to call attention to their causes. The overlapping bomb campaigns cause a national atmosphere of terror.

AUGUST 7, 1969:

Bomb Blast Rip Banks in Financial Area   1969-08-21 NYT

A blast rips through the eighth floor of the Marine Midland Building, injuring at least twenty and littering the area with shattered glass, torn plaster, and wrecked furnishings.

AUGUST 8, 1969:

Explosion Wrecks U.S. Offices   1969-09-20 NYT

An explosion shatters the United States Department of Commerce offices on the 40th floor of the one-year-old Federal Building at Foley Square.

OCTOBER 7, 1969:

Draft Center Damaged by Blast   1969-10-8 NYT

An explosion devastates the fifth floor of the Armed Forces Induction Center at 39 Whitehall Street.

OCTOBER 14, 1969:

Sixth Bomb Planted in Macy's—Two
Detectives Injured   1969-10-15 NYT

A small bomb explodes in Macy's Herald Square store as two members of the Police Department's bomb squad attempt to dismantle the device. The Puerto Rican nationalist group FALN takes credit.

MAY 1, 1971:

The Nation's First Bomb Dogs Join NYPD Bomb Squad

The Squad begins the EDC (Explosive Detection Canine) program. Brandy, a German Shepherd, and Sally, a golden Lab, become the nation's first two bomb dogs.

MARCH 7, 1972:

Bomb Dogs Find Explosive on Plane

"There was four suitcases in that cockpit—pilot, co-pilot, the engineer's. Whose is that? Nobody's. On the suitcase—it was the same identical suitcase as all those pilots had. On the suitcase was 'please leave on plane.' Well, when the dog sat on that one, I really didn't believe that. Some say I disbelieved it—I don't know whether this is so or not. Then I cut in the bag and there was 4.5 pounds of C-4. And then there was the clock mechanism. And we had something like the first initial call was at 1:00. It was to explode—it was like ten minutes before the hour."*

SEPTEMBER 11, 1976:

Police Officer Brian Murray Killed by Terrorist Bomb

At the Rodman's Neck Bomb Range, Police Officer Brian Murray is killed and Sgt. Terry McTigue is seriously injured while trying to render safe a small bomb that had been planted in a locker in Grand Central Station by Croatian terrorists.

"It was just Brian and I. So we went over, and I think I was front. We started to squat down like a baseball pitcher. . . . Everything seemed okay. And then Brian was a half a step behind me and squatting down too. And then [claps his hands] blew. Just like that. Hadn't even touched it . . . I was blinded instantly. I had terrible pain in my face and my hands. I felt the blood rushing down my throat. I remember being just thrown back, tumbled back. I couldn't hear much. I was trying to say, 'Take care of my boys, take care of my boys. I'm okay.' But the words weren't coming out. My mouth wasn't hinged on this side at all. This was just flapped open.

"I heard the guy say, 'How is he?'

"He just said, 'No pulse.'

"I knew I had a pulse, so I knew it was Brian."†

* *Det. Bill Schmidt (Rtd. NYPD Bomb Squad)*
†*Sgt. Terry McTigue (Rtd. NYPD Bomb Squad).* Interview by authors.

1978:

The Bomb Squad Moves to Greenwich Village

Through 2004 it remains in this suite of shabby offices above a busy police precinct in the heart of one of the city's most vibrant communities.

DECEMBER 31, 1982:

New Year's Eve Bombing

Three officers are critically injured when four FALN bombs explode at government buildings. A fifth is defused by Sgt. Charlie Wells, NYPD Bomb Squad.

> "All I remember is a loud explosion. According to witnesses I was blown
> fifteen feet off the ground. I sustained some serious injuries. I lost my
> right eye. My whole face is reconstructed. I lost my ear drums. My hip
> was broken. I suffer from a severe case of vertigo, and a severe case of
> post-traumatic stress disorder."*

JANUARY 4, 1983:

Introduction of Robots   1983-01-04 NYT

As the injured detectives clung to life following the New Year's Eve blast, Mayor Edward I. Koch held a press conference where he described the bombers as "among the vilest people on earth." Koch proposed using robots as a way to perform remote entry into suspicious packages. The robots turned out to be as significant a development as the X-ray in protecting bomb technicians. "Remote Whenever Possible," became the bomb tech mantra.

MARCH 2, 1983:

Bomb Squad Debuts New Robots   1983-03-04 NYT

At a press event at Rodman's Neck, the Bomb Squad shows off its new robots.

APRIL 21, 1983:

Robot First Used on Suspicious Package   1983-04-21 NYT

The robot is first used on a suspicious package at the corner of Lexington Avenue and 48th St. It picks up a briefcase, places it inside the Pyke La-Guardia truck, and the case is then transferred to Rodman's Neck. The case contains telephone repair tools.

---

* *Det. Anthony Senft, NYPD Bomb Squad.* Interview by authors.

1992:

PAN Disrupter Introduced Sandia Labs Interview

Sandia National Laboratory creates the Percussion Actuated Non Electric (PAN) Disrupter. Basically a water cannon, the PAN fires a powerful high-speed jet of water into the heart of a bomb's mechanism before it can trigger an explosion. It soon becomes a primary tool for disabling conventional bombs while keeping the bomb technician at a distance from danger. The PAN uses shotgun shells to propel its jets of water or sand.

Foreign Terror . . .

FEBRUARY 26, 1993:

First World Trade Center Bombing

Bomb Squad Detective Donald Sadowy and ATF explosives expert Joe Hanlin crack the case when they find the hidden identification number of the rental van that carried the bomb into the parking garage of the World Trade Center. This discovery soon leads to the arrests of the bombing suspects.

SEPTEMBER 11, 2001:

Bomb Squad Detective Claude "Danny" Richards Killed

Detective Danny Richards races into the collapsing towers to attempt rescues. He never comes back out.

2004:

"The White Devil"—The Backscatter Van Is Introduced

A breakthrough in X-ray detection technology, the Backscatter Van (ZBV) is an extremely maneuverable screening system built into a commercially available delivery van. The X-ray detection technology allows the operator to see through walls and inside cargo containers, trucks, buses, and cars. The system's unique "drive-by" capability allows one or two operators to conduct X-ray imaging of suspect vehicles and objects while the ZBV drives past.*

★ American Scientific and Engineering materials, describing in general the effectiveness of the backscatter system.

APPENDIX II

Commanding Officers,
NYPD Bomb Squad
1903–2004

The CO doesn't mean anything, what's he going to do,
tell me how to kill myself? He was someone to sign my paperwork.
—Bill Schmidt

Lt. Giuseppe Petrosino, Italian Squad   1903–1909

Giuseppe Petrosino, one of the first Italians on the New York City police force, is selected to head the squad. Its mission is to hunt down Black Hand extortionist bombers. He is assassinated in Sicily, where he had gone to visit Italian authorities and exchange information on the gangsters. In 2006 he remained the only New York police officer killed overseas in the line of duty.

Lt. Arthur Gloster, Italian Squad   1909–1910

Gloster is acting commander of the squad following Petrosino's death.

Lt. Antonio Vachris, Italian Squad   1910–1911

Vachris, who ran the Brooklyn branch of the Italian Squad, is appointed commander. He serves until Commissioner Waldo abolishes the squad in September, 1911.

Sgt. Michael Fiaschetti, Italian Squad   1920–1922

Joining the force in 1908, Fiaschetti learned much from his mentor, Petrosino. He was successful in fighting both the Black Hand and later, as a private investigator, police corruption. He earned and was proud of his nickname "Treat 'Em Rough Fiaschetti."* His autobiography was entitled *You Gotta Be Rough*.

Lt. Thomas J. Tunney, Bomb Squad   1914–1917

August 1, 1914, Police Commissioner Arthur Woods creates the Bomb Squad. Thomas J. Tunney is its first commander.

---

* *You Gotta Be Rough,* Doubleday and Doran, 1930.

285

Lt. James J. Gegan — 1919–1926

Gegan ran the squad when it hunted so-called "radicals" and Bolsheviks in New York City. Under Gegan, the squad earned an unsavory reputation as a group of thugs.

Lt. Charles Newman — 1926–1936

Labor unrest, union actions, radicals, and racketeers keep the squad busy:

1. A racketeer bomb explodes a block away from the John D. Rockefeller Jr. Fifth Avenue mansion. July 1930
2. An attempt is made to bomb the railroad tracks at Park Avenue and 144th St., February, 1930
3. Tear gas canisters are released on Wall Street August 4, 1933
4. "Stench" bombs are left in numerous theaters as part of union protest

Newman broadens range of squad investigative skills. Starting in 1935, twice a month, Newman and members of the squad study cryptography and how terrorists might use "paper, inks, mystic symbols, perforations, and signatures" to get secret messages to their cohorts.

Three months after he died in 1982, the Bomb Squad was called to his brownstone at 333 East 51st Street. They found and removed three sticks of old crystallized dynamite he had stored in his basement. Not even Bomb Squad members are immune from hoarding souvenirs.

Lt. James Pyke — 1936–1943

Following the deaths of detectives Socha and Lynch while they attempted to dismantle a bomb at the 1940 World's Fair, Lt. Pyke designed, tested, and put into service the first total containment vehicle. It was designed to carry bombs away from congested areas so they could be dismantled with no risk to the public and no hurry on the part of the technicians. Pyke had been a driver for Lt. Gen. John J. Pershing in World War I. He had been severely burned while trying to dismantle a German incendiary. At the onset of World War II he returned to the military. This time he served in the U.S. Navy.

Lt. Charles W. Beakey — 1944–1951

Following a September 1944 bazooka explosion in the Bronx that seriously injured five young boys, Beakey's squad was given the monumental task of collecting war souvenirs.

Acting Commanding Officer Sgt. Pete R. Dale — 1951–1956

Dale grew up around dynamite—both his father and grandfather were rock blasters—the *New York Times* claimed that "dynamite for him, [is] what a pocket knife is to most youngsters."* Never officially named commander, Dale ran the squad effectively. During presidential visits, Dale would ride on top of all the elevators in the President's hotel to check that the shafts were free of bombs. In 1948 he used listening devices to examine some 2,000 closed lockers at James Madison High School following a phone threat of a time bomb. Nothing was found. In 1951 he looked through 3,000 lockers at Grand Central Station after another anonymous phone call—again, nothing. On March 10, 1954, Dale had his right hand mangled after a grenade he was holding went off. He had been checking into a cache of arms from a "Cuban conspiracy ring."

Lt. Jim Falahe   1956–1957
Falahe led the squad through the end of the Mad Bomber investigation.

Lt. Kenny O'Neil   1958–1976
O'Neil spent half his thirty-five-year police career as head of the bomb squad. Known as "The Silver Fox," he was a quiet commander who brought with him to the squad an extensive background in chemistry. Astute at handling the media, the day-to-day needs of the squad, and as a natural leader, he was content most of the time to leave the defusing of bombs to his technicians.

As squad commander, he led the investigation into the explosion at La-Guardia Airport on December 30, 1975, which took place as hundreds of TWA passengers were retrieving their luggage. Eleven people were killed and seventy-five seriously injured in the blast. It was caused by a bomb with the power of twenty-five sticks of dynamite that had been placed in a locker.

Sgt. Terry McTigue and Sgt. Jim Helbock   1976–1981
Seriously injured on Sept 11, 1976 while standing next to the device that killed Officer Brian Murray, McTigue was named head of the squad. It was an honorary title. His injuries prevented him from returning to work. Sgt. Jim Helbock ran the squad as acting CO.

Lt. Charlie Luisi, Acting Commanding Officer   1981–1985

Lt. Bill McCarthy   1985–1986

---

* *New York Times*, December 26th, 1956.

Lt. Walter Boser   1986–1993
Lt. Boser was a thirty-year veteran police officer when the World Trade Center was first attacked. It was under his command that Dct. Donald Sadowy and ATF agent Joe Hanlin discovered the hidden VIN number in the rental van that the bombers had used to transport their 1,200-pound bomb onto level B-2 of the World Trade Center garage. This information directly led to the arrest of a number of the bombers.

Lt. Michael White   November 1993–2000
Mike White led the team though the TWA 800 investigation in Long Island.

Lt. Jerry Sheehan   July 2000–September 2002
Jerry Sheehan led the bomb squad through the aftermath of Sept 11—a time when suspicious packages were spotted dozens of times each day on every street corner in New York.

Lt. Mark Torre   September 20, 2002–present
Lt. Torre joined the bomb squad as a sergeant in March 1993, within a week of the WTC I bombing.

APPENDIX III

Former Members of the
NYPD Bomb Squad
1903–2004

On your left as you enter the Bomb Squad Base, there is a wall board covered with passport-size pictures. The pictures are there to honor past members of the Bomb Squad. In 101 years about 225 officers have served on the squad. During the same 101 years, more than 500,000 have served in the New York City Police Department.

The Roster 1903–2004
This roster, as completely as historical records allow, lists those officers in the order in which they joined the squad, from 1903 through 2004.

Giuseppe Petrosino	Theodore Hesig	Francis D. Murphy
John Duane	William Dickerson	John Lannig
Peter Hayias	Charles O'Malley	Roger Reddin

Edward Thomas

Robert J. Kelly

Archibald Woods

Thomas Burke

William Miller

Louis Muscatello

James Pyke

Chris F. Kelly

Ferdinand Socha

John Stevenson

Joe McLaughlin

Joe Lynch

Thomas Collins

William McBride

John Petrizzo

James Dooley

John Barry

Peter Dale

Harold Keichlin

Ed Moroney

Michael Sheehan

Ed Dobler

Phil Creamer

Kenneth Ryan

John Tracy

Dominick Pereca

William Schmidt

Oscar Dahlstrom

George Hearle

Joseph Jove

Frank Pietromonaco

William Foley

Edward Tennis

Donald Collins

Joseph Rothengast

John O'Brian

Andrew Sweeny

Herbert Wilson

Albert Gleason

Donald Cerbelli

Wes Somerville

Ken O'Neill

Jordan Tansey

Arthur Hornidge

Terrance McTigue

John J. Heslin

William Suchoski

James Graham

Kenneth Dudonis

Ronald Kerney

Christopher Hayes

Francis Toomey

Thomas Cousins

Joseph Mulligan

Neil Monaco

James O'Connor

John Kelleher

Frank DeCecco

Vincent Connolly

Andrew Haufman

Brian Murray

Charles Wells

Henry Dworkin

Ronald Mclean

John Shlagler

James Helbock

William J. Carroll

Daniel Buckley

John Kelly

Edward Carney

Peter Major

Joseph Cipriano

William Sullivan

Hugh McGowan

Frank Guerra

Kenneth Kelly

George Murphy

Daniel Boldi

Michael Castallano

Robert Noll

Richard Scattaglia

Peter Perrotta

Richard Pastorella

Anthony Senft

Walter Breslin

Charles Newman

John Santos

Charles Luisi

Donald Hurly

John Panicci

James Hatcher

William O'Carrol

Denis Mulcahy

Victor Solis

Kevin Barry

Joseph Ahern

Brian Murphy

Mike Barge

Peter J. Dalton

Daniel Kiely

Brian Tuohy

Donald Sadowy

Miles Harrington

William McCarthy

Edward Hayes

Chris Brauer

Guy Renzi

Anthony Ruggirello

Glenn Welsh

Gerard Hoag

Charles Epps

John Lanigan

Paul Ragonese

Fred Lange

Steve Dodge

Gerald Brennan

Phil Brown

James Corbett

Mike Murray

Claude Richards

Dennis Hunt

Daniel McNally

Dennis Martin

Steve Berberich
John Donahue
Walter Boser
William Valentine
Tim Dinan
Joseph P. Putkowski
Richard Hackford
Robert Treston
Thomas Connolly
Karen Engdahl
James Carrano
Richard Teemsma
John Harvey
Keith Mulcahy
Mark Torre
Charles Hill
Paul Yurkiw

Michael White
Michael Kelly
Richard Kauke
Kenneth Silva
Faith Beiser
Richard Vergara
Gerald Fitzpatrick
Brian Hearn
Jeffery Oberdier
Jack Gunshanan
Raymond Clair
Barry Nagelberg
Robert Nolan
Thomas Sullivan
George Wich
Patrick O'Connor
Andrew Rea

Michael Walsh
Michael DeMarfio
Gerald Sheehan
Brian Coughlan
James Hunt
Thomas O'Riordan
Michael Oldmixon
Raymond Butkiewicz
William Popper
Anthony Biondolilo
Joseph Dolan
Craig Collopy
Daniel Condon
Joseph Cornetta
Kenneth Dean
Michael Klippel

APPENDIX IV

Squad Deaths
1903–2004

Fidelis ad Mortem
1903–2004

There are six portraits hanging in the squad room. They depict squad members who lived up to the Police Department motto, "loyal unto death."

Lieutenant Giuseppe Petrosino, March 12, 1909
Detective Ferdinand A. Socha, July 4, 1940
Detective Joseph J. Lynch, July 4, 1940
Detective Vincent David Connolly, December 3, 1973
Detective Brian James Murray, September 11, 1976
Detective Claude Danny Richards, September 11, 2001

APPENDIX V

Significant Terrorist
Bomb Incidents
1945–2003

1945

October 31, Rome, Italy

Two bombs in suitcases left by Jewish Irgun terrorists explode at the British embassy. No casualties.

1946

July 22, Jerusalem, Palestine

Eighty are killed and more than one hundred are wounded when Jewish terrorists blow up the King David Hotel in Jerusalem. The hotel was home to British government and military offices. The terrorists held workers at pistol point while they planted explosives in the basement.

1947

September 29, Haifa, Palestine

Jewish Irgun terrorists bomb a police station in Haifa, Palestine, killing four British and four Arab policemen, as well as two Arab civilians. Forty-six are injured.

December 12, Palestine

Twenty Arabs, five Jews, and two British soldiers are killed and thirty are wounded in Jewish terrorist bomb attacks on buses in Haifa and Ramleh, Palestine. British mandate to rule Palestine ends on 15 May, 1948; state of Israel established.

December 29, Jerusalem, Palestine

Jewish Irgun terrorists throw grenades from passing taxi into café near the Damascus gate, killing eleven Arabs and two British policemen.

1948

March 11, Jerusalem

Headquarters of the Jewish Agency is destroyed by an Arab car bomb, killing thirteen and injuring eighty-four.

July 22, New York, NY

Pro-peace activist Stephen J. Supina, piloting a small private plane, drops a homemade bomb on United Nations headquarters in Lake Success, New York. The missile explodes harmlessly in midair. He later surrenders to the authorities.

1955

April 1, Cyprus

Greek Cypriot EOKA (National Organization of Cypriot Fighters) terrorist campaign for independence begins with a series of bomb explosions on British-controlled Cyprus.

1960

August 29, Amman, Jordan

Jordanian prime minister and eleven others are killed by a bomb in the foreign ministry building. Two of the bombers fled to safety and eleven others are sentenced to death for the attack.

1961

September 9, Aube, France

Organisation Armée Secrète (Secret Army Organisation/OAS) terrorists attempt to assassinate French President Charles De Gaulle in Aube, France. The roadside bomb they planted fails to explode.

1966

August 4, Bogotá, Colombia

An American and two Colombians are killed by a bomb planted by left-wing rebels in the Binational Centre, Bogotá, Colombia.

November 22, Aden, Saudi Arabia

A DC-3 aircraft explodes up in midair near Aden, Saudi Arabia. All twenty-eight aboard are killed. The bomb had been hidden in the luggage compartment.

1967

October 12, Turkey

A British European Airways Comet airliner is destroyed by a bomb smuggled into the passenger cabin. All sixty-six on board died.

1968
September 4, Tel Aviv
Three bombs explode in central Tel Aviv. One person dies and seventy-one are wounded.

1969
February 21, Jerusalem
Palestinian terrorists bomb a crowded supermarket in Jerusalem, killing two and injuring twenty.

October 22, Haifa, Israel
Four civilians are killed, and twenty wounded by Palestinian bombs planted in two apartments.

December 12, Milan, Italy
Left-wing terrorists kill sixteen and wound ninety when they blow up a bank in Milan.

1970
February 21, Zurich, Switzerland
The Popular Front for the Liberation of Palestine blows up a Swiss airliner on takeoff, killing all forty-seven on board.

1971
December 4, Belfast, Northern Ireland
Protestant Ulster Volunteer Force (UVF) terrorists explode bomb in Catholic area, killing fifteen civilians.

1972
February 22, Aldershot, England
An Irish Republican Army bomb attack on the British Parachute Regiment Officers dining hall in Aldershot, England, kills seven.

March 4, Belfast, Northern Ireland
Two are killed and 131 injured when Protestant terrorists bomb the Abercorn restaurant.

May 5, Florence, Italy
Italian terrorist and publisher Giangiancomo Feltrinelli blows himself up while planting a bomb.

July 21, Belfast, Northern Ireland
"Bloody Friday." An Irish Republican Army (IRA) bomb attack kills eleven and injures 130.

July 31, Claudy, Ireland
Three IRA car bomb attacks leave six dead.

September 9, London, England
A member of the Israeli embassy staff is killed by a Palestinian letter bomb.

1973

December 17, Rome
Five terrorists begin a bloody assault when they pull weapons from their luggage in the terminal lounge at Rome's international airport, killing two persons. They then attack a Pan American 707 bound for Beirut and Tehran, destroying it with incendiary grenades and killing twenty-nine persons, including four senior Moroccan officials and fourteen American employees of ARAMCO, the oil industry giant. They herd five Italian hostages into a Lufthansa airliner and kill an Italian customs agent as he tries to escape. In Athens, the hijackers demand the release of two Arab terrorists. In order to convince Greek authorities to comply with their demands, the hijackers kill a hostage and throw his body onto the tarmac. The terrorists force the pilots to fly to Kuwait, where the terrorists release their hostages in return for passage to an unknown destination. The Palestine Liberation Organization disavows the attack. No other group claims responsibility.

February 4, England
The Irish Republican Army explodes a bomb on a coach packed with British soldiers on the M62 motorway in England, killing twelve.

March 8, London
Two IRA car bombs explode outside London's Old Bailey courthouse and the agriculture department headquarters, killing one and wounding more than 150.

August 4, Bologna, Italy
Twelve are killed and forty-eight injured when neo-fascists explode a bomb on a train approaching Bologna.

August 5, Athens, Greece
A Black September suicide squad attacks passenger terminals at Athens Airport, killing three and injuring fifty-five.

December 17, Rome, Italy
Palestinian terrorists bomb a Pan Am office at Fiumicino Airport. Thirty-two are killed and fifty injured. The terrorists then took seven Italian policemen hostage and hijacked an aircraft to Athens, Greece. After killing one of the hostages, they flew on to Kuwait. The terrorists eventually surrendered.

December 20, Madrid, Spain
Basque Fatherland and Liberty (ETA) terrorists kill Spanish Prime Minister Admiral Luis Carrero Blanco, in a spectacular bomb attack.

1974
October 5, London
Two IRA bombs explode in pubs in the London suburb of Guildford; five die, more than fifty are injured.

November 21, Birmingham, England
Two IRA bombs kill nineteen and wound more than 180.

May 17, Dublin, Ireland
A car bomb explodes, killing twenty-two. Protestant Northern Ireland terrorists blamed.

1975
January 24, New York City
The Puerto Rican nationalist terror group FALN bombs Fraunces Tavern, killing four and injuring more than fifty.

January 29, Washington, D.C.
The Weather Underground claims responsibility for an explosion in a bathroom at the U.S. Department of State in Washington, D.C.

January 21, Bihar, India
Indian railway minister Narayan Mishra is blown up in Bihar, India, by Anang Marg terrorists.

April 24, Stockholm, Sweden
German left-wing terrorists seize the German embassy in Stockholm, Sweden, and take twelve staff hostage to force the release of Baader-Meinhof gang terrorists. One hostage is murdered and a terrorist killed when explosives go off by accident. From this incident the so-called Stockholm Syndrome theory is developed. The theory holds that hostages start to sympathize with their captors.

1976

July 21, Dublin, Ireland
British ambassador to the Irish Republic, Christopher Ewart Briggs, is killed when an Irish Republican Army landmine destroys his car.

September 11, New York City
A TWA airliner flying from New York to France is hijacked by Croatian terrorists. The terrorists surrender in Paris but Bomb Squad member Brian Murray is killed by a bomb left by the terrorists in a locker in Grand Central Station.

September 21, Washington, D.C.
Chilean exile Orlando Letelier is assassinated by a bomb in his car.

1978

February 17, Comber, Northern Ireland
Irish Republican Army kills twelve civilians when they explode a bomb in a restaurant.

May 25, Evanston, Illinois
One person is hurt in a package bomb explosion at Northwestern University. This is now designated as the first attack by the Unabomber, Theodore Kaczynski.

1979

March 30, London
British politician Airey Neave is killed when a bomb planted under his car explodes in the car park of the House of Commons. The IRA takes credit.

August 27, County Sligo, Ireland

Lord Louis Mountbatten is killed when an IRA bomb explodes on his boat, the *Shadow V.* The IRA claims credit.

August 27, Warrenpoint, Northern Ireland

Eighteen British Parachute Regiment soldiers are killed by two bombs near Warrenpoint, Northern Ireland. The IRA detonated the bombs by remote control from across the border in the Irish Republic.

November 15, United States

Twelve are injured in a bomb explosion on an American Airlines flight in the United States, which is blamed on the so-called Unabomber.

1980

June 1, South Africa

African National Congress bombs strategic oil-from-coal plants in South Africa, causing $7 million worth of damage.

August 1, Bologna, Italy

The Bologna railway station is devastated by a massive bomb believed to have been planted by right-wing terrorists linked to rogue elements in the country's Intelligence services. Eighty-five are killed and three hundred injured.

October 3, Paris, France

Four Jews are killed and twelve injured in Palestinian bomb attack on synagogue.

October 6, Chicago, Illinois

The president of United Airlines is injured in a bomb attack. The Unabomer is blamed.

October 26, Munich, West Germany

Neo-Nazi bomb attack at October beer festival leaves thirteen dead and seventy-two wounded.

1981

August 31, Rammstein Air Force Base, West Germany

Twenty are injured when the Red Army explodes a bomb at the U.S. Air Force Base at Rammstein.

October 8, Salt Lake City, Utah
Unexploded bomb found and made safe at the University of Utah, Salt Lake City. The Unabomber is linked to the attack.

October 10, London
Irish Republican Army bomb kills two civilians and injures forty others outside Chelsea Army Barracks.

October 17, London
A bomb injures British Lieutenant-General Sir Steuart Pringle, a Royal Marines officer, outside his home in London.

1982

July 2, Berkeley, California
A professor is injured in a bomb attack at the University of California, Berkeley. The Unabomber is suspected.

July 20, London
Two IRA bombs in Hyde Park and Regents Park kill eleven British soldiers and wound more than forty others, mostly civilians.

September 14, Beirut, Lebanon
Lebanese president Bashir Gemayel assassinated by a massive car bomb.

November 11, Tyre, Lebanon
Israeli military headquarters is destroyed by Islamic suicide bomber. Seventy-five Israeli soldiers are killed, as are fifteen Lebanese and Palestinian prisoners.

December 6, Ballykelly, Northern Ireland
Seventeen are killed and sixty are injured when an IRA bomb destroys a bar.

1983

April 18, Beirut, Lebanon
Sixty-three are killed and 120 are wounded when a four-hundred-pound suicide truck-bomb explodes outside the U.S. Embassy. The Islamic Jihad claims responsibility.

October 9, Rangoon, Burma
North Korean agents blow up a delegation from South Korea, killing twenty-one and injuring forty-eight.

October 23, Beirut, Lebanon

Simultaneous suicide truck-bomb attacks are made on American and French compounds in Beirut, Lebanon. A 12,000-pound bomb destroys the U.S. compound, killing 242 Americans. Meanwhile, fifty-eight French troops are killed when a four-hundred-pound device destroys a French base. Islamic Jihad claims responsibility.

December 17, London

An IRA car bomb explodes outside Harrods department store, killing six and wounding about one hundred.

1984

April 12, Torrejon, Spain

Eighteen U.S. servicemen are killed and eighty-three are injured in a bomb attack on a restaurant near a U.S. Air Force Base in Torrejon, Spain.

October 12, Brighton, England

The IRA targets a conference of the ruling Conservative Party, killing five and wounding twenty-four. The attack narrowly misses Prime Minister Margaret Thatcher.

1985

June 23, Atlantic Ocean

A bomb destroys an Air India Boeing 747 over the Atlantic, killing all 329 aboard. Both Sikh and Kashmiri terrorists are blamed. Two cargo handlers are killed at a Tokyo airport, when another Sikh bomb explodes in an Air Canada aircraft en route to India.

1986

March 30, Athens, Greece

A Palestinian splinter group detonates a bomb as TWA Flight 840 approaches Athens Airport, killing four U.S. citizens.

April 5, Berlin, Germany

Two U.S. soldiers are killed and seventy-nine American servicemen are injured in a Libyan bomb attack on a nightclub in West Berlin. In retaliation, U.S. military jets bomb targets in and around Tripoli and Benghazi.

September 14, Seoul, South Korea
North Korean agents detonate an explosive device at Kimpo Airport, killing five and injuring twenty-nine.

1987
July 5, Sri Lanka
A member of the Liberation Tigers of Tamil Eelam (LTTE), as the Tamil Tigers are formally known, drives an explosive-laden truck into an Army camp housed at a school in Nelliady. Forty government troops are killed. This is the first use of a suicide bomb by the Tigers.

April 24, Athens
Sixteen U.S. servicemen aboard a Greek Air Force bus near Athens are injured in a bombing attack carried out by the revolutionary organization known as November 17.

November 29, Indian Ocean
North Korean agents plant a bomb aboard Korean Air Lines Flight 858. It crashes into the Indian Ocean. One hundred fifteen passengers and crew members are killed.

December 26, Barcelona, Spain
Catalan separatists bomb a Barcelona bar frequented by U.S. servicemen. One U.S. citizen is killed.

1988
April 14, Naples, Italy
The Organization of Jihad Brigades explodes a car bomb outside a USO Club in Naples, killing one U.S. sailor.

June 28, Athens, Greece
The defense attaché of the U.S. Embassy is killed by a car bomb outside his Athens home.

December 21, Lockerbie, Scotland
Pan American Airlines Flight 103 is blown up over Lockerbie, Scotland, by a bomb believed to have been placed aboard by Libyan terrorists in Frankfurt, West Germany. All 259 on board are killed.

1989
September 19, Sahara Desert, Niger
A bomb destroys UTA Flight 772 over the Sahara Desert in southern Niger during a flight from Brazzaville to Paris. All 170 aboard are killed. Six Libyans are later found guilty in absentia and sentenced to life imprisonment.

September 22, Kent, England
The IRA bombs the Royal Marines School of Music, killing ten soldiers and wounding more than thirty.

1990
January 15, Lima, Peru
The Túpac Amaru Revolutionary Movement bombs the U.S. Embassy in Lima.

May 13, Central Luzon, Philippines
The New People's Army (NPA) kill two U.S. Air Force personnel near Clark Air Force Base in the Philippines.

1991
January 18, Indonesia
Iraqi agents plant bombs at the U.S. ambassador to Indonesia's home residence.

February 7, London
The IRA fires three homemade mortar shells at 10 Downing Street, the prime minister's official residence in London. There are no injuries.

February 18, London
The IRA explodes a bomb at Victoria Station in London; one person is killed and over forty injured in the attack.

March 2, Colombo, Sri Lanka
Defense minister Ranjan Wijeratne is among the nineteen killed when a car bomb explodes.

May 21, Tamil Nadu, India
A female suicide bomber from the LTTE (Liberation Tigers of Tamil Eelam) kills former Prime Minister Rajiv Gandhi and sixteen others by detonating

an explosive vest after presenting a garland of flowers to Gandhi during an election rally.

1992

March 17, Buenos Aires, Argentina
Hezbollah claims responsibility for the bombing of the Israeli Embassy in Buenos Aires that killed 29 and wounded 242.

April 10, London
An IRA truck bomb in London's financial district kills three and causes hundreds of millions of dollars of damage.

1993

February 26, New York City
A powerful car bomb planted by Islamic terrorists explodes in an underground garage at the World Trade Center. The bomb leaves six dead and one thousand injured. The men carrying out the attack are followers of Umar Abd al-Rahman, an Egyptian cleric who preached in the New York City area.

March 20, Warrington, England
An IRA bomb hidden in a garbage can in the shopping district of Warrington, northwest England, kills two boys, ages three and twelve.

May 1, Colombo, Sri Lanka
Sri Lankan President Ranasinghe Premadasa and twenty-three others are killed by a suicide bomber.

1994

October 24, Colombo, Sri Lanka
Sri Lankan Opposition leader Gamini Dissanayake and fifty-six others are killed by a suicide bomber.

1995

April 19, Sri Lanka
Tamil Tiger suicide bombers attack two Navy gunboats at the port of Trincomalee, killing eighteen sailors.

March 2, Tokyo, Japan
Twelve persons are killed in a Sarin nerve gas attack on a crowded subway station. A similar attack occurs nearly simultaneously in the Yokohama subway system. The Aum Shinri-kyo cult is blamed for the attacks.

April 20, Oklahoma City, Oklahoma
Right-wing extremists Timothy McVeigh and Terry Nichols destroy the Federal Building in Oklahoma City with a massive truck bomb that kills 166, including 19 nursery school children.

August 21, Jerusalem
HAMAS claims responsibility for the detonation of a bomb onboard a Jerusalem bus. The bomb kills six and injures over one hundred, including several U.S. citizens.

September 13, Moscow, Russia
A rocket-propelled grenade is fired through a window of the U.S. Embassy in Moscow, ostensibly in retaliation for U.S. strikes on Serb positions in Bosnia.

November 13, Riyadh, Saudi Arabia
The Islamic Movement of Change plants a bomb in a Riyadh military compound. One U.S. citizen and several foreign national employees of the U.S. government are killed. Over forty are injured.

November 19, Islamabad, Pakistan
A suicide bomber drives a vehicle into the Egyptian Embassy compound, killing at least sixteen and injuring sixty. Three militant Islamic groups claim responsibility.

1996

January 31, Colombo, Sri Lanka
Members of the Liberation Tigers of Tamil Eelam (LTTE) ram an explosive-laden truck into the Central Bank, killing ninety and injuring more than fourteen hundred others.

February 9, London
An IRA bomb detonates in London, killing two and wounding more than one hundred.

APPENDICES

February 15, Athens, Greece
Unidentified assailants fire a rocket at the U.S. Embassy compound in Athens, causing minor damage.

February 26, Jerusalem
A suicide bomber detonates aboard a bus, killing twenty-six.

March 4, Tel Aviv
HAMAS and the Palestine Islamic Jihad (PIJ) both claim responsibility for a bombing outside of Tel Aviv's largest shopping mall that kills twenty and injures seventy-five.

June 11, Moscow
A homemade bomb explodes in a subway car, killing four and injuring twelve. Opponents and supporters of President Boris Yeltsin blame each other for the attack, which comes four days before the first round of presidential elections.

June 15, Manchester, England
An IRA bomb containing an estimated 3,300 pounds of explosives is detonated at a Manchester shopping center, wounding 206 persons. Overall, 538,000 square feet of retail space and 269,000 square feet of office space is destroyed.

June 25, Dhahran, Saudi Arabia
A large vehicle bomb explodes outside the U.S. military housing facility in Khobar Towers, in Dhahran. Nineteen U.S. military personnel are killed and 515 persons are wounded. Several groups claim responsibility.

July 11–12, Moscow, Russia
Two bomb attacks in twenty-four hours on Moscow trolley-buses leave about thirty injured. The attacks occur soon after Yeltsin is reelected president. The government blames Chechen separatists. But some suggest it might have been the work of Russian mafia in the wake of a presidential decree to stamp out crime.

July 20, Reus, Spain
A bomb explodes at Tarragona International Airport in Reus, Spain, wounding thirty-five. The Basque Fatherland and Liberty (ETA) organization is suspected.

July 27, Atlanta, Georgia
At 1:25 A.M. a bomb explodes in Atlanta's Centennial Olympic Park, killing one and injuring more than one hundred.

December 3, Paris
A bomb explodes aboard a Paris subway train as it arrives at the Port Royal station, killing four. Eighty-six are injured. No one claims responsibility. Algerian extremists are suspected.

1997

January 2–13, Egyptian Letter Bombs
A series of letter bombs with Alexandria, Egypt, postmarks are discovered at *Al-Hayat* newspaper bureaus in Washington, D.C., New York City, London, and Riyadh. Three similar devices, also postmarked in Egypt, are found at a prison facility in Leavenworth, Kansas. Bomb disposal experts defuse all the devices but one. It detonates at the *Al-Hayat* office in London, injuring two security guards and causing minor damage.

January 16, Sandy Springs, Georgia
At about 9:30 A.M a bomb explodes at Northside Family Planning Clinic in Sandy Springs. At 10:37 A.M, as the parking lot fills with investigators, a second bomb, buried in a flower bed, explodes, injuring seven.

February 21, Atlanta, Georgia
At about 9:50 P.M an explosion injures four at the Otherside Lounge, an Atlanta nightclub. Investigators find and detonate a second bomb, hung in shrubbery overlooking the parking lot.

July 12, Havana, Cuba
A bomb explodes at the Hotel Nacional in Havana, injuring three. A previously unknown group calling itself the Military Liberation Union claims responsibility.

September 4, Jerusalem
Three HAMAS suicide bombers detonate in the Ben Yehuda shopping mall in Jerusalem, killing eight, including the bombers, and wounding nearly two hundred.

1998

January 25, Kandy, Sri Lanka
Suicide bombers devastate the country's holiest Buddhist shrine, killing sixteen.

January 29, Birmingham, Georgia
A bomb is detonated by remote control at a clinic that performs abortions in Birmingham, killing off-duty police officer Robert Sanderson. Nurse Emily Lyons is severely injured.

March 5, Colombo, Sri Lanka
A bus bomb attack in Colombo's commercial area of Maradana kills 37 and wounds 250.

August 1, Banbridge, Northern Ireland
A five-hundred-pound car bomb planted by the Real IRA explodes outside a shoe store and injures thirty-five.

August 7, East Africa U.S. Embassy Bombings
A bomb explodes at the rear entrance of the U.S. Embassy in Nairobi, Kenya, killing 12. Approximately five thousand are injured. The Embassy building sustains extensive structural damage. Simultaneously a bomb detonates outside the U.S. Embassy in Dar es Salaam, Tanzania, killing ten. Seventy-seven are injured. The explosion causes major structural damage to the Embassy. The U.S. holds Osama bin Laden responsible.

August 15, Omagh, Northern Ireland
A five-hundred-pound car bomb planted by the Real IRA explodes outside a local courthouse and, killing 29 and injuring more than 330.

September 11, Jaffna, Sri Lanka
Twelve people, including the mayor, are killed when a bomb blast rocks the municipal council building.

October 18, Colombia
A National Liberation Army (ELN) bomb explodes at an oil pipeline plant, killing approximately seventy-one persons and injuring at least one hundred. The pipeline is jointly owned by the Colombia State Oil Company Ecopetrol and a consortium including U.S., French, British, and Canadian companies.

1999

August 31, Moscow, Russia
One person is killed in a bomb attack on a shopping center near the Kremlin.

September 8, Moscow, Russia
Ninety-four are killed and 150 are injured when a nine-story apartment building is destroyed by a bomb planted in its lobby. The bomb is estimated to have been made of 650 to 900 pounds of explosives.

September 13, Moscow, Russia
A large bomb explodes at an apartment on Kashirskoye Highway in southern Moscow. The eight-story building is flattened. One hundred eighteen die and two hundred are wounded.

2000

January 5, Colombo, Sri Lanka
At least twelve are killed and twenty-four wounded when a woman suicide bomber detonates explosives strapped to her body outside the office of Prime Minister Chandrika Bandaranaike.

January 21, Madrid, Spain
Two car bombs explode in Madrid, killing at least one person and wounding a child. Basque separatists are suspected.

June 7, Colombo, Sri Lanka
A suicide bomber assassinates Industrial Development Minister C. V. Gooneratne, killing twenty-five others and injuring twenty-seven. (The bomber detonated explosives strapped to his body after embracing the minister on a crowded parade route. The parade was held to collect contributions for thousands of government troops fighting Tiger rebels in the island's north.)

August 1, Jakarta, Indonesia
A bomb kills two and seriously injures the Philippine ambassador to Indonesia.

August 8, Moscow, Russia
Thirteen are killed when a bomb explodes in an underground walkway near Pushkin Square.

September 20, London
IRA dissidents fire rocket-propelled grenades at the headquarters of the British domestic security agency MI5.

September 13, Jakarta, Indonesia
A car bomb explodes inside the garage of the Jakarta Stock Exchange building, killing ten and injuring sixteen.

October 1, Dushanbe, Tajikistan
Militants detonate two bombs in a Christian church, killing seven and injuring seventy.

October 2, Muttur, Sri Lanka
A suicide bomber kills twenty-three, including Muslim candidate Baithullah eight days before elections.

October 12, Aden, Yemen
A small dingy packed with explosives rams the destroyer *USS Cole*, putting a forty-by-forty hole in the side of the boat, killing seventeen sailors and injuring thirty-nine. Al Qaeda is suspected.

December 24, Indonesia
Bombs explode at eleven churches on Christmas Eve, killing nineteen and injuring about one hundred. The attacks are blamed on Jemaah Islamiah.

December 30, Manila, Philippines
A bomb explodes in a plaza across the street from the U.S. Embassy in Manila, injuring nine. The Moro Islamic Liberation Front is allegedly responsible.

2001
March 4, London
A car bomb explodes at midnight outside of the British Broadcasting Corporation's main production studios. One person is injured. British authorities suspect the Real IRA.

March 4, Netanya, Israel
A suicide bomb attack in Netanya kills three and wounds sixty-five. HAMAS claims responsibility.

March 9, Hernani, Spain
Two policemen are killed by the explosion of a car bomb. The ETA is suspected.

April 22, Kfar Saba, Israel
A member of HAMAS detonates a bomb at a bus stop, killing one and injuring sixty.

June 1, Tel Aviv
A Palestinian suicide bomber kills at least twenty and wounds more than one hundred at a Tel Aviv nightclub.

July 24, Colombo, Sri Lanka
Tamal Tiger rebels stage a devastating suicide attack against the main air base and only international airport in Sri Lanka, destroying thirteen aircraft and leaving twelve dead.

August 9, Jerusalem
A HAMAS-planted bomb detonates in a Jerusalem pizzeria, killing fifteen and wounding more than ninety.

September 9, Nahariya, Israel
The first suicide bombing by an Israeli Arab kills three. HAMAS claims responsibility.

September 9, Khvajeh Ba Odin, Afghanistan
Two al Qaeda–linked suicide bombers posing as journalists fatally wound Ahmed Shah Massoud, a leader of Afghanistan's Northern Alliance, and a key U.S. ally.

September 11, New York City
Two hijacked airliners crash into the twin towers of the World Trade Center. The Pentagon is struck by a third hijacked plane. A fourth crashes into a field in southern Pennsylvania. The attacks kill 3,025. President Bush and his cabinet state that Osama bin Laden and al Qaeda are the prime suspects. They declare that the United States is now in a state of war with international terrorism.

October 1, Jammu and Kashmir, Indian Controlled Kashmir
A suicide car bomber forces open the gate of the state legislature. Two gunmen enter the building and hold off police for seven hours before being killed. Forty are killed. Jaish-e-Muhammad claims responsibility.

October 21, Sri Lanka

Five suicide bombers die in an attack against two Navy gunboats off the island's northern coast.

October 29, Colombo, Sri Lanka

A suicide bomber detonates explosives strapped to his body as he is questioned by the police guarding Prime Minister Ratnasiri Wickremanayake in Colombo. A policeman and a civilian are killed, and sixteen others are wounded.

December 1, Jerusalem

Two suicide bombers attack a Jerusalem shopping mall, killing 10 and wounding 170.

December 2, Haifa, Israel

A suicide bomb attack aboard a bus in Haifa, Israel, kills fifteen and wounds forty. HAMAS claims responsibility.

December 22, Over the Atlantic

Richard Reid is arrested for attempting to destroy a passenger airliner by igniting plastic explosives hidden in his shoes. He is found guilty of terrorism charges at a federal court in Boston and sentenced to life in prison.

2002

January 22, Jammu, Kashmir

A bomb explodes in a crowded retail district, killing one and injuring nine.

January 27, Jerusalem

A suicide bomb attack in Jerusalem kills the bomber and one victim, and wounds one hundred. The incident is the first suicide bombing carried out by a Palestinian woman.

February 16, West Bank, Israel

A suicide bombing in an outdoor food court kills four and wounds twenty-seven. The Popular Front for the Liberation of Palestine (PFLP) claims responsibility.

February 28, Amman, Jordan
A time bomb placed underneath the car belonging to Ali Bourjak, the head of Jordan's anti-terrorism unit at the intelligence services, kills two of his neighbors.

March 7, West Bank, Israel
A suicide bombing in a supermarket in the settlement of Ariel wounds ten.

March 9, Jerusalem
At least nine are killed in a suicide blast at a crowded central Jerusalem café close to Prime Minister Ariel Sharon's residence.

March 17, Islamabad, Pakistan
Militants throw grenades into the Protestant International Church during a service attended by diplomatic and local personnel. Five persons are killed and forty-six are wounded. The Lashkar-e-Tayyiba group is suspected.

March 20, Lima, Peru
Three days before President George W. Bush visits Peru, a car bomb explodes at a shopping center near the U.S. Embassy in Lima. Nine are killed and thirty-two wounded. The dead include two police officers and a teenager. Peruvian authorities suspect either the Shinning Path rebels or the Tupac Amaru Revolutionary Movement.

March 21, Jerusalem
A suicide bomber kills three and wounds eighty-six.

March 27, Netanya, Israel
A suicide bombing in a noted restaurant in Netanya kills 22 and wounds 140. The Islamic Resistance Movement (HAMAS) claims responsibility.

March 30, Kashmir, India
A bomb at a Hindu temple kills ten. The Islamic Front claims responsibility.

March 31, West Bank, Israel
A suicide bombing near an ambulance station in Efrat wounds four.

April 11, Tunisia
A suicide bomber detonates a truck loaded with propane outside a historic synagogue in Tunisia, killing sixteen. Twenty-six German tourists are injured. The Islamic Army for the Liberation of the Holy Sites claims responsibility.

April 12, Jerusalem
A female suicide bomber kills six in Jerusalem and wounds ninety others. The al-Aqsa Martyrs' Brigades claims responsibility.

May 8, Karachi, Pakistan
A car bomb explodes near a Navy shuttle bus in Karachi, killing twelve and wounding nineteen. Al-Qaeda is suspected.

May 9, Kaspiisk, Dagestan
A remote-controlled bomb explodes near a May Day parade in Kaspiisk, Dagestan, killing 42 and wounding 150. Fourteen of the dead and fifty of the wounded are soldiers. Islamists linked to al Qaeda are suspected.

May 17, Kashmir
Two bombs explode, killing two and wounding twenty-two.

June 14, Karachi, Pakistan
A car bomb explodes near the U.S. Consulate and the Marriott Hotel in Karachi. Eleven are killed and fifty-one wounded. Al Qaeda is suspected.

June 19, Jerusalem
A suicide bombing at a bus stop in Jerusalem kills six and wounds forty-three. The al-Aqsa Martyrs' Brigades claim responsibility.

July 17, Tel Aviv
Two suicide bombers attack the old bus station in Tel Aviv, killing five and wounding thirty-eight. The Islamic Jihad claims responsibility.

July 31, Jerusalem
A bomb hidden in a bag in the Frank Sinatra International Student Center of Jerusalem's Hebrew University kills nine and wounds eighty-seven. The Islamic Resistance Movement (HAMAS) claims responsibility.

August 4, Safad, Israel
A suicide bomb attack on a bus kills nine and wounds fifty. Many of the wounded are soldiers returning from leave. HAMAS claims responsibility.

September 19, Tel Aviv
A suicide bomb attack on a bus in Tel Aviv kills six and wounds fifty-two. HAMAS claims responsibility.

October 6, al-Dhabbah, Yemen
An explosive-laden boat rams the French oil tanker *Limburg*, anchored five miles off the coast of al-Dhabbah, Yemen. One is killed and four are wounded. Al Qaeda is suspected.

October 12, Bali, Indonesia
A car bomb explodes outside the Sari Club Discotheque, killing 202 and wounding 300. Most of the casualties, including eighty-eight of the dead, are Australian tourists. Al Qaeda claims responsibility.

October 23–26, Moscow, Russia
Fifty Chechen rebels led by Movsar Barayev seize the Palace of Culture theater in Moscow to demand an end to the war in Chechnya. They take more than eight hundred hostages and threaten to blow up the theater. During a three-day siege they kill a Russian policeman and five hostages. On October 26, Russian Special Forces pump an anesthetic gas through the ventilation system and storm the theater. All of the rebels are killed, but ninety-four hostages also die, many from the effects of the gas. A group led by Chechen warlord Shamil Basayev claims responsibility.

November 21, Jerusalem
A suicide bomb attack on a bus on Mexico Street in Jerusalem kills eleven and wounds fifty. HAMAS claims responsibility.

November 24, Kashmir
Armed militants attack the Reghunath and Shiv temples in Kashmir, killing thirteen and wounding fifty. The Lashkare-e-Tayyiba claim responsibility.

November 28, Mombasa, Kenya
A suicide car-bomb attack on the Paradise Hotel in Mombasa, Kenya, kills fifteen and wounds forty. Three of the dead and eighteen of the wounded are Israeli tourists; the; the others are Kenyans. Near Mombasa's airport, two SA-7 shoulder-fire missiles are lauched at an Arkia Airlines Boeing 757 carrying 261 passengers back to Israel. Both missiles miss. Al Qaeda, the Government of Universal Palestine in Exile, and the Army of Palestine claim responsibility for both attacks.

December 5, Sulawesi, Indonesia
A bomb explodes outside a McDonald's restaurant on Sulawesi Island, killing three and injuring eleven. Jemaah Islamiah–linked militants are blamed for the blast.

December 27, Groznyy, Chechnya

Two explosives-laden trucks are driven into the offices of the pro-Russian Chechen government in Groznyy. The suicide attack kills more than 80 and wounds 210. According to a Chechen Web site run by the Kavkaz Center, Chechen warlord Shamil Basayev claims responsibility.

2003

JANUARY 5, TEL AVIV

Two suicide bomb attacks kill twenty-two and wound at least one hundred. The Al-Aqsa Martyrs' Brigades claim responsibility.

February 7, Bogotá, Colombia

A car bomb explodes outside a nightclub in Bogotá, killing 32 and wounding 160. No group claims responsibility. Colombian officials suspect the Colombian Revolutionary Armed Forces (FARC) of committing this, the worst terrorist attack in the country in a decade.

March 5, Haifa

A suicide bomber aboard a bus in Haifa kills fifteen and wounds forty.

March 30, Netanya, Israel

A suicide bombing in a cafe in Netanya wounds thirty-eight, but only the bomber is killed. Islamic Jihad claims responsibility.

May 12, Riyadh, Saudi Arabia

Suicide bombers attack three residential compounds for foreign workers in Saudi Arabia. The thirty-four dead include nine attackers, seven other Saudis, nine U.S. citizens, and one citizen each from the United Kingdom, Ireland, and the Philippines. Another American dies on June 1. It is the first major attack on U.S. targets in Saudi Arabia since the end of the war in Iraq.

May 12, Znamenskoye, Chechnya

A truck bomb demolishes a government compound in Chechnya, killing fifty-four. Russian authorities blame followers of a Saudi-born Islamist named Abu Walid. President Vladimir Putin says he suspects that there was an al Qaeda connection.

May 12, Chechnya

Two female suicide bombers attack Chechen administrator Akhmed Kadyrov during a religious festival. He escapes injury but fourteen others are killed and forty-three are wounded. Chechen rebel leader Shamil Basayev claims responsibility.

May 16, Casablanca, Morocco

A team of twelve suicide bombers attacks five targets in Casablanca, killing forty-three and wounding one hundred. The Moroccan government blames the Islamist al-Assirat al-Moustaquim (the Righteous Path), but foreign commentators suspect an al Qaeda connection.

May 16, Jerusalem

A suicide bomb attack on a bus in Jerusalem's French Hill district kills seven and wounds twenty. The bomber is disguised as a religious Jew. HAMAS claims responsibility.

May 19, Afula, Israel

A suicide bomb attack by a female Palestinian student kills three and wounds fifty-two at a shopping mall. Islamic Jihad and the al-Aqsa Martyrs' Brigades claim credit.

July 5, Moscow, Russia

Two female suicide bombers, at least one of Chechen origin, kill twenty and injure thirty at a Moscow rock concert.

July 10, Moscow, Russia

A Chechen woman fails in an attempt to blow up a restaurant in central Moscow, but a bomb disposal expert dies trying to defuse the explosive device in her rucksack.

July 11, Jerusalem

A suicide bombing aboard a bus in Jerusalem kills seventeen and wounds seventy. HAMAS claims responsibility.

August 1, Northern Ossetia, Russia

A suicide truck bomb destroys a Russian military hospital, killing fifty. Russian authorities attribute the attack to followers of Chechen rebel leader Shamil Basayev.

August 5, Jakarta, Indonesia

A car bomb explodes outside the Marriott Hotel in Jakarta, killing 10 and wounding 150. Indonesian authorities suspect Jemaah Islamiah.

August 7, Baghdad, Iraq
A car bomb explodes outside the Jordanian Embassy, killing nineteen and wounding sixty-five.

August 12, Israel
The first suicide bombings since the June 29 Israeli-Palestinian truce take place. One attack in a supermarket at Rosh Haayin, Israel, kills and wounds fourteen. A second, at a bus stop in the West Bank, kills one and wounds three. The al-Aqsa Martyrs' Brigades claim responsibility for the first; HAMAS claims responsibility for the second.

August 19, Baghdad, Iraq
A truck loaded with surplus Iraqi ordnance explodes outside the United Nations headquarters in Baghdad's Canal Hotel. The twenty-three dead include UN Special Representative Sergio Viera de Mello. More than one hundred are wounded.

August 19, Jerusalem
A suicide bombing aboard a bus in Jerusalem kills twenty and injures at least one hundred. HAMAS and Islamic Jihad claim responsibility.

August 29, Najaf, Iraq
A car bomb explosion outside the Shrine of the Imam Ali in Najaf, Iraq kills at least 81 and wounds at least 140. The dead include the Ayatollah Mohammed Bakir al-Hakim, one of four leading Shi'ite clerics in Iraq. Al-Hakim had been the leader of the Supreme Council for the Islamic Revolution in Iraq (SCIRI) since its establishment in 1982, and SCIRI had recently agreed to work with the U.S.-sponsored Iraqi Governing Council.

September 9, Tsrifin, Israel
Two suicide bombings take place in Israel. The first, at a bus stop near Tsrifin Army Base southeast of Tel Aviv, kills seven soldiers and wounds fourteen and one civilian. The second, at a café in Jerusalem's German Colony neighborhood, kills six and wounds forty. HAMAS claims responsibility.

September 22, Baghdad, Iraq
A suicide car bomb attack on the UN headquarters in Baghdad kills a security guard and wounds nineteen others.

October 4, Haifa, Israel

A Palestinian woman suicide bomber in Haifa kills nineteen and wounds at least fifty-five in a restaurant. Islamic Jihad claims responsibility.

October 12, Baghdad, Iraq

Two suicide car bombs explode outside the Baghdad Hotel, which houses U.S. officials. Six are killed and thirty-two wounded.

October 15, Gaza Strip, Israel

A remote-controlled bomb explodes under a car in a U.S. diplomatic convoy in the northern Gaza Strip. Three security guards are killed. A fourth is wounded.

October 26, Baghdad, Iraq

Iraqis use an improvised rocket launcher to bombard the al-Rashid Hotel, killing one U.S. Army officer and wounding seventeen. Deputy Secretary of Defense Paul D. Wolfowitz, who is staying at the hotel, is not injured.

October 27, Baghdad, Iraq

A series of suicide car bombings in Baghdad kills at least 35 and wounds at least 230. Four attacks are directed at Iraqi police stations; the fifth and most destructive is directed at the International Committee of the Red Cross headquarters, where at least twelve are killed. A sixth attack fails when the car bomb does not explode.

November 8, Riyadh, Saudi Arabia

A suicide car bombing in the Muhaya residential compound kills 17 and wounds 122. U.S. officials say al Qaeda was probably responsible.

November 12, Nasiriyah, Iraq

A suicide truck bomb destroys the headquarters of the Italian military police, killing eighteen Italians and eleven Iraqis, and wounding at least one hundred.

November 15, Istanbul, Turkey

Two suicide truck bombs explode outside the Neve Shalom and Beth Israel synagogues, killing twenty-five and wounding at least three hundred. The initial claim of responsibility comes from Turkish militants. Turkish authorities blame al Qaeda. The London-based newspaper *al-Quds al-Arabi* receives an e-mail in which an al Qaeda branch called the Brigades of the Martyr Abu Hafz al-Masri claims responsibility.

November 15, Bogotá, Colombia
Grenade attacks on two bars frequented by Americans kills one. The FARC is suspected.

November 20, Istanbul, Turkey
Two suicide truck bombings devastate the British HSBC Bank and the British Consulate General in Istanbul, killing 27 and wounding at least 450. The dead include Consul General Roger Short. Officials suspect al Qaeda.

November 20, Kirkuk, Iraq
A suicide car bombing kills five.

November 29–30, Iraq
Iraqi insurgents step up attacks on members of the Coalition. An ambush in Mahmudiyah kills seven out of a party of eight Spanish intelligence officers. Iraqi insurgents kill two Japanese diplomats. Another ambush kills two South Korean electrical workers and wounds two more. A Colombian employee of Kellogg Brown & Root is killed and two are wounded in an ambush near Balad.

December 5, Rostov-on-Don, Russia
A suicide bomb kills 42 and wounds 150 aboard a Russian commuter train in south Russia. Russian officials suspect Chechen rebels; President Putin says the attack was meant to disrupt elections. Chechen rebel leader Aslan Maskhadov denies any involvement.

December 9, Moscow, Russia
A female suicide bomber kills five and wounds fourteen outside Moscow's National Hotel.

December 15, Iraq
Two days after Saddam Hussein is captured, two suicide car bombers attack Iraqi police stations. Eight are killed and twenty-seven are wounded.

December 19, Baghdad, Iraq
A bomb destroys the Baghdad office of the Supreme Council of the Islamic Revolution in Iraq, killing a woman and wounding at least seven others.

December 24, Irbil, Iraq
A suicide car bomb attack on the Kurdish Interior Ministry kills 5 and wounds 101.

December 25, Rawalpindi, Pakistan

Two suicide truck bombers kill fourteen as President Musharraf's motorcade passes through Rawalpindi, Pakistan. Pakistani officials suspect Afghan and Kashmiri militants. On January 6, 2004, Pakistani authorities announce the arrest of six suspects who are said to be members of Jaish-e-Muhammad.

December 25, Petach Tikva, Israel

A Palestinian suicide bomber kills four at a bus stop near Petach Tikva, Israel. The Popular Front for the Liberation of Palestine claims responsibility for the attack, in retaliation for Israeli military operations in Nablus that had begun two days earlier.

December 31, Baghdad, Iraq

A car bomb explosion outside Baghdad's Nabil restaurant kills eight and wounds thirty-five. The wounded include three *Los Angeles Times* reporters and three local employees.

2004

February 6, Moscow, Russia

A rush hour bombing hits the Moscow subway five weeks before presidential elections, killing forty-one.

February 11, Madrid, Spain

A series of bomb blasts on commuter trains in Madrid kill 191 and injure almost 2,000.

July 7, Colombo, Sri Lanka

A woman blasts herself to pieces while being questioned at the Kollupitiya police station, killing four policemen and wounding thirteen others.

September 9, Jakarta, Indonesia

A suicide car bomb explodes outside the Australian Embassy in the capital in Jakarta, killing eleven and wounding one hundred others. Six alleged members of the regional al Qaeda–linked Jemaah Islamiah terror group have been convicted over the attack.

October 8, Sinai, Egypt

A triple attack against part of the Egyptian Sinai peninsula, popular with Israeli tourists, kills thirty-four.

2005

May 22, New Delhi, India
One person is killed and forty-nine are wounded when blasts rock two cinemas in New Delhi that are screening a controversial film condemned by Sikhs.

June 24, Srinagar, India
Nine Indian soldiers are killed and seventeen wounded when a powerful car bomb explodes, as a bus carrying troops drives past a popular tourist attraction in revolt-torn Indian Kashmir.

July 20, Srinagar, India
A car bomb claimed by Islamic rebels explodes in the heart of Indian Kashmir's summer capital, Srinagar, killing four soldiers and a civilian and injuring twenty-one others.

July 28, Lucknow, India
An explosion rips through a long distance passenger train in northern India, killing twelve.

July 7, London
Four blasts on public transport in London kill fifty-six, including four presumed suicide bombers.

July 22–23, Sharm el-Sheikh, Egypt
A series of bombings in the Egyptian Red Sea resort of Sharm el-Sheikh kills sixty-eight, including seventeen foreigners.

August 7, Guwahati, India
Rebels in India's northeastern state of Assam destroy an oil pipeline, killing four.

August 12, Guwahati, India
One person is killed and six others are injured in a grenade attack by rebels in India's northeast. It is one in a wave of attacks before India's August 15 Independence Day.

September 4, New Delhi, India
At least twenty-four paramilitary soldiers are killed in a powerful landmine blast triggered by suspected Maoist rebels in eastern India. The three-decade-old conflict has claimed thousands of lives.

September 29, Srinagar, India

Seven die and twenty are injured when a grenade explodes outside a shopping mall in Indian Kashmir.

October 1, Bali, Indonesia

Bombs explode at three crowded restaurants on the tourist island, killing at least thirty-two, including one Australian, and wounding scores of others.

October 8, Jharkand, India

An explosion believed to have been set by Maoist rebels kills twelve policemen in the eastern Indian state of Jharkand.

October 29, New Delhi, India

At least 61 are killed and 188 injured when three bombs explode in the Indian capital of New Delhi.

November 9, Amman, Jordan

At least fifty-six die in Amman when three bomb blasts tear through hotels in the Jordanian capital.

Acknowledgments

There are many men and women from the ranks of police departments, fire departments, state police, the federal government, and military organizations within the United States and England who selflessly assisted us in the research that went into this book. There are men from the ranks of retired members of several of those services, and there are family members of bomb technicians who gave us their time. We are grateful and proud to have met each one of you; to each one of you, our thanks.

There are some we want to single out for a special acknowledgment:

- New York City Police Commissioner Raymond W. Kelly. He granted our request for unfettered access to the NYPD Bomb Squad.
- Former NYPD Deputy Commissioner for Public Information Michael O'Looney. Michael endorsed our project, shepherded its approval past the senior members of his police department, and lent us his ongoing support.
- NYPD Deputy Commissioner for Public Information Paul Browne and the incredibly helpful members of his unit, especially Detective Walter Burnes and civilian television specialist Jason Post, for their continued assistance.
- Sergeant John Santos of the Arson and Explosion Squad; Sergeant Joe Blozis of the Crime Scene Unit; Deputy Chief Denis McCarthy of the Forensic Investigations Division; Assistant Chief John Colgan of the Counter Terrorism Division; Assistant Chief Phil Pulaski, Deputy Chief Robert Giannelli, and Chief George Brown of the Detective Division.
- Federal Bureau of Investigation former Assistant Director in Charge of the New York field division Pasquale D'Amuro, and his public information officer, Joe Valiquette. From its inception they endorsed our project within the FBI. Special Agent Anne Todd: Anne tirelessly worked to convince the FBI to accept us into the Hazardous Devices

School in Huntsville, Alabama. David Jernigan, who runs that school, generously shared his time and expertise with us.

- Kevin Miles, the FBI's senior special agent bomb technician.
- Lieutenant Tom Fitzpatrick, our good friend, invaluable resource, and, as commander of the Philadelphia Bomb Squad, an asset to the safety of that city beyond all measure. Thanks also for his technical reading of the manuscript.
- Floyd Pirtle, Paul Carter, and the other instructors and staff at HDS. They unstintingly gave of their time, knowledge, and experience.
- Robert Hunt of the Public Affairs staff of the United States Army was invaluable in getting both the Army and the FBI to agree to the same things at the same time during our stay at the HDS School.
- James Neilson, commander of the Austin, Texas, Bomb Squad; the bomb technicians of the LA County Sheriff's Department and the LAPD for their assistance on the explosives used by the FALN; Ed Kittel, chief of the Explosives Division of the Transportation Safety Administration for his explanation of the national security questions; the Bellevue Washington Fire Department; the Bergen County, New Jersey, Bomb Squad; the British military retired Major Barry Taylor, as well as retired Major Graham Lightfoot; and the City of Boston Bomb Squad for their generous assistance.
- The members of the International Association of Bomb Technicians and Investigators, especially Jerry Dennis, former international president of the IABTI, and board members Kevin Barry and Frank Tabert.
- The Bureau of Alcohol, Tobacco and Firearms—especially Sheree Mixell, Rich Marianos, Tom Hill, and Joseph Green—for the national bomb data they provided and their ongoing assistance.
- To retired NYPD Sergeant Mike Bosak and the researchers of the U.S. Secret Service for assisting us in historical research.
- Lisa Schwartz of the ABC research department, for her detailed answers to numerous queries and her skills in checking our facts. And to her colleague, Sheelagh McNeill, for assisting in the fact-checking process.
- To our colleagues at ABC News and ABC News/Nightline, our gratitude for their understanding, encouragement, and support from the beginning through the end of the research, writing, and publishing process. Special thanks to Ted Koppel and Leroy Sievers for allowing us to produce the two *Nightline* reports that led to this book; to Sara Just at *Nightline*, who brought us together with the publisher, Hyperion, after those broadcasts aired; and to Tommy Fasano, who edited those two broadcasts.
- To ABC Vice President for News Mimi Gurbst, who endorsed this project.

ACKNOWLEDGMENTS

- To Kerry Smith at ABC Standards and Practices, who approved it.
- To retired NYPD Bomb Technicians Wes Somerville, William Schmidt, Arthur Hornidge, Neil Monaco, Jim Helblock, Pete Major, and Faith Beiser.
- To William Polignani, for his research into his grandfather, early Bomb Squad member Amadeo Polignani.
- To Assistant Brooklyn District Attorney Joseph Petrosino for research into his great uncle, Giuseppe Petrosino.
- To Senior Police Administrative Aide Antoinette Giovino, who welcomed us into the Bomb Squad each time we showed up.
- To all the current members of the NYPD Bomb Squad, named and unnamed in this book, who gave us their friendship, humor, knowledge, and trust. Thank you very much.
- To David Black, our literary agent.
- To our parents, Marie and Richard Esposito and Mel and Gayle Gerstein.
- And last but not least, to our daughters, Emily Brown Gerstein and Tatiana Maria Esposito. They are our biggest supporters and their dads' biggest fans.

Index